Dish

MARION KANE

Canada's best-read food columnist

Dish

memories, recipes and delicious bites

**A COLLECTION OF FAVOURITE COLUMNS
FROM THE *TORONTO STAR***

whitecap

Edited by Alison Maclean
Proofread by Sonnet Force
Design by Roberta Batchelor
Illustrations by Kirsten Horel

Printed and bound in Canada

LIBRARY AND ARCHIVES CANADA CATALOGUING IN PUBLICATION

Kane, Marion
    Dish/Marion Kane.

    Includes index.
    ISBN 1-55285-646-1

    1. Food. 2. Cookery. 3. Kane, Marion. I. Title.
    TX355.K348 2005   641   C2005-900152-6

The publisher acknowledges the financial support of the Government
of Canada through the Book Publishing Industry Development
Program for our publishing activities.

www.marionkane.com

The inside pages of this book are 100% recycled, processed chlorine-free
paper with 100% post-consumer content. For more information, visit
Markets Initiative's website: www.oldgrowthfree.com.

Table of Contents

Introduction

✳ HOW DID I WIND UP CHATTING CHEERFULLY about rice pudding with a New York mobster-turned-cookbook author who's under the witness protection plan?

What's the scoop on my getting the only Toronto print interview with screen legend Sophia Loren when she was in town touting her cookbook? A meeting, by the way, that turned out to be a magnificent, intimate, three-hour Italian lunch for two.

And what quirk of fate reunited me and my darling nanny when she recognized me on TV, more than 50 years later, promoting a cookbook I'd written?

These are among the stories that have made fine fodder for me as a food columnist for Canada's largest newspaper, the *Toronto Star*. They, and dozens of other stories, are included in this book: a collection of favourite columns accompanied by many of my absolute best recipes.

Yes, writing about food is a peachy gig. It connects me with people wherever I go. I talk to cabbies about favourite dishes from their homes, be they in Canada, India, Turkey, Iran or Somalia. My daughter's friends, many of whom are from far-flung countries, are used to being grilled about their national dishes. Sometimes, I stop in at a homeless shelter where a hot lunch and someone to share it with soothes many a body and soul. Nearly always, those I'm with are as excited as I am to talk about food. Usually, they're happy and proud to wind up in my column.

Writing about food means, for me, writing about life. And what a privilege, as well as a supreme pleasure, it is. I hope you enjoy my stories. I also hope my book makes you want to cook—whether it's a simple salad, a pot of steaming soup or a loaf of chocolate chip-laced banana bread. Best of all, you can eat the results.

The real pleasure, as I'm sure you know, is enjoying food at leisure with family and friends.

--⌒ *Chapter One* ⌒--

PERSONAL BEST

✳ I WAS WELL INTO MY 30S WHEN, BY FLUKE, I became a food writer. Happily, this career has turned out to be my natural niche. As with most things, it all dates back to childhood.

Some people recall clearly where they were, who was with them or what they were wearing at key moments in their lives. For me, it's all about the food. I come by this affinity honestly.

Mine was a rootless, often chaotic, never-dull family in which mealtime was one of the few sure things. What made our repasts particularly memorable was the delicious food, which I learned to appreciate from an early age. On those rare occasions when it was accompanied by good vibes, all was well in my otherwise shaky world.

My father, Mel Schachter, a medical researcher and university physiology professor, was a brilliant, inwardly tender, but volatile man brimming with feelings he had trouble controlling. The primary emotion, unfortunately, was rage, the result of growing up in a rough, often cruel, working class family of Russian Jewish immigrants in The Main neighbourhood of Montreal.

My mother, Ruth, is a biologist who spent many years teaching high school. Calm and collected on the surface, she bears emotional scars from fleeing the Holocaust as a Jewish teenager in Latvia, where all her extended family was killed. Her cultured refinement and lack of emotion belie the pain of survivor guilt and the struggles of being a refugee. Hers was an odd, striking contrast to my dad's persona and left the children in our family to negotiate a confusing, sometimes scary familial minefield.

For me, food was a soothing pleasure. Dinner was always at 6 P.M. and my mother, a fantastic self-taught cook with an eclectic, mostly European, repertoire, would produce a delicious spread complete with healthy components: a big salad, for which I always made the vinaigrette, and glasses of milk for me and my two younger brothers.

My father, whose best quality was a razor-sharp sense of humour, could be extremely funny when in the mood and often brandished his somewhat cynical wit at the table. He loved to eat and was accomplished in the kitchen, having put himself through medical school at McGill by working as a short-order cook. One of my favourite memories is of clambering into the car with him on weekends to visit Zlotnik's, a popular Jewish deli in our North London suburb, to pick up bagels, cream cheese, lox and other ingredients from his youth.

Occasionally, he would drive us to an eatery in Golders Green that specialized in his beloved childhood staple, smoked meat or salt beef as it was called in England in those days. But Melly, as Mum called him, really came to life on the Sunday mornings he decided to cook. He would grandiosely clear the kitchen, carefully line up ingredients and, with much fanfare, meticulously produce his amazing French toast, immaculate salami and eggs or, my favourite, a perfect toasted bacon sandwich.

The bill of fare in our home may have been comforting and delectable to me. However, it stood out like a sore thumb in an almost totally Anglo milieu in which my friends had never seen, let alone tasted, schnitzel, rye bread, salami or plum kuchen. I, in turn, rebelled against my mother's gourmet ways and yearned for British staples like Toad-in-the-Hole, the currant-studded steamed pudding Spotted Dick and—yes, believe it—Spam fritters, all highlights of my school's daily hot lunch. However, even these paled beside the luxurious array of dishes my mother would prepare for my happiest times at home: dinner parties at which my parents were quintessential hosts.

As a teenager, I loved to chit-chat with my parents' actor friends, mingle with my dad's handsome graduate students, and even hobnob with famous colleagues, like Andrew Huxley and Miriam Rothschild, at our convivial soirees. My ruse of moving among the crowd offering wine, holding a tray of hors d'oeuvres and offering coffee in small cups, honed the entertaining skills I'm glad to possess today.

Food looms large in many pivotal moments of my life. Some involve memories that are particularly sweet. Take the tale of my erstwhile nanny, Evelyn Smail. My parents had often talked about the teenage girl from a St. Lawrence Valley farm who looked after me when I was a baby in Montreal. You can imagine my surprise—and joy—when she contacted me in 1998 after seeing me talk about my most recent cookbook on TV. A few weeks later, I was at the front door of her lace-curtained farmhouse surrounded by cornfields. After 50 years, it was a beautiful reunion for us both, filled with laughs and a few tears. That day, we went to the local orchard and picked raspberries. The next morning, we baked her famous Raspberry Cream Pie.

I took a trip further back in time when I unearthed the story of Joe Martinson, a distant relative on my mother's side and a coffee merchant in New York's Greenwich Village in the early 1900s. He started small, with a wagon for selling the beans he roasted in his mother's oven, but soon became a huge success. Martinson Coffee is still a popular brand in parts of the U.S. What's more, he's the source, so the story goes, of the well-known phrase "cup of Joe."

My daughter Ruthie pops up in many a column. A regular taster of my cooking and baking, with an impeccable palate, she loves to cook, especially the healthy Wheat Berry Salad on page 244, which she likes to make for a tasty, nutritious high-school lunch. Ruthie's interest in food inspired an annual potluck party that started on a whim and became a huge hit. About a dozen of her girlfriends gathered at our house one civic holiday, a dish of homemade food in hand. I'll never forget the heartwarming sight: a bevy of gorgeous, smiling teenagers of every size, shape and colour seated around our long kitchen table laden with Asian noodles, Indian samosas, Caribbean fruit salad and a Vietnamese jellied dessert. A lovely reflection of cosmopolitan Toronto's delicious diversity. And you guessed it, it's a column.

⤜⧆⤛

BAKEWELL TART BROUHAHA

※ BAKEWELL, DERBYSHIRE—"This is the home of the Bakewell Pudding," replies the manager of The Rutlands Arms Hotel with mock reproach when asked where in town to find the best Bakewell Tart. Then, flashing me a wicked grin, she adds cheekily, "The tarts just live here." Oka-a-ay! Point taken. Lesson learned. One soon confirmed by other locals who insist the word "tart" does not apply to the original confection born many moons ago in this historic market town nestled at the heart of the Peak District National Park in a lush valley on the River Wye.

Bakewell is beloved and, at this time of year, besieged by two groups of people: back-packing, ruddy-cheeked hikers, and comparatively pale-faced folks like moi motivated by that less wholesome attribute—a sweet tooth. And it turns out I've just had my first taste of the culinary controversy to come. As I check out the few cobbled blocks where four busy, well-stocked bakeries specializing in Bakewell Pudding—and, yes, even the politically incorrect Bakewell Tart—sell their wares, I unearth a mouthwatering mystery that remains unsolved.

For the second year in a row, I'm accompanied by my trusty 80-year-old mum for this, our latest foray into Britain's north country to check out the birthplace of a traditional sweet. Last year, it was the tiny Lancashire town of Eccles, home to the currant-laden, flaky pastry called Eccles Cake. Sadly, the bakery from which it hails is long gone and it was left to the stalwart Marks & Spencer's in nearby Manchester to serve up a delicious, definitive version.

Here, far from finding a dearth of sources, a couple of bakeries loudly proclaim they are originators of the Bakewell Pudding. (We'll get to that pesky tart later.) In fact, so heated has the battle become over this claim to fame, owners of two local establishments recently wound up in court.

One was trained chef Marion Wright, who has operated Bloomers Original Bakewell Puddings since purchasing it 10 years ago. It's a sunny mid-morning when I sit down with Marion in the bakery's coffee shop over cappuccino and a slice each of Bakewell Pudding and Tart to chew over this baking brouhaha. First, she explains the difference between the two desserts. The pudding, which resembles a large, flat butter tart with pallid puff pastry as its base, is, she says, "filled with a sort of egg custard with ground almonds in it on a layer of strawberry or raspberry jam." I find it less attractive than the much-maligned, tastier tart, which, says Wright, came into being about 150 years ago. The reason: "It's cheaper to make a sponge mixture than the custard," she notes, "and you can use almond essence instead of ground almonds."

The lawsuit was launched five years ago by the owners of the nearby Old Original Bakewell Pudding Shop. That bakery and Wright's both claim to have a copy of the original recipe dating back to the 1860s. It was handed over, so the story goes, by The Rutland Arms Hotel where the pudding came about when an inexperienced cook made a mistake in assembling a strawberry jam tart. The court case won national attention in the British press, but remains unresolved. "There were $100,000 in legal costs, which we split," says Wright wearily. "There's no date on my recipe and they don't have the technology to date it accurately. The Pudding Shop says they have a recipe but no one's seen it."

Later that day, I ponder all this as I savour a luscious wedge of deep-dish Bakewell Tart nearby at the recently opened Bakewell Tart Shop. Its rich, crunchy crust is filled with tangy jam and a lusciously sweet almond cake. Served warm and bathed in silky, warm custard, it tastes divine. All this is still on my mind back in Toronto where I discover The Brick Street Bakery at 55 Mill St. Here, owner Simon Silander proudly shows me his rendition of Bakewell Tart—a dark, rich dessert made with unblanched almonds—along with a slew of other British-inspired pies, cookies, bread and cakes. Good as it is, the tart pales beside the bakery's delectably sticky, currant-studded Somerset Lardy Cake. Soon I'm on the phone to Mum. Looks like I've found our culinary mission for next summer!

Bakewell Tart

I've combined elements from several recipes for this excellent version. Serve warm or at room temperature with warm custard, ice cream, whipped cream or thickened yogurt.

PASTRY

1¼ cups (300 mL) all-purpose flour
⅓ cup (75 mL) icing sugar
Pinch of salt
½ cup (125 mL) cold unsalted butter, cubed
2 egg yolks
1 tbsp (15 mL) water

FILLING

¾ cup (175 mL) raspberry jam
½ cup (125 mL) unsalted butter, at room temperature

½ cup (125 mL) icing sugar
3 eggs
¼ tsp (1 mL) almond extract
1¼ cups (300 mL) ground almonds
⅓ cup (75 mL) all-purpose flour
1 tsp (5 mL) baking powder

GLAZE

⅓ cup (75 mL) peach, apple or apricot jelly
1 tbsp (15 mL) lemon juice
½ cup (125 mL) icing sugar

1. For pastry: Combine flour, icing sugar and salt in bowl. Using hand-held wire pastry blender, cut in butter until mixture resembles coarse crumbs. (Or, using food processor, combine dry ingredients, then cut in butter by pulsing several times.) Add egg yolks; mix lightly with fork. (In food processor, add yolks and pulse briefly.) Add water; gather into ball. Cover in plastic wrap and chill about 30 minutes.

2. Preheat oven to 350°F (180°C).

3. Reserve about ⅛th of the pastry for lattice. Press remaining pastry onto bottom and about halfway up the sides of an 8-inch (20 cm) spring-form pan. Bake about 20 minutes or until pastry is barely golden around edges. Cool completely. Leave oven on.

4. Spread jam over bottom of cooled pastry shell.

5. For filling: Use an electric mixer to beat together butter and sugar until light and smooth. Beat in eggs, one at a time, until fluffy. Add almond extract.

6. In small bowl, combine almonds, flour and baking powder. Stir into egg mixture until smooth. Pour into pastry shell; spread evenly over jam layer. Roll reserved pastry out between two sheets of plastic wrap into an

8-inch (20 cm) circle. Remove top layer of plastic wrap. Using a sharp knife, cut pastry into six strips. Working quickly, lay three strips over tart in one direction and three strips on top in opposite direction.

7. Return tart to oven. Bake for 50 to 55 minutes, or until golden brown. Cool completely.

8. For glaze: Place jelly in small bowl; warm in microwave about 60 seconds on High. Pour over top of tart; smooth evenly with back of spoon.

9. In small bowl, combine lemon juice and icing sugar. Place mixture in piping bag or plastic bottle with squirt tip and make abstract swirls over top of tart.

MAKES 8 SERVINGS.

A CUP OF JOE

❋ WHO WOULD HAVE THOUGHT I'M RELATED—albeit distantly—to the "Joe" of that famous coffee drinkers' phrase? It all began, as is often the case, almost by accident.

I was in Las Vegas attending a four-day gathering of food writers from across North America. One evening, at a cocktail soiree atop one of The Strip's glitzy casinos, I was chatting with a colleague, Suzanne Martinson, food editor of the *Pittsburgh Post-Gazette*, and her investigative journalist husband, Bob.

During our conversation, I asked if they were related to the Martinsons of Martinson Coffee, a popular American brand of that trusty brew. The pair answered "No," although they knew the coffee well, and I thought that was that. My reason for asking was a long-shot that resulted from some recent rooting around I'd been doing to unearth my family tree.

My Martinson connection dates back to the summer of 1940. That was when my mother, at age 17, arrived in Seattle with her parents and younger sister, having fled the Holocaust that was soon to decimate their large Jewish family in Riga, Latvia. Their escape, which took one year, was via Sweden, the Trans-Siberian Railway to Japan and across the Pacific Ocean to the United States. Having omitted to get their passports stamped in Vancouver, the family was refused visas to enter the U.S. They were imprisoned and would have been returned to Europe had not my wealthy oil tycoon grandfather, Aaron Nisse, contacted an attorney called Paul Martinson—a relative of my grandmother's who lived and, at age 94, still resides in New York. As my mother succinctly recalls, "He sprung us from jail and saved our lives."

The foursome subsequently stayed for six months in a residential hotel on Manhattan's Upper West Side before moving to Montreal. When urged to tell this story, my mother remarked that the Martinson family was in the coffee business. Fast-forward to Las Vegas where newspaper scribe Bob Martinson has returned to his hotel room to surf the Internet in search of Martinson Coffee. The result of his sleuthing and mine goes back to that cup of joe and is as follows:

There was, it turns out, a man called Joe Martinson who was the attorney Paul's uncle. Joe, whose family immigrated to the United States from Mitau, Latvia, in the late 1800s, began his career in coffee at age 16. A resourceful lad, he had the idea of roasting several kinds of high-quality coffee beans separately before blending them—an intricate, labour-intensive *modus operandi* rarely used then or now—in his mother's kitchen.

"Joe maximized flavour by discovering and using the ideal roast for each particular type of bean," explains John Martinson, Paul's son and co-owner of the u.s. tea company China Mist. "That was what set his coffee apart from others and made it so popular," says John, speaking to me by phone from his home in Phoenix, Arizona. Joe, he continues, then sold the freshly roasted whole beans from a pushcart to his neighbours on Manhattan's Lower East Side. The formula was an immediate success, says John, and the coffee aroma emanating from Joe's cart as he made his popular door-to-door deliveries gave birth, word has it, to the expression "cup of joe."

"Joe was a pioneer in marketing," says John enthusiastically. "He bought a small fleet of Rolls Royces in the 1930s. He had the back seats removed, painted the Martinson logo on them and sent out salesmen and delivery guys dressed as chauffeurs to deliver the coffee to upscale hotels and restaurants in Manhattan." Ahead of his time, the clever entrepreneur also used small airplanes to streak across the Big Apple skyline trailing banners, and served free coffee on Wall Street in the thick of winter from a Martinson bus. By the 1940s, the company was in full swing.

Joe died in 1949, just before the completion of his large new roasting and blending warehouse at 190 Franklin St. in Greenwich Village. Since then, the company has been sold several times. In our most recent phone chat, John Martinson tells me he's heard via the grapevine that Martinson Coffee may once again be for sale. "I should give them a call," says John, adding, "The coffee would need to be improved and marketed the way Joe did."

By the way, to make a terrific cup of coffee, use my method: Using a paper filter, pour 1 cup (250 mL) of boiling water over 1½ tablespoons (22 mL) of my favourite blend: half Brazilian Santos and half espresso beans, ground fine.

Here's a great cake to accompany your cup of joe.

Sour Cream Coffee Cake

Based on the recipe by Toronto's cooking and baking maven in her book Lillian Kaplun's Kitchen, *I like to bake this in a small bundt or tube pan—about 8 inches (20 cm) in diameter—as it gives the prettiest shape. You can use chopped walnuts instead of chocolate chips, if desired. Best served—with a cup of joe, of course—the day it's baked.*

1 cup (250 mL) sour cream
1 tsp (5 mL) baking soda
2 cups (500 mL) cake and pastry flour
Pinch of salt
2 tsp (10 mL) baking powder
1/2 cup (125 mL) unsalted butter
1 cup (250 mL) less 2 tbsp (30 mL)
   granulated sugar
2 eggs
1 tsp (5 mL) vanilla extract

FILLING
1/4 cup (50 mL) brown sugar
2 tbsp (30 mL) cocoa powder
1 tsp (5 mL) ground cinnamon
1/2 cup (125 mL) semisweet chopped
   chocolate or chocolate chips
   (optional)
Icing sugar for dusting

1. Preheat oven to 350°F (180°C).
2. In small bowl, combine sour cream and baking soda.
3. In medium bowl, sift together flour, salt and baking powder.
4. In large bowl, using electric mixer, cream butter until soft. Add granulated sugar; beat until light and fluffy. Beat in eggs, one at a time, then vanilla. Fold in dry ingredients alternately with sour cream mixture.
5. In small bowl, combine filling ingredients.
6. Grease and lightly dust with flour an 8-inch (20 cm) bundt pan, 9-inch (23 cm) square baking pan or 9-inch (23 cm) round springform pan. Spread half of batter in pan; sprinkle filling mixture on top. Spread with remaining batter.
7. Bake for about 40 minutes or until tester comes out clean. Cool in pan on wire rack. Invert onto plate. Dust with icing sugar.

MAKES 8 TO 10 SERVINGS.

HEARTBURN AND HEARTACHE IN MOTOR CITY

❊ I RETURNED FROM A RECENT VISIT TO Detroit beset by two feelings: heartburn and heartache.

The former was the result of this city's definitive culinary experience: a spicy, late-night chili dog consumed at American Coney Island—a huge, neon-lit, 24-hour fast food emporium located at the heart of what remains of Detroit's downtown.

The bittersweet emotion came from exploring and embracing a once famously vibrant metropolis now struggling to recover from decades of decay.

Here, what some call "fabulous ruins" have replaced a once-booming Motor City in which the pulsing vibe of Motown had its home and where big money lavishly constructed some of the most stunning art deco edifices I've seen. Instead, there are now boarded-up buildings scrawled with graffiti, half-finished construction sites and derelict, deserted stores at every turn. Still, I can't wait to go back. In just three days, Detroit captured and enraptured me, body and soul.

My trip was inspired by friend, fellow food writer and proud Detroiter, Patty LaNoue Stearns. "I want to show you my Detroit," she vowed as we met up in places like Atlanta, New York and Las Vegas at various conferences for food journalists in recent years. Stearns grew up in Allen Park, a Detroit suburb she calls "a white-bread, 'Leave It to Beaver' bungalow community of solid, middle-class families."

A journalist for 30 years, she spent many of them writing about food for the *Detroit Free Press* while residing in the city's hub. Today, she lives with her husband, Joe, in Traverse City—a resort in northern Michigan—where she's a freelance writer at *Traverse* magazine. But she still loves, and misses, her hometown. "For the longest time, Detroit was known as 'the murder cap'tal,' especially in the '70s," Stearns begins. "Even though many cities have surpassed it, it still has that scary reputation. But I've never been scared here." She cites the loss of business by major car manufacturers to Japan, a large exodus that followed and the tragic five-day race riot in 1967 as key causes of an economic demise that's in stark contrast to the spectacular boom of earlier decades. For Stearns, "Detroit has a raw, industrial energy that I love. It can be bleak but, at times, it makes you believe anything can happen here."

The city is more than 80 percent African-American. "There were no black people where I grew up," she explains. "I've always found their culture exciting, rich and friendly." Which goes for Detroit in general. "I love its grittiness," she continues. "It has a very diverse population of no-nonsense people." Patty cites a lively Arab population that includes "the largest community of Iraqis outside Baghdad" and insists we stop by the hugely popular, Lebanese-owned La Shish restaurant—one of two locations—in the suburb of West Dearborn.

Here, two big rooms are abuzz at early dinner. Low-slung lampshades dripping with coloured beads, lush wall-hangings and an open hearth where sweet-smelling pita rounds are baking, make us feel at home. Lemon-laced tabbouleh, succulent roast lamb and killer kebabs are among the best Middle Eastern fare I've tasted.

The next day, we wander from our downtown hotel to Greektown where Monroe St. gives new meaning to the term "restaurant row." At the New Parthenon, our server gives the traditional "Opa!" whoop as he delivers the luscious flaming cheese called saganaki. Later, I nibble on chocolate pistachio baklava from the neighbouring Astoria Pastry Shop. This syrupy, crunchy delicacy may entice me back to Detroit for it alone.

I haven't finished gazing at the gorgeous—and wondrously subversive— murals in the Detroit Institute of Arts' giant atrium commissioned by Henry Ford's son Edsel and painted by Mexican socialist Diego Rivera in the 1930s. And I can't wait to sip coffee again in the lobby of the beautifully restored art deco Fisher Theatre. And to dine at upscale soul food restaurant Sweet Georgia Brown.

Then there are those "Coneys," Detroit's most famous food. Dan Keros, the affable, garrulous man whose grandfather opened American Coney Island in 1917, owns and operates this busy landmark where his son Chris also works. He lists famous customers like Eminem, Bill Cosby, Jeff Daniels and Mike Ilitch along with the city's late African-American mayor Coleman Young. "He came here for 20 years," Keros notes. "He used to say, 'This was the only place, when I was being raised, that would treat us equal.'" Keros cites the grilled frankfurter "made from 80 percent beef, 10 percent pork and no lips, snouts or tails—just cuts of meat—in a lamb casing" as key to the hot dog's "great taste and snap." Belgian-style yellow mustard, sweet Vidalia onions, no-bean chili and a steamed bun, washed down with a mandatory beer, have "limos lined up here at night," he says.

"Where else can you get waited on by a waiter or waitress and get a hot dog?" Dan asks with a grin. I'll be back for one of his famous Coneys, but this time I'll nosh on my fiery chili dog at lunch.

Michigan is the top U.S. producer of cherries. Here's a recipe from Patty LaNoue Stearns's cookbook *Cherry Home Companion*.

Patty's Zippy Pork Tenderloin

Two 12 oz (375 g) pork tenderloins
1¹/₂ cups (375 mL) orange juice
Grated rind of 1 orange
¹/₄ cup (50 mL) dried cherries, chopped

1 jalapeno pepper, seeded, finely chopped
2 tbsp (30 mL) extra-virgin olive oil
Vegetable oil
Salt and freshly ground pepper
3 tbsp (45 mL) whipping cream

1. Slice each tenderloin down the centre almost, but not right through; open each like a book. Place in shallow glass baking dish.

2. In small bowl, whisk together orange juice, rind, cherries, jalapeno and olive oil. Pour over tenderloins. Turn to coat. Cover with plastic wrap. Chill 2 to 4 hours.

3. Preheat broiler. Grease rack in broiler pan with vegetable oil.

4. Remove tenderloins from marinade; reserve marinade. Place tenderloins on prepared rack. Sprinkle with salt and pepper. Place pan several inches from broiler. Broil 6 to 8 minutes per side, or until meat is almost cooked through.

5. Pour reserved marinade into small saucepan. Bring to boil over medium-high heat; cook until reduced by half, about 7 minutes. Reduce heat to low. Stir in cream. Cook, stirring, until slightly thickened, about 2 minutes. Add salt and pepper to taste. Slice tenderloins on diagonal. Pour sauce over top.

MAKES 4 SERVINGS.

ECCLES TAKES THE CAKE

"*The Eccles Cake is a small round cake made of buttery flaky pastry with a filling of currants. It takes its name from Eccles, a town in Greater Manchester (a notable baking area), and was reputedly invented by the cookery writer Elizabeth Raffald (1733–81), who spent most of her working life in Manchester.*" – *A Gourmet's Guide* by John Ayto.

❋ I LOOKED AROUND FOR MY MOTHER. She'd stopped dead in her tracks behind me a few steps from the check-out counter at the giant Marks & Spencer's in downtown Manchester where we'd just made our purchase: one freshly baked Eccles Cake from the bakery section. Holding her half of that small pastry in one hand and letting a few stray currants drop to the ground, my diminutive, silver-haired mum fixed her baby blues on me and announced, complete with pregnant pause, "You know dear, I think this is the best thing I've ever eaten."

For some reason, this grandiose statement made us break into uncontrollable giggles. It was a wonderful moment. We had bonded over my latest culinary mission: the search for the ultimate Eccles Cake.

It all began at the beginning of my two-week visit to the U.K. in August. While planning a couple of expeditions in the living room of Mum's North London home, I had expressed a wish to visit Manchester: a place where neither of us had been. That formerly bleak industrial town known for its once "dark Satanic mills," the musical Gallagher brothers, ladism and a popular football team, had, I'd heard, experienced a recent facelift and, more important, become a haven for foodies and budding chefs.

Ever the avid collector of newspaper clippings, my mum pulled out a two-page spread she'd culled from the *Observer*. This guide to Manchester included tips on where to stay (we took their advice and spent a wondrous night at the centrally located, French-owned Malmaison), how to catch a glimpse of Victoria and David Beckham at tony boutiques Geese and Oyster, and the following short item. For a food sleuth like moi, its words were irresistible: "For food, head for Eccles, find the Old Bradburn Bakery (now Hampsons) where you can buy Manchester's answer to sachertorte—the Eccles Cake."

Which explains our visit to Marks & Sparks, the first stop on our cake-sleuthing itinerary and a place recommended for this mission by a young woman at Manchester's downtown tourist information office. 'Twas she who told us the Eccles Cake's nickname is "dead fly pie" because of its currant filling.

Next, it was on to the town of Eccles. It's the last stop on the GO-style train that travels to several small towns and villages on Manchester's outskirts, including Salford, home to the famous gallery displaying the works of the late local artist L.S. Lowry. Newspaper clipping in hand and mother in tow, I headed to the tiny "main street" of Eccles in search of Hampsons bakery. There it was—a small, sanitized outlet of a Lancashire chain specializing in all things pie. Meat pies, sausage rolls, Cornish pasties and fruit pies filled its shelves. And yes, they had Eccles Cakes—but a rather dry, tasteless specimen, Mum and I mused as we each munched on one, compared with the flaky, flavour-packed version from M & S.

Freshness is key, I soon discovered, when it comes to this dessert. In fact, I'll say it now: A fresh Eccles Cake is a beautiful thing. A stale one is to be avoided at all costs. Noting that the *Observer's* comparison with the lofty sachertorte was ringing a tad hollow, I decided to scour the town of Eccles for a better representative of the pastry that bears its name.

"You could try the supermarket, Morrison's, right next to the railway tracks," said an elderly woman helpfully when pressed for info. Sure enough, this spacious supermarket's bakery department—testimony to the British people's sweet tooth—was a dessert sleuth's nirvana. It yielded three brands of jam roly-poly, Bakewell Tarts in five flavours, all manner of puddings from sticky toffee to Spotted Dick and—you guessed—four brands of Eccles Cakes. Leaving a trail of currants, Mum and I nibbled our way through all of them. The best by far, made in nearby Wigan by Lowthers, came in a package of four small pastries and cost a mere $2.

Back in London, I was having lunch with British food writer Nigel Slater later that week when talk turned to my favourite topic. "You have to try the Eccles Cake at St. John restaurant," he insisted. The next day, Mum and I found ourselves perusing the menu at this elegantly simple but pricey eatery near Smithfield Market, dedicated to foods British in general and things offal in particular.

On which matter, a word of advice: Don't order, as my poor mum did, the Stinking Bishop and Potatoes—a large mound of soft, smelly cheese with a side dish of boiled fingerling potatoes. I can't speak for Rolled Pig's Spleen and Bacon, Deep-Fried Sand Eels or Duck Neck with Green Beans. However, the Eccles Cake, served with a large slice of tangy Lancashire cheese, is top-notch—a biggish, round pocket of crisp puff pastry encasing a deeply deli-cious currant mixture spiked with lemon juice and allspice. At $3 a pop, the cakes are available to take home from the restaurant's bakery.

By the way, my mother's last words to me as I approached the min-cab en route to Heathrow were, "I think I'll heat up that last Eccles Cake, dear, and have it with a cup of tea." You, too, can savour this sweet experience with the help of my recipe. Here it is—and darned good, too, if I say so myself.

Eccles Cakes

If you're a pastry chef or want to be a hero, you can make the dough. However, perfectly good frozen pastry dough is sold in most supermarkets. The pastry chef at St. John restaurant lets the currant mixture sit overnight, once cooked, to let flavours mellow.

1 tsp (5 mL) unsalted butter
1½ cups (375 mL) currants
⅓ cup (75 mL) chopped mixed peel
1 tsp (5 mL) ground nutmeg
1 tsp (5 mL) ground allspice
1 tsp (5 mL) ground ginger

Juice of ½ a lemon
14 oz (397 g) package frozen puff
  pastry
1 egg white, lightly beaten
Fruit (superfine) sugar for dusting

1. Preheat oven to 425°F (220°C).

2. In a saucepan, melt butter. Add currants, mixed peel, nutmeg, allspice, ginger and lemon juice. Stir to combine.

3. Roll pastry to about ⅛-inch (3 mm) thickness on floured surface. Using a drinking glass, cut circles 3 to 4 inches (8 to 10 cm) in diameter to make about 20. Place a rounded tablespoonful of currant mixture in middle of half the pastry circles and moisten edges of each with water. Place remaining circles on top, crimping edges to seal. Brush tops with beaten egg white; dust with fruit sugar. With sharp paring knife, cut two or three parallel slits on top of each.

4. Brush large baking sheet(s) with water. Place Eccles Cakes on sheets and bake about 15 minutes, or until puffed and golden.

MAKES ABOUT 20.

MY NANNY'S RASPBERRY PIE

❋ EVELYN SMAIL HAS BEEN DRIVING HER aging, slightly rickety Ford sedan slowly along the bumpy country road for several miles. I'm her lucky passenger, happy to be sitting beside her on this sunny midsummer afternoon, glad to be along for the ride amid the gorgeous countryside of the St. Lawrence Valley about 60 kilometres south of Ottawa and an hour's drive from the Quebec border. I'm content to savour the peace and quiet while she points out an occasional landmark: the wood-frame, one-room school she attended; the little church hall where she helps out at strawberry socials and turkey suppers; and big mounds of freshly bailed hay that dot the fields belonging to friends she's known all her life.

She has just stopped at the home of one such buddy, Alan Groves, to ask directions. Our destination: a farm, located in the tiny village of Lunenburg, which my grandparents once owned and where I spent a few summers as a young child. Moments later, a ruddy-cheeked man emerges from the compact farmhouse and, smiling, comes to greet us. As he leans into the car on Evelyn's side, she shares some small talk. Then, after a pregnant pause, she cuts to the chase:

"Al, remember the time I went to Montreal to mind that baby all those years ago?"

"Yep, I think I do," Al replies with an affable grin.

"Well," she continues, speaking slowly and turning to me with perfect dramatic timing, "Here she is."

I don't know who felt more proud at that moment, Evelyn or I, but I will say it was one of the sweetest moments of my life.

It turns out Al knows the way to the farm of my childhood and informs us it's only a kilometre or two away. At this point, Evelyn's recall of our itinerary kicks in and we're away to the races—at about 40 km an hour, that is.

Sure enough, I can vaguely remember the big verandah and gingerbread second-floor balcony of the farmhouse my grandfather Aaron Nisse bought soon after he settled in Montreal, having fled Latvia during the Holocaust. He bought the place in 1942 from a fellow Jewish refugee called Ben Baikowitz who was having trouble making enough money from the small mixed farm to buy feed for his animals.

My tall, handsome grandfather, known for his business acumen and the wicked twinkle in his bright blue eyes, had a favourite adage: "Do me ein favour, I'll do you ein favour," which I recall him uttering often in his distinctive German/Russian accent. In keeping with this tried-and-true strategy, he paid Baikowitz a nominal sum for the farm on one condition: that our family be allowed to spend summers there.

It was during one such visit that my parents met Evelyn, who had a job cleaning and shopping for the Baikowitzes. My father, then a medical student, had the bright idea of asking her to come to Montreal as a nanny for me, with whom my mother was pregnant.

Although Evelyn's parents, Nolan and Pearl Rupert, were nervous about sending their daughter off to the "big smoke," the pretty, auburn-haired 17-year-old arrived later that summer to live with us at my grandparents' elegant home in Snowdon. She had never seen an escalator and, she adds shyly, "never even drunk a Coke," but soon took to city life and stayed almost two years.

"I loved it," Evelyn recalls. "I had a friend from Cornwall who was looking after a baby next door and we would take the bus downtown, go shopping and walk to Mount Royal."

She and I became so close that my mother now admits she was jealous. But when my dad got a job in Halifax, Evelyn decided to return home. She began working at the nearby linen mill in the small town of Iroquois and soon met Will Smail whom she married in 1949.

They moved to his family's farm in the tiny village of Brinston not far from where she grew up. The couple raised purebred Holstein dairy cattle and grew corn, hay and oats to feed them.

If you're wondering how Evelyn and I connected after more than 50 years, it was her doing.

I was in the studio of an Ottawa TV station about five years ago to talk up my cookbook *The Best of Food* when a middle-aged cameraman wearing a baseball cap squeezed a crumpled piece of paper into my hand. On it were the names and phone numbers of Evelyn and her daughter Kathy. The reunion a few months later at her Brinston home was tender and tearful. These days, I visit each summer. We keep in touch by phone and the memories are sweet when I bake her wonderful country version of Raspberry Cream Pie.

Raspberry Cream Pie

To streamline, use store-bought frozen pie shell and instant custard powder. Use homo or 2 percent milk, not skim. Egg whites should be at room temperature before beating for meringue. This is best eaten the day it's made.

9-inch (23 cm) unbaked pie shell
2 large eggs, separated
2 tbsp + 1 tsp (35 mL) cornstarch
2 cups (500 mL) milk
1/2 cup (125 mL) granulated sugar
1 tsp (5 mL) vanilla extract

Pinch of salt
2 cups (500 mL) fresh raspberries

MERINGUE
2 tbsp (30 mL) granulated sugar
1/4 tsp (1 mL) cream of tartar

1. Preheat oven to 400°F (200°C).

2. Prick pie shell all over bottom and sides with fork. (If dough puffs up after 5 minutes, prick more holes.) Bake about 8 to 10 minutes or until golden brown. Cool.

3. In medium bowl, whisk together egg yolks and cornstarch until smooth.

4. In medium saucepan, cook milk, sugar, vanilla and salt over medium heat, whisking at intervals, until mixture just begins to bubble. Gradually add about one-third of mixture to egg yolk mixture in bowl, whisking constantly. Return to milk mixture in saucepan; cook over medium heat, whisking constantly, until mixture just begins to bubble again. Reduce heat to low; cook, whisking constantly, until slightly thickened, about 3 minutes. Transfer to bowl; let custard cool at least 30 minutes.

5. Spread half of cooled custard into pie shell; smooth top. Arrange raspberries on top in even layer. Spread remaining custard over raspberries.

6. For meringue: In medium bowl, using electric or hand mixer, beat egg whites, sugar and cream of tartar until stiff peaks form. Spread mixture evenly on top of pie. Return to oven; bake 5 to 8 minutes or until peaks are browned. Chill in fridge at least 30 minutes before serving.

MAKES ABOUT 6 SERVINGS.

GIRLS JUST WANNA HAVE FOOD

✳ I UNLOCKED AND OPENED THE FRONT door, as usual. As usual, I stepped inside. I hung my jacket on the usual hook. That was when my usual homecoming ritual came to an abrupt end.

Looking down, I glimpsed 10 pairs of running shoes lined up in raggle-taggle rows against the wall. As I entered the hallway, the thumping bass and raw male voices of hip-hop music emanating from the living room stereo assailed my ears. Approaching the kitchen, I saw the source: The girls were in the house.

Suddenly, I remembered something a slightly scatter-brained woman with a lot on her plate can be forgiven for forgetting: This was a PD day at my daughter Ruthie's downtown high school and she had gathered a gaggle of Grade 10 girlfriends at this, the appointed time, for a potluck meal. How could I—who frequently and passionately urges anyone who'll listen to celebrate community, friendship or just being together over heaping plates of good food—be anything but joyful at the sight before my eyes?

Even as I nervously eyed the array of half-empty Tupperware containers and wondered what my kitchen would look like at meal's end, my heart melted when 10 beautiful, smiling faces turned toward me and, almost in unison above the musical din, chanted, "Hi, Ms. Kane!"

That said, the lively medley of noise—hip-hop mingled with screams and laughter—quickly inspired me to hot-foot it to the downtown Y. When I returned, the kitchen was spotless and I sat down for a chat with this terrific group of teens.

Darakhshan Ansari supplied samosas—a three-cornered, deep-fried pastry encasing spicy meat and/or vegetables—as appetizer for the communal repast. Although she was born here, her parents are both from India and cook all manner of curries, roti and rice dishes. "My family loves to entertain," she says. "For special occasions, we have dishes like biryani and my father sometimes makes samosas." Ansari concedes this "takes a long time. He makes the dough for the wrappers ahead, then fills them with spiced potatoes. We sometimes buy samosas at Brar Sweets on Islington Ave. in Rexdale."

Karen Nguyen (pronounced "Win"), whose parents are from Vietnam, was also born here. Dinner at her home "is based around steamed rice" and often consists of stir-fries made with meat, vegetables, fish or tofu and a small bowl of broth on the side. On Saturday, about 20 family members gather at her grandmother's house for dinner at which the traditional Vietnamese noodle soup *pho* is a staple. For the potluck, Nguyen brought pink squares of tasty "Vietnamese jell-o" made with gelatin, coconut milk, vanilla and what she calls "a sweet leaf."

Ana-Maria Yoon, born in Buenos Aires, came here as a young child. Her parents are Korean and so is most of the food at home. Rice, she says, is mandatory at meals. It's usually accompanied by the wonderful Korean spiced cabbage *kimchee*, some kind of stir-fry and all manner of condiments such as pickles and dried seaweed squares. Yoon's potluck contribution was Korean deep-fried potato pancakes traditionally eaten with soy sauce and/or ketchup for dipping.

Canadian-born Marwa Eldardiry's parents hail from Egypt. Having tried her mother's wonderful stuffed grape leaves and other goodies, I know that some pretty fine Middle Eastern cooking goes on in the home. I didn't get too far asking how to make the delicious dessert—"coconut squares made with milk"—that Eldardiry brought that day. Says she, "I don't know how my mom makes it—I just eat it."

Natali Luzardo, born in Havana, has an exotic heritage. Her mother, with whom she lives, is from St. Petersburg, Russia; her father is Cuban. She came to Canada at age 4. "My mom is a trained chef," she says proudly. "She cooks Russian food—pierogi like I brought today, borscht with lots of vegetables in it, smoked salmon with pickles and cheese—and Cuban dishes like beans with rice, very good guacamole and lots of things with jalapeños."

Born in her parents' hometown of Tirane, Albania, Blerina Fani came here four years ago. She tells me, "Albania is a small country next to Italy." This explains her mother's Mediterranean style of cooking: "At meals, there's usually pasta or rice. We often eat stuffed peppers and the dish I brought to the potluck: baked eggplant stuffed with feta, eggs and parsley."

Although Corinne Aberdeen was born in Toronto, most of her family still lives in her mother's native country, Grenada. Not surprisingly, much of the food her mom cooks includes Caribbean dishes like curried chicken, roti and, she notes, "rice and peas every Sunday." On visits to Grenada, she says with a smile, "It's lots and lots of mangoes." She brought a big fruit salad to the feast. Aberdeen especially enjoys Caribbean cuisine, she adds, "because it's a link that reminds me of my roots."

This sentiment is echoed by Samitha Sundarajah, whose parents are from Madras, India, where she was born. She and her mother are vegetarians so "lots of rice, *dahl* (curried lentils) and spiced vegetables like potatoes, greens and cauliflower" are staples at home where both parents cook. Sundarajah, who enjoys cooking, brought fried potatoes and fish cutlets to the potluck. "A lot of people, especially my parents' friends, don't think I'm Indian enough because I don't speak the language," she explains, "so, by being able to make Indian food, it's a substitute. It helps me know my culture."

Sylvia Kim came here from South Korea at age 8 and lives with her father and brother. Her single dad does the cooking. "He makes Korean food," she says, "mostly big bowls of soup with noodles, fish or meat." She contributed chicken teriyaki with green and red peppers to the group meal and is learning to prepare dishes from a Korean cookbook her dad bought. "My family— uncles, aunts, cousins—expect me to cook Korean dishes like *kimchee* from scratch because it's traditional. Sometimes they're appalled I don't know how to cook all the dishes yet. I will learn. I just need my dad's patience."

The last word goes to the potluck host—my Canadian-born offspring Ruthie Anderson—whose mother is Jewish and father a fifth-generation Anglo-Canadian. She relishes the chance to share food experiences with her diverse group of friends. "I try as often as possible to stay over or have dinner at friends' houses," she explains. "I try new dishes that other Canadians might not. My Asian friends are surprised I can use chopsticks and many are surprised I'm open to trying unusual foods." The potluck was a way to bond while breaking bread. "Keeping up with schoolwork and extra-curriculars, it's very hard to get everyone together to relax and chill," she adds. "When it does happen it leaves me—and, I know, many of my friends—with a very good feeling."

And that includes me. Here are two recipes from that lovely event.

Samosas

2 medium new potatoes, scrubbed
1 tbsp (15 mL) fennel seeds
1 tbsp (15 mL) ground cumin
1/2 tsp (2 mL) ground turmeric
2 tbsp (30 mL) vegetable oil
1 onion, finely chopped
2 to 3 fresh hot green chiles (e.g.
   jalapeno), seeded, finely chopped
3 cloves garlic, finely chopped
2 tsp (10 mL) finely chopped fresh
ginger root
1/2 cup (125 mL) frozen peas
Salt and freshly ground pepper to
   taste

10 sheets phyllo dough
1/2 cup (125 mL) unsalted butter,
   melted

YOGURT DIPPING SAUCE
3/4 cup (175 mL) plain yogurt
2 tbsp (30 mL) each finely chopped
   fresh coriander and mint
1 hot green chile (e.g. jalapeno),
   seeded, finely chopped
1 1/2 tsp (7 mL) fresh lemon juice
1/4 tsp (1 mL) salt

1. For dipping sauce: In a bowl, whisk together all ingredients. Chill.

2. For samosas: In saucepan, place potatoes in cold, salted water to cover and bring to a boil. Reduce heat to low; simmer until soft, about 15 minutes. Cool. Cut into 1/4-inch (5 mm) cubes.

3. In large skillet, toast fennel seeds, cumin and turmeric over medium heat, stirring, until fragrant, about 3 minutes. Stir in oil, onion, chiles, garlic and ginger root. Reduce heat to medium-low; cook about 3 minutes. Stir in cooked potatoes and 1/4 cup (50 mL) water; cook for 2 minutes, stirring. Remove from heat. Stir in peas. Cool. Add salt and pepper.

4. Preheat oven to 400°F (200°C).

5. Place 1 sheet of phyllo on work surface. Brush with melted butter. Top with second sheet of phyllo; brush with melted butter. Cut crosswise into 5 strips. Place 1 tbsp (15 mL) filling near one corner of each strip; fold corner over to enclose filling and form a triangle; continue folding strip, maintaining triangle shape. Place seam side down on greased, rimmed baking sheet. Continue with remaining phyllo, melted butter and filling. Place on baking sheets. Brush tops with melted butter. Bake in centre of oven about 10 minutes or until golden. Serve with dipping sauce.

MAKES 25.

Tropical Fruit Salad

This recipe can be halved or doubled easily. I often add brandy and/or orange liqueur. To toast coconut, cook in large skillet over medium-low heat 5 minutes or until golden. Serve with vanilla ice cream or thickened, sweetened yogurt made by straining plain yogurt through a coffee filter set over a cup for about 30 minutes, then adding a little vanilla extract and maple syrup.

2 medium mangoes, peeled, diced
1 pineapple, peeled, cored, diced
2 cups (500 mL) hulled strawberries, halved
4 kiwifruit, peeled, quartered
1 tbsp (15 mL) fresh lemon juice
1/3 cup (75 mL) unsweetened mango or other tropical juice

1 tbsp (15 mL) liquid honey or maple syrup
1 tsp (5 mL) grated fresh ginger root, (optional)
3/4 cup (175 mL) unsweetened dried flaked coconut, toasted

1. Place fruit in large serving bowl.
2. In small bowl, whisk together lemon juice, mango juice, honey and ginger root (if using). Add to fruit. Stir gently to coat. Just before serving, sprinkle with toasted coconut.

MAKES 8 TO 10 SERVINGS.

ℰℬ

DIET DÉJÀ VU ALL OVER AGAIN

✻ WHEN IT COMES TO THAT PESKY, all too prevalent Atkins diet, mine is a clear case of "been there, done that."

In fact, I may have been one of the first people to try this questionable weight loss plan more than 30 years ago when its creator, the late Dr. Robert Atkins, first published his low-carb, high-protein regimen as the *Dr. Atkins Diet Revolution.*

I had just given birth to my older daughter, Esther, and felt this would be the ideal way to shed some of the 22 kilos I'd gained during a blissful pregnancy. I say blissful because I had the healthy resilience of youth and a body that relished having a bun in the oven. I surrendered happily to food cravings in the belief that, if I was going to be spherical in shape, I may as well enjoy it. And spherical I became.

The extra weight, comprised mostly of a huge bulge in the middle of my short frame, was caused by two things: regular servings of french fries and a daily wedge of coconut cream pie consumed at the Chinese-Canadian diner on the main street of the small Northern Ontario town in which I lived. (A disclaimer: I don't recommend these two items as diet staples. I'm just telling the truth to make a point.)

One late night, a frantic visit to the local french fry truck announced the imminent birth of my beautiful daughter. Almond-eyed, with a thick shock of black hair, she weighed in at a dainty 3 kilos. A few months later, I embraced the Atkins diet: plenty of protein-packed meat, poultry, fish, eggs and cheese with nary a worry about fat. Carbs weren't allowed, so no bread, potatoes, grains or sugary foods, including carrots and fruit. No-carb veggies like cabbage, greens and eggplant were okay.

For a few weeks, I loved my meals of bacon and eggs, steak with gorgonzola sauce, crispy chicken wings and salad doused in dressing. Then one afternoon, I found myself leaning on the walls of my home for support. I got into my car, which drove me to the nearby 7-11. I snatched a Sara Lee chocolate cake from the freezer, took it home and ate the whole thing.

Although I had lost a good chunk of excess weight, I vowed never to diet —this or any other way—again.

Like most women, I have days when I wish I resembled Catherine Zeta-Jones—a star with at least some flesh on her bones—but I have no truck with support meetings, food diaries or any eating plan that excludes most of my favourite foods. But whaddya know, the Atkins diet is back in vogue. With the likes of Jennifer Aniston and Gerri Halliwell touting its virtues, it's a horrible case of diet déjà vu. All this in the face of expert warnings that it may be dangerous to your health. Not to mention the fact that the weight usually returns once a more balanced diet is resumed.

So here's the positive part of today's rant:

I urge all those who aren't unhealthily overweight to stay away from diets. Enjoy your food by choosing tasty, fresh, locally grown and, when possible, organic ingredients. With them, prepare balanced meals loaded with taste and texture that will satisfy both body and soul. Main course salads like a wonderful chicken Caesar, Asian beef or wheat berry bean made with lots of veggies and some kind of protein are a great idea.

Here's one that's tried and true. Easy to make, it uses green beans, a high-fibre and high-flavour veggie. Great served with hunks of wholegrain bread.

Salade Nicoise

You could use grape or cherry tomatoes, whole or halved. Romaine or leaf lettuce, or a mixture, would be fine.

1 lb (500 g) unpeeled baby new
  potatoes, scrubbed
12 oz (375 g) green beans, stems
  removed
1 head Boston lettuce, torn
  about 5 cups (1.25 L)
5 plum tomatoes, cut in wedges
Half small red onion, thinly sliced
3 cans (each 170 g) chunk white
  tuna, drained
¼ cup (50 mL) pitted, cured black
  olives

3 hard-boiled eggs, peeled, quartered
6 anchovy fillets, rinsed, drained
  and patted dry (optional)

DRESSING
¼ cup (50 mL) wine vinegar
1 tbsp (15 mL) Dijon mustard
1 clove garlic, minced
¼ tsp (1 mL) each salt and freshly
  ground black pepper
½ cup (125 mL) extra virgin olive oil

1. In saucepan, bring potatoes to boil in salted water to cover. Cook 12 to 15 minutes or until tender. With slotted spoon, transfer to bowl. Add green beans to saucepan. Return to boil; cook about 4 minutes, or until tender-crisp. Drain. Refresh under cold running water; drain.

2. For dressing: In small bowl, whisk together vinegar, mustard, garlic, salt and pepper. Gradually add oil; whisk until blended.

3. Toss lettuce with 3 spoonfuls of dressing. Arrange lettuce on large serving platter or in decorative bowl. Halve potatoes. Arrange mounds of potatoes, green beans, tomatoes, onions and tuna chunks on lettuce. Scatter olives over top. Arrange eggs around edge. If using anchovies, place in X pattern on top. Drizzle with remaining dressing.

MAKES 4 TO 6 MAIN COURSE SERVINGS.

FRIDGE ARTIFACTS

✳ It is 1976.

The year the Parti Québecois is voted into power for the first time in Quebec, Rene Levesque becomes premier of that province and the Summer Olympics are held in Montreal.

Mao Zedong, chairman of the People's Republic of China, dies and Jimmy Carter is elected 39th president of the United States.

"Rocky", "Taxi Driver" and "All the President's Men" are among the year's hot movies, and "One Flew Over the Cuckoo's Nest" cleans up at the Academy Awards.

The Montreal Canadiens beat the Philadelphia Flyers to win the Stanley Cup.

Caesar Salad, pasta primavera and carrot cake are popular foods.

But more important to me—and utterly amazing, I've realized, to family and friends—1976 was the year my mother gave me a big jar of her home-made brandied cherries, some of which are alive, well and still residing in my fridge!

It was my recent, annual clean-out-the-fridge routine—the only New Year's ritual with which I have any truck—that yielded the ever-dwindling stash of these wondrously well-preserved fruit. And, as I opened the small glass bottle, allowing the sweet, boozy aroma within to waft my way, I popped a couple of these still delectable, firm-textured morsels into my mouth as I do each year at fridge-cleaning time.

"I can barely remember making them," replied my mother when I called her at her home in London, England, to chat about these amazing vintage confections. Then the high-school biology teacher in her kicked in as she recalled the recipe she'd used from her well-worn copy of *The Settlement Cookbook* compiled for the Milwaukee Public School Kitchens by Mrs. Simon Kander. "There are two reasons those cherries could last all these years," she began. "Both the sugar syrup I used and alcohol from the brandy would kill any bacteria cells. Nothing could survive in there." Then came the real surprise. "You know, dear," she added sweetly, "you didn't need to keep those cherries in the fridge. As long as the lid was tightly closed, they'd be fine

---

stored in the kitchen on a shelf." As I hung up the phone and slowly spat out the pits from a few more cherries, I tried to digest this fact. Then I got on with the purge of my fridge.

Right at the back, behind the slew of mustards, sauces, jellies and jams, were two small jars of capers that I neatly consolidated into one and resolved to use in my next batch of pasta puttanesca. The many aging veggies in the crispers, I promised myself, would be roasted and used in soup. As for the five tubs of bananas I'd frozen at least a year ago that were languishing in the dark depths of my freezer, those would wind up fruitfully as chocolate-spiked banana bread.

My recent discussions with friends about their fridges yielded similar themes. One, a brilliant cook and part-time caterer, has a big fridge. "It has practically my whole life in it for the past five years," she claims with a chuckle. As is often the case, condiments loom large. "I recently found a jar of bright green relish I once used on barbecued hot dogs," she explains, "and a bottle of salsa with fur on top."

Another friend echoes this theme. "Lots of old pestos, capers, molasses— whoever uses all of it?—and a bottle of beet juice I once bought on a health kick" are in the far reaches of her fridge. She was surprised recently to discover "a bowl of fat from a goose I roasted in 2001." She reckons "everyone has an old container of tofu in their fridge," and speaks for many when she adds, "I know the minute I throw out one of these foods, I'll be using a recipe that calls for it."

Sometimes, an attachment to a vintage food can run deep. One Jewish friend tells how her mother's sister escaped the Holocaust when she left her home in Morocco, entered the medical corps and assumed a new identity. After 50 years and much sleuthing, this friend found her aunt living in Toulouse. "She had a fig tree in her garden and sent me delicious homemade jam from it for several years," she explains. When the aunt moved to an apartment with no such tree, the jam gifts stopped. Today, my friend keeps a little of that precious preserve in her fridge.

Here are some tips on how to recycle forgotten foods in your fridge and freezer, followed by some great recipes.

• SOUP: Start by sautéeing a couple of chopped onions and some chopped garlic, then add whatever veggies you have on hand, cut in chunks, along with seasoning and stock or water to cover. Cook until soft and purée all or part of soup. Add chopped leftover meat, if desired, and cook until heated through. Leftover salad, with its dressing, can be added, too.

• ROASTED VEGETABLES: Carrots, parsnips, rutabaga, beets, fennel and onions are great cut in uniform chunks, tossed with oil and seasonings, then roasted in a single layer at 425°F (220°C) for about 40 minutes. Eat as is, add to salads, soup or pasta sauce, or use in vegetable lasagna.

• STIR-FRIES: Stir-fry leftover meat or seafood in hot wok. Remove meat, then stir-fry vegetables, adding hardest ones first. Return meat to wok; add sauce made by combining: 1 tsp (5 mL) each: hoisin, oyster and soy sauces, and cornstarch and 1 tbsp (15 mL) Chinese cooking wine with a little granulated sugar and black pepper. Cook until thickened.

Here are three great recipes for recycling some common fridge finds, followed by the prescription for those famous cherries.

Hot and Sour Soup

I slightly adapted this recipe from avid, ace cook Sarah Ramsey. I used half chicken stock, half water. Feel free to add leftover chicken, shredded or cut in chunks, and canned water chestnuts or bamboo shoots for a nice crunch. Dried shiitake or wood ear mushrooms, soaked for 20 minutes in warm water, are traditional in this. They and the black vinegar are sold in Chinatowns or Asian food markets.

2 tbsp (30 mL) vegetable oil
2 tbsp (30 mL) grated fresh ginger
   root
2 cloves garlic, chopped
2 cups (500 mL) mushrooms, sliced
6 cups (1.5 L) chicken or vegetable
   stock or water
3 tbsp (45 mL) Chinese black or
   rice vinegar
3 tbsp (45 mL) soy sauce

1 to 2 tsp (5 to 10 mL) hot sauce, or
   to taste
2 tbsp (30 mL) granulated sugar
1 tsp (5 mL) sesame oil
1 cup (250 mL) fresh or frozen peas
1 cup (250 mL) tofu (soft or firm),
   cubed
1 egg, lightly beaten
Salt and pepper to taste
4 green onions, chopped

Heat oil in large saucepan over medium heat. Add ginger root and garlic; cook, stirring, until soft, about 2 minutes. Add mushrooms; cook, stirring, 2 to 3 minutes more. Add stock or water, vinegar, soy sauce, hot sauce, sugar, sesame oil and peas. Cook until heated through; add tofu. Add egg in thin stream, stirring, until it forms threads, about 1 minute. Add salt and pepper, if necessary. Serve at once, garnished with green onion.

MAKES 4 TO 6 SERVINGS.

Banana Bread

I searched high and low for a tasty, nutritious loaf that uses as many bananas as possible and found this version in The Complete Canadian Living Cookbook *by Elizabeth Baird and* The Canadian Living Test Kitchen. *I made it with both frozen and fresh bananas that were over-ripe, and I found frozen ones made the most deliciously moist—almost pudding-like—bread. I used a left-over bittersweet chocolate bar broken into chunks. Substitute soy protein powder (sold in health food stores) for 1 cup (250 mL) of the flour for a terrific nutrient boost. You could use vegetable oil instead of butter, and feel free to add toasted chopped nuts, raisins and/or flaked coconut. To make about 12 muffins, spoon into paper-lined muffin cups and bake about 25 minutes.*

2 cups (500 mL) all-purpose flour
¼ cup (50 mL) granulated sugar
2 tsp (10 mL) baking powder
1 tsp (5 mL) baking soda
Pinch salt
1 cup (250 mL) semisweet chocolate
   chunks or chips

2 cups (500 mL) mashed ripe
   bananas (about 5)
½ cup (125 mL) unsalted butter,
   melted
¼ cup (50 mL) milk, buttermilk or
   plain yogurt
2 eggs

1. Preheat oven to 350°F (180°C).

2. In large bowl, combine flour, sugar, baking powder, baking soda and salt. Add chocolate chunks or chips.

3. In another bowl, whisk together bananas, butter, milk and eggs. Add to flour mixture; stir just until blended. Spread batter in greased 9 x 5-inch (23 x 13 cm) loaf pan. Bake in centre of oven about 50 minutes, or until tester inserted in middle comes out clean. Cool on wire rack 15 minutes. Turn loaf onto wire rack; cool completely.

MAKES 1 LOAF.

Brandied Cherries

Here it is—from The Settlement Cookbook. *Wait until local cherry season in early summer and use big, dark red, sweet cherries.*

5 lb (2.2 kg) cherries
5 cups (1.25 L) granulated sugar
2 cups (500 mL) water
2 cups (500 mL) brandy

1. Wash cherries. Place in very large bowl.

2. In heavy saucepan, bring sugar and water to boil over medium heat; reduce heat to low and cook 8 minutes, until clear syrup forms. Pour over cherries. Let sit overnight.

3. Drain syrup from cherries into large heavy saucepan; bring to boil. Add cherries; reduce heat to low; cook 8 minutes. Using slotted spoon, transfer cherries to clean glass jars with tight-fitting lids. Bring syrup to boil; reduce heat to low and cook until thickened, about 5 minutes. Add brandy; pour mixture over cherries at once, filling to top of jars. Seal with lids.

MAKES ABOUT 15 CUPS (3.75 L).

CONFECTIONS OF A BRITISH SCHOOLGIRL

✳ LONDON—"I REMEMBER YOU NOW," I said jubilantly after failing to place the voice at the other end of the phone for the first few minutes. "I used to eat your cheese and marmalade sandwiches." Initially nonplussed, my former schoolmate Julie Ward (onward Duncan), calling from her home in Philadelphia to ask if I was coming to our high school reunion, suddenly twigged to this item of culinary memorabilia. "That's right," she chuckled, "my mother used to make them for my packed lunch. I didn't like them so I gave them to you."

Then Ward-Duncan evoked a story that only vaguely registered with me. "Do you remember climbing out of the window during Frankie's French class?" she asked, referring to one of my favourite teachers, Frank (known to all as Frankie) Stabler, the school's effervescent language pro. Perhaps not wishing to admit participation in such an unruly act (I'm not sure why not, since I was known at school for being a tad wayward), I claimed no recollection.

Instead, as I explained on the phone, the Frankie link that's as clear as day to me is of another nature. It's of cheesecake—an exotic dessert in England in those days but one my family often ate—which I used to bake from a recipe in my mother's 1950s edition of the *Joy of Cooking* and sell to Frankie upon request. My first—and, mercifully, successful—attempt at baking this gave me the confidence to try chocolate mousse, apple pie and even apricot soufflé. It's not surprising that, faced with the prospect of a high school reunion, most of my associated memories involve food. Or that a cheesecake for Frankie was high on my list of plans for attending that nostalgic event held during a visit to England, land of my formative years and now home to my retired parents.

The school I attended from age 11 to 18, and the reunion's venue, was Minchenden Grammar School, located in Southgate, a leafy old suburb of North London. Although the school of 600-plus students housed in what was then a beautiful old mansion (in rough shape these days, it's now an adult education college) was a 30-minute bus ride from my house, my parents chose it over closer ones because of its reputation for high academic standards and an enlightened headmaster. Among its famous alumni are multi-millionaire movie producer Lord David Putnam and Lynne Franks— the inspiration for Edina, that wacky character played by Jennifer Saunders in the hilarious British TV series *Absolutely Fabulous*.

Although Minchenden has had several reunions since my graduation, I didn't hear of them. This is probably because I returned to Canada, land of my birth, in 1965 and have been in touch with only one former schoolmate: my good buddy and sometime partner-in-crime, Frances Ainger (now Carter). It was she who informed me of the July gathering. And, as I contemplated the upcoming reunion, food memories came flooding back.

I have appreciated food—in all its wondrous forms, from humble to haute —since I was a mere pup. Growing up, I was especially drawn to the English fare enjoyed by my peers. Alien to me, it was deliciously fascinating compared to the menu at home where my European Jewish mother specialized in the likes of wiener schnitzel, Beef Stroganoff, Linzertorte and open-faced sandwiches made with rye bread. I'm also the proud owner of a hearty appetite, an attribute that enabled me to scarf down those dainty, crustless cheese and marmalade sandwiches intended for pal Ward-Duncan—and then devour a two-course, hot school lunch.

Oh, hot school lunch! How sweet the memory of what we called "school dinners"—much maligned by others but dearly beloved by me. Rib-sticking meals comprised of good British grub—subsidized, pre-Thatcherite repasts, a shilling a pop, based on a rotating menu featuring delectable dishes my mother refused to make. Shepherd's pie smothered in thick brown gravy. Steaming hunks of steak and kidney pudding sharing a plate with overcooked greens. And my favourite: greasy Spam fritters accompanied by an amorphous mound of mashed potatoes complete with lumps.

The luscious lunch experience featured feisty and sometimes fierce, hair-netted "dinner ladies" wielding giant ladles over vast vats of food amid the din of rowdy students speed-eating through a whirlwind sitting of 15 minutes. Desserts ran the gamut from Spotted Dick (a steamed vanilla dessert dotted with currants) to rice pudding garnished with a blob of jam. Warm, runny custard in an array of hues—white, pink or brown—were hot sweets' mandatory adornment. Cold ones were crowned with fake cream made, I later found out, by combining dried milk, sugar and lard.

And so, as I entered the huge, hot roomful of people from my past at Minchenden Grammar School one recent, mid-July, I came bearing cheesecake. And there, among the noisy, boisterous sea of faces was the unmistakable Frankie, chatting up a storm and easily recognizable 35 years later—only his hair had changed from blond to gray—as the person who taught me French, German and, unsuspectingly, a love of cooking.

Here's the recipe for Toad-in-the-Hole (a Minchenden School dinner staple) and for the cheesecake Frankie inspired, only slightly new and improved by the addition of a recipe for my sweet-tart Berry Glaze.

Toad-in-the-Hole

1¹/₂ cups (375 mL) milk
2 eggs
1¹/₂ cups (375 mL) all-purpose flour

¹/₂ tsp (2 mL) salt
¹/₄ tsp (1 mL) freshly ground pepper
1 lb (500 g) pork sausages

1. Preheat oven to 425°F (220°C).
2. In bowl, whisk together milk and eggs. Whisk in flour, salt and pepper until blended but lumpy. Let mixture stand in fridge about 1 hour.
3. Place sausages in 8-inch (20 cm) square baking dish. Bake in centre of oven, turning several times, for about 15 minutes, or until browned on all sides. Drain off any excess fat, leaving just enough to cover bottom of baking dish.
4. Pour batter evenly over sausages in baking dish. Return to oven; bake 25 to 30 minutes or until nicely browned. Pudding may fall as it cools.

MAKES 4 TO 6 SERVINGS.

Marion's Cheesecake

The best cheesecake I've ever made. Don't be alarmed if the batter is runny but be sure to use a springform pan with a tight-fitting base, so it doesn't leak. Delicious made with National brand cream cheese, but use deli-style cream cheese such as Mandel's or Daiter's if available.

CRUST
3/4 cup (175 mL) graham cracker
   crumbs
3 tbsp (45 mL) unsalted butter,
   melted
1 tbsp (15 mL) granulated sugar

FILLING
1 lb (500 g) cream cheese, at room
   temperature

3 eggs
2/3 cup (150 mL) granulated sugar
Grated rind of 1 lemon
2 tbsp (30 mL) fresh lemon juice
1/2 cup (125 mL) sour cream

TOPPING, OPTIONAL
1 cup (250 mL) sour cream
3 tbsp (45 mL) granulated sugar
2 tbsp (30 mL) fresh lemon juice

1. Preheat oven to 350°F (180°C).
2. For crust: In bowl, combine graham crumbs, melted butter and sugar.
3. Press into bottom of 9-inch (23 cm) springform pan. Chill while preparing filling.
4. For filling: In bowl, and using an electric mixer, beat cream cheese until fluffy. One at a time beat in eggs. Beat in sugar, lemon rind, and juice until smooth. Stir in sour cream. Pour into chilled crust.
5. Bake 30 to 35 minutes or until puffed around edges, but still slightly jiggly at centre. Meanwhile, prepare topping, if using.
6. For topping: Combine sour cream, sugar and lemon juice in bowl. Spread mixture evenly over hot baked cheesecake. Return to oven; bake 5 minutes more.
7. Cool cheesecake to room temperature on a wire rack. Refrigerate overnight. Serve topped with fresh berries, finely shredded lemon rind or berry glaze (recipe follows).

MAKES 10 SERVINGS.

Berry Glaze

300 g package frozen unsweetened
   raspberries, strawberries or blueberries
3 tbsp (45 mL) granulated sugar
2 tsp (10 mL) cornstarch

Place frozen berries in strainer set over bowl; thaw. Measure drained liquid; add enough cold water to make 1 cup (250 mL). In another bowl, stir together sugar and cornstarch; stir in 2 tbsp (30 mL) berry juice to make a smooth paste. Bring remaining berry juice to boil in a small saucepan. Whisk in cornstarch mixture; return to boil, whisking constantly. Remove pan from heat. Cool. Stir in thawed berries. Spoon over cheese-cake, or serve on the side.

MAKES ABOUT 1$\frac{1}{2}$ CUPS (375 ML).

MY TASTY HIATUS

※ Believe it or not, it wasn't easy adjusting to what is loving-ly called a "life of leisure."

In fact, my leave of absence, which began as six months and wound up being one year, had a rocky start. For me, a workaholic food editor used to having plenty on her plate, the prospect of having no fish to fry made me seriously doubt my raison d'être.

However, after days spent forlornly lounging around the house in my dressing gown, lamely watching daytime TV and generally sinking into a state of existential angst, I decided to get a grip. Not surprisingly, the self-imposed therapy that ensued revolved around food and cooking. First, I tidied my spice cupboard—as it turned out, the perfect plan.

How soothing it felt to remove the cluttered assortment of small bottles and plastic packages that had accumulated on one large kitchen shelf. And what satisfaction—after much sniffing and the realization that some items were almost as old as me—in banishing to the composter withered sticks of cinnamon, fossilized lumps of nutmeg and an entire tin of ancient turmeric. Replacing them with a new selection, neatly lined up on a small rack I installed myself, was icing on the cake.

Next, on the advice of a friend who suggested I take time out "to decom-press," I rented a room overlooking the falls in the lovely Muskoka town of Bracebridge. Amid vibrant fall colours, I spent four days vegging out with the help of a few books and a bottle or two of robust red wine. My days began with a bracing jog down the hill to Tim Hortons to sit and discreetly scan the steady, motley stream of locals and travellers as I nibbled on sugar-dusted and, in this popular spot, always tender, freshly baked Timbits. My dinner ritual was a drive down that same hill for roast chicken with sidekicks at Swiss Chalet.

I made more forays into rural Ontario and became a regular in Stratford. With apologies to culture vultures convinced the play's the thing, I'm drawn to this humble burg like a bee to honey because of the food. Home to the Stratford Chefs School—a constant source of budding talent—this friendly place offers delectable edibles at every turn. Between sumptuous meals, I sipped strong coffee at cozy Balzac's and slowly savoured a cone of the rich Rolo ice cream I first came upon at Scooper's.

In Montreal, I made a pilgrimage to The Main for lunch at Schwartz's: the favourite dining haunt of my dear late dad, who grew up nearby in what was then that city's working-class Jewish enclave. Few meals come close to Schwartz's Special Combo: a heaping helping of steak, smoked meat, kosher dills and crispy fries. Not far away, at Persian restaurant Byblos, I tried two exotic omelettes: one inundated with creamy dates, the other laced with feta cheese and fresh herbs.

Back on home turf, I joined the downtown Y. What a relief for body and soul to feel the rush of endorphins induced by a rigorous Runfit class led by Murray—leader of our loyal band of sweaty stragglers who follow him around the gym like baby ducks imprinted on their mom. After class, a crunchy oatmeal cookie made from a secret recipe (even I, recipe mooch *par excellence*, couldn't extract it from the powers-that-be) and purchased at the Y's snack bar hits the spot.

All over town, I picked the brains of cooks, chefs and food merchants. In Kensington Market, Omar Houmani, a chef who works part-time at busy bulk-food store Casa Acoreana and makes the best cappuccino in town (I've conducted a year-long survey), shared the tricks of his trade and agreed to show me how to make the couscous and aromatic mint tea of his native Algeria.

I used my sabbatical to learn.

At the Symposium for Professional Food Writers held at The Greenbrier—a lavish resort nestled in the rolling hills of White Sulphur Springs, West Virginia—I met and became a fan of witty egghead Chris Kimball, publisher and editor of the clever *Cook's Illustrated* magazine, to which I now subscribe.

In Toronto, I attended a basic class at The Cookworks, a west-end cooking school operated by chef Donna Dooher who, with her husband, owns the adjacent restaurant, Mildred Pierce. That enjoyable evening, I mastered nifty knife skills and almost perfected the art of flipping mushrooms with one-handed dexterity in a sauté pan.

Naturally, I took in some screen cuisine. Among Food Network's many cooking shows, I enjoy two British offerings: the series by hottie chef Jamie

Oliver ("The Naked Chef") and Nigella Lawson. But it's on WTN that I found a homegrown TV show that takes the cake. "Loving Spoonfuls" host David Gale is almost as appealing as the ethnically diverse grandmothers who laugh, banter and dance with him, all the while contagiously cooking up a storm.

And, of course, I cooked.

This was not the harried, rush-hour cooking of former work-week dinners. I've had time to peruse cookbooks, try new recipes, bake a sour cream coffee cake laced with bittersweet chocolate bits and invite friends over for a casual lunch or dinner.

I shopped for food almost every day and became a regular in Chinatown to buy items like my latest find: hefty, flavour-packed Chinese greens. I slice these diagonally, stir-fry with grated ginger, chopped garlic, chunks of chicken and tomato wedges, then douse in chicken stock and soy sauce to serve over brown rice.

I grew fresh herbs, which I tossed into fragrant ratatouille, a simple mixed bean salad with wheat berries and my vegetable dish du jour: a toothsome sauté of onions, garlic, tomatoes and sweet peppers of every hue. I made a point of seeking out organic produce, preferably Ontario-grown, doing my small bit to save this planet.

Here are two recipes from my year off.

Cheese Shortbreads

Tasty snacks to serve with cocktails from The Cookworks where they sandwich homemade red pepper jelly between two shortbreads. I serve them singly with store-bought jelly on the side. You can freeze dough logs and slice into rounds just before baking. Instead of shaping into logs, you can roll dough out and cut into desired shapes.

2½ cups (625 mL) all-purpose flour
½ tsp (2 mL) cayenne pepper
1 tsp (5 mL) each paprika and salt

1 cup (250 mL) unsalted butter, at room temperature
2 cups (500 mL) grated cheddar cheese

1. In bowl, combine flour, cayenne pepper, paprika and salt.

2. In food processor, cream butter until light and fluffy. Add cheddar; process with a few short pulses until combined. Add flour mixture in three batches, processing after each addition, until dough begins to form ball. (It may be a bit crumbly.) Turn onto work surface. Divide in half. Place one half on sheet of plastic wrap; using plastic wrap, roll up into log about 1½ inches (3.5 cm) in diameter. Fold plastic wrap over ends to enclose. Repeat with other half of dough. Chill logs 1 hour or until firm.

3. Preheat oven to 350°F (180°C).

4. Slice dough logs into rounds about ¼-inch (5 mm) thick. Place on ungreased baking sheet(s). Bake about 20 minutes on middle rack of oven or until golden brown. Cool on wire rack(s).

MAKES ABOUT 6 DOZEN.

Roast Chicken My Way

*I've been making this ever since California chef Wolfgang Puck suggested stuff-
ing herbs and garlic under the skin of a chicken when I interviewed him in the
1980s; I've added goat cheese. Use poultry shears (or a cheap pair of kitchen
scissors) to butterfly chicken. Feel free to use other herbs, omit cheese, etc.*

3 to 4 lb (1.5 to 2 kg) chicken
¹/₄ cup (50 mL) soft goat cheese
¹/₄ cup (50 mL) fresh herbs
   (rosemary, thyme, sage or a
   combo), finely chopped
2 large cloves garlic, minced

¹/₂ tsp (2 mL) each salt and freshly
   ground pepper
Juice of half a lemon
³/₄ cup (175 mL) chicken stock,
   preferably homemade
Salt and pepper to taste

1. Preheat oven to 400°F (200°C).

2. To butterfly chicken, slice through bones along each side of backbone;
remove it and reserve for stock or other use. Place chicken, breast side up,
in a wide roasting pan or baking dish; press hard on breastbone so chicken
lies flat.

3. In bowl, combine cheese, herbs and garlic. Stuff a bit more than a quarter
of mixture under skin of each chicken breast; press on breast to distribute
mixture. Repeat with thighs using remaining mixture. Sprinkle salt, pepper
and lemon juice over chicken.

4. Roast chicken in oven 40 minutes. Pour stock around chicken, return
to oven and roast about 10 minutes more or until juices run clear when
pierced with fork. Transfer chicken to warmed platter. For sauce, scrape up
browned bits from pan; skim off fat and add salt and pepper to pan juices.

MAKES 4 TO 6 SERVINGS.

MOTHER'S DAY

❋ TODAY IS MOTHER'S DAY AND THIS is a tribute to the person who first inspired my love of food and cooking—my mum.

I call her "Mum" because of the formative years—from age four to 19—I spent living with my parents and two brothers in London, England. It was by phone from the North London home she shared with my dad until his death two years ago that my mother recently told me about the food of her childhood, learning to cook and what breaking bread with others means to her.

My mother Ruth Schachter (née Nisse) has a bachelor's and a master's degree in science from McGill, taught high school biology for many years, speaks five languages and has worked as a translator from Russian and German into English. She's a bookworm who likes to read Goethe's poetry, in German, with her morning coffee—"I find it soothing," she says shyly—and enjoys a Proust or Dostoevsky novel at bedtime, in the original.

She's also a fantastic cook who knows how to welcome guests into her home like few others.

A Holocaust refugee, who once told me to watch Vittorio De Sica's magnificent, heart-wrenching film *The Garden of the Finzi-Continis* to best understand her past, she grew up in a wealthy, educated Jewish family in Riga, Latvia. Today, through the veil of survivor guilt, she recalls a "golden childhood" that suddenly ended in 1939. That was the year she, her parents and younger sister left for North America, spending a year en route that included stays in Sweden and Japan. The hope of my oil tycoon grandfather, Aaron Nisse, was to help the many relatives still at home escape. Sadly, they all perished at the hands of the Nazis.

Still, my mother's memories of life at the family's 10-room, art nouveau apartment on elegant Elizabetes St. in downtown Riga and at their nearby seaside summer house—the dacha—border on idyllic. Cuisine in the Nisse household, where a large extended family and many friends were frequent visitors, was, says my mum, "a fusion of Russian, German, Latvian and Jewish fare." When there were guests, meals were leisurely and long. "We grew up with a culture of feasting and festivity," she recalls fondly, "with people of all ages sitting around the table—often for several hours."

As a child, she remembers having "ersatz coffee" at breakfast along with "little rolls, smoked fish and cheese." Lunch was "a hefty midday meal." Among the German entrées were *sauerbraten* (marinated, braised beef), *rouladen* (stuffed, rolled-up beef), sausages and *wiener schnitzel*. Favourite Russian dishes were little meat pies called *pirozhki*, beef stroganoff, *coulibiac* (salmon in puff pastry), meat patties called *kotleti*, borscht and a gelatin dessert made with fruit called *kissel*. At Friday night dinner, Jewish standards like chicken soup, gefilte fish, chopped liver and chopped herring were *de rigueur*.

"It seems odd now," my mother notes, "but red caviar was an everyday hors d'oeuvre. On the other hand, tinned sardines, chicken, and turkey were real treats. Our family only had tinned pineapple when there were guests." At that time, Latvia was, she says, "a land of milk and honey." Fresh ingredients like cranberries, all manner of fish, sour cream and butter were of top quality and plentiful. The Latvian staple of salt herring with boiled potatoes and sour cream is still, she says, her "favourite dish of all time." She grew up with no idea of how to cook. Things didn't improve when, living in Stockholm at age 17, she took cooking classes. "The food we made was supposed to go to a deli," she says with a laugh. "Mine had to be thrown out."

Once settled in Montreal, she picked up the *Joy of Cooking* by Irma and Marion Rombauer and baked a cheesecake that failed miserably. Her new husband, my dad, by now a doctor, took charge and produced a perfect cake. Able to laugh at it now, she says, "He told me I didn't know how to do accurate work." When he took a job teaching physiology at Dalhousie University in Halifax, she honed her cooking skills on friends. "We had elaborate dinner parties," she says. "I got very ambitious."

After the move to England, the home entertaining began in earnest. Soon, our family was known for gatherings at which good food and lively conversation reigned supreme.

My mother says she learned her hosting talents from her grandmother, Marianne Berner, after whom I'm named. "My granny was a terrific cook who poured all her goodness into her food," she explains. "I love to have people come and enjoy themselves, to feel welcomed and a bit spoiled." On a daily basis, she had an appreciative audience. "Cooking for your dad was sheer pleasure," she says of the corpulent, rambunctious man with whom she shared 55 years. "He loved food. You kids, too."

These days, my mother's eclectic culinary repertoire includes European baking from kugelhopf and Linzer torte to strudel and kuchen. She makes a mean lamb curry, delicious roast duck with red cabbage, all kinds of stir-fries and a yummy prawn rice salad.

But she hasn't forgotten her Eastern European roots and often prepares what is arguably Russia's most famous dish: beef stroganoff. This version is adapted from her favourite, well-worn cookbook: *How to Cook and Eat in Russian* by Alexandra Kropotkin.

Beef Stroganoff

My mum is adamant that this is a quick, pan-fried dish, not a stew as it often is in restaurants. Also, you must use top-notch beef like tenderloin, sirloin or New York steak. She likes to use brown mushrooms. Don't use low-fat sour cream or yogurt; they may curdle. This is delicious served over egg noodles.

1½ lb (750 g) beef tenderloin
1 lb (500 g) mushrooms, halved
½ tsp (2 mL) each salt and freshly
   ground black pepper
3 tbsp (45 mL) vegetable oil
1 small onion, chopped
1 tbsp (15 mL) all-purpose flour

1 cup (250 mL) beef or chicken stock
1 tbsp (15 mL) Dijon mustard
⅓ cup (75 mL) sour cream or
   plain yogurt
Salt and freshly ground pepper to
   taste
Chopped fresh parsley

1. Cut beef into strips about 2 inches (5 cm) long, 1 inch (2 cm) wide and ½ inch (1 cm) thick. Sprinkle with salt and pepper.

2. Heat 1 tbsp (15 mL) of oil over medium-high heat in large heavy skillet. Add mushrooms. Sprinkle with salt and pepper; cook, stirring, until browned, about 4 minutes. Transfer to bowl.

3. Add remaining 2 tbsp (30 mL) of oil to skillet. Using tongs, add only enough beef to fit in single layer. Cook, in batches if necessary, turning once, until browned on both sides, about 3 minutes. Transfer to bowl.

4. Reduce heat to low. Add onion to skillet. Cook, stirring, until soft, about 2 minutes. Add flour. Cook, stirring and scraping up browned bits from bottom of skillet, about 1 minute. Whisk in stock and mustard; cook, whisking for about 2 minutes or until thickened.

5. In small bowl, combine sour cream and 2 tbsp (30 mL) of sauce from skillet. Add to sauce in skillet; cook, stirring, until heated through, about 1 minute. Return mushrooms and beef to skillet. Stir to coat with sauce. Cook until heated through, about 1 minute. Taste; add salt and pepper if necessary. Garnish with parsley.

MAKES 6 SERVINGS.

Linzer Torte

My mother's trademark European dessert is now a favourite with me. Once you've tried this, you'll never look back.

1¹/₄ cups (300 mL) whole unblanched
 almonds, skins on
³/₄ cup (175 mL) unsalted butter, at
 room temperature
¹/₂ cup (125 mL) granulated sugar
2 egg yolks (reserve 1 white)
1 tsp (5 mL) grated lemon rind

1 tbsp (15 mL) fresh lemon juice
1 cup (250 mL) all-purpose flour
1 tbsp (15 mL) cocoa powder
¹/₂ tsp (2 mL) ground cinnamon
Pinch ground cloves
About 1 cup (250 mL) good quality
 raspberry jam

1. In food processor, chop almonds, pulsing with on/off motion, just until ground.

2. In large bowl, using electric mixer, cream butter and sugar until fluffy. Add egg yolks, lemon rind and lemon juice. Beat until smooth.

3. In separate bowl, combine flour, cocoa, cinnamon, cloves and chopped almonds. Stir into butter mixture to form soft dough. Gather into ball, wrap well in plastic and refrigerate at least 1 hour or overnight. (If chilling overnight, bring to room temperature 30 minutes before using.)

4. Preheat oven to 350°F (180°C).

5. With floured hands, evenly pat two-thirds of dough on to bottom and up sides of 9-inch (23 cm) springform pan or fluted flan ring with removable bottom. Carefully spread jam over dough.

6. On floured surface, roll remaining dough into an oval ¹/₄ inch (5 mm) thick. Cut into strips ³/₄ inch (2 cm) wide; arrange in lattice on top of jam, pressing edges into edge of torte. (If strips break, simply press them back together.)

7. In small bowl, lightly beat reserved egg white. Brush on to lattice strips and edges of torte.

8. Bake in centre of oven about 45 minutes or until pastry is well browned. Cool completely in pan on wire rack. Remove sides of pan. Dust with icing sugar before cutting in narrow wedges. Serve with vanilla ice cream, sweetened plain yogurt or crème fraîche.

MAKES ABOUT 10 SERVINGS.

Text inside illustration: Passion for LIVING ♥♥ LIVING & EATING — Break Bread — Julia Child Domestic Goddess — be who you are

—◈ *Chapter Two* ◈—

FAMOUS FOODIES

✳ MUCH AS I LOVE MY JOB, it rarely makes me shed tears of joy. However, that's what happened in Toronto one magical April morning in 1991: the day Julia Child came to town. Her whirlwind, one-day visit to our city as a guest of the *Toronto Star* was a dizzying day during which she and I became firm friends. Seeing this amazingly down-to-earth, life-loving woman in action made it crystal clear why she has such a devoted following among professional chefs, fellow foodies and plenty of ordinary folk.

I had several more meetings with Julia over the next few years, some fleeting at food conferences and professional gatherings, others intimate and special. My last contact with her was by email a few months before her death in August, 2004. Not realizing how frail she had become after major knee surgery a couple of years earlier, I was stricken on hearing my dear friend was gone, but comforted by her famous assertion that she was not afraid of death.

Another fearless foodie is celebrated political satirist, travel writer and humourist Calvin Trillin, who humbly claims food writing is "a sideline." However, his unfailingly witty, populist approach to the genre, along with an obvious love of food, make him one of my main mentors. Happily, as with Child, arranging a meeting with this surprisingly approachable celebrity was sweet and simple.

It was 2003 and *Feeding a Yen*, a collection of Trillin's food articles from the *New Yorker*, had just been published. I emailed to say I had plans to be in New York and could we meet? He replied with his home phone number, address and a suggestion we go to lunch. Lunch was effortless and delightful.

As for food writers in the U.K., no one writes as evocatively about food and cooking as *Observer* writer and cookbook author Nigel Slater. Having made the initial request to meet some years ago, I now regularly join him for lunch when I cross the pond each summer to visit my mother in North London.

Slater cooks up a storm in his London home, with a penchant for simple, bold flavours. His weekly columns are all about imparting the urge to cook easy-to-prepare, mouth-watering food in a way that does not intimidate or mystify. He insists on offering recipes that give rough amounts and plenty of leeway in their method. His goal is to impart the confidence to home cooks to trust in their own palates. In my opinion, no one does it better.

Talking of expertise, American cookbook author Pam Anderson has plenty. As with many famous foodies I've encountered, she and I met via a promotional book tour. Over French fries at Mildred Pierce Restaurant, one of my favourite Toronto dining haunts and a spot known for its delectably skinny frites, we discussed the perfect way to make this delicacy at home.

My experiences with these people are more proof (as if we need more proof!) that breaking bread is the best way to bond with others, be they regular folk or famous foodies.

GOODBYE, MY DEAR FRIEND

❀ THE FIRST MEETING WITH MY MAGNIFICENT mentor and dear friend Julia Child began inauspiciously. The date was March 31, 1991. The place: Toronto Pearson International Airport.

I was a bundle of nerves when I arrived at the appointed time to welcome North America's celebrated doyenne of cuisine. The carefully orchestrated plan was to accompany her to the Four Seasons Hotel, Yorkville, with a brief stop at my home for snacks and a glass of wine.

Child, then 78, was in good health and brimming with energy. She had already expressed enthusiasm for the following day's action-packed schedule. Dubbed "April Food Day", it included a book signing at The Cookbook Store, a glitzy lunch with Toronto's movers and shakers prepared by five of our city's top chefs, followed by a cooking demo by her at George Brown College. This highly anticipated one-day visit, hosted by the *Toronto Star*, was the result of a phone interview earlier that year for an article about famous foodies and their favourite home-cooked meal. I recall Child citing Boeuf Bourguignon, Potatoes Anna and "a nice pear with cheese for dessert."

Then, in typical fashion, she turned the tables, questioning me about my job and life in Toronto. I asked if she'd ever been here. Her response: "No one's invited me." A quick visit to my publisher's office was followed by a return call to Child. She immediately accepted the *Star's* offer to bring her here and play host.

At Pearson's arrivals area, I began to panic. I was obviously at the wrong gate. Child was nowhere to be seen. Suddenly, I turned around and there she was. Totally unmistakable, more than 6 feet tall, though slightly stooped, and ferreting through her purse for my phone number. She was travelling alone—no handlers, no entourage, not even her trusty assistant Stephanie Hersh with whom I'd discussed details of this trip. Breezily, Child brushed off my profuse apologies and jauntily joined me in the limo, one small travel bag in hand. Soon we were cheerfully sharing Asian-inspired munchies and a bottle of Alsace Riesling at my kitchen table.

Child pulled out her powder compact when the *Star* photographer's flash began to pop—a momentary interruption between questions about me, my two daughters and Canadian food.

That night, we both stayed at the hotel, Child in a penthouse suite, I on a lower floor. Before heading to her room, my new buddy invited me to join her for breakfast. That morning, I made an embarrassing confession: I had a phobia of being alone in elevators (several years of psychotherapy later, this is now cured) and was stumped about reaching her top-floor abode. In minutes, Child was at my door. As the two of us made our ascent, she offered gently in a motherly tone, "You know dear, you should ask your daughter to help with your fear. I'm sure she could." This lovely woman had remembered our conversation about my elder offspring Esther, now a full-fledged psychotherapist, who was studying psychology.

We ate, then Child excused herself to phone her beloved husband Paul who was in a nursing home after suffering several strokes. "He's got the dwindles," she'd told me the day before. The affection was palpable in her inimitable voice coming from the other room. "I'm up in Canada, dear— with the heavy book," she told him, a reference to the hefty tome which she considered her definitive work: *The Way to Cook*. That morning, Child carefully, calmly and caringly signed books for more than 800 excited fans.

After a magnificent lunch at the hotel, she stood up to speak, raving about the food and Reserve Ice Wine from Inniskillin. "I love Toronto; you're a real food town," she said to a table of beaming faces. "It's a shame we don't know more about you in the u.s. You should do more P.R."

During the meal, I overheard Dave Nichol, then Loblaws high-profile president, asking Child to put her stamp of approval on his popular chocolate chip cookies. "I don't endorse things," she told him kindly but firmly. "It destroys your credibility." However, she was a practical soul and later wrote asking me how to contact "that wealthy supermarket executive" so she could request financial support for her pet project, the American Institute of Wine and Food.

As we stood to leave, Child asked me to bring her to the kitchen to meet the chefs. I'll never forget their faces as we approached the glassed-in chef's office where all five were chewing on baguettes stuffed with salami nor their joy as she heartily shook hands and sincerely thanked each one.

After her stellar demo performance at George Brown, hampered by glitches with some blunt knives, we returned to our hotel. I was a tad pooped, though high on life. Child, full of vim and vigour, felt like a bite to eat so we sat down in the lobby lounge. She requested two favourite foods from the motherly waitress who did not recognize the celebrity guest: a large, dry martini on the rocks in a big wine glass with a twist of lemon and a hamburger, rare to medium-rare. As Child devoured the burger, which was extremely well-done, I ventured, "How is it?" "Edible," came the reply. "And the martini?" I asked with trepidation. Child's answer was short and sweet: "Perfect!" I wrote about this and heard afterwards that heads had rolled at the hotel. I'm sure Child would have been upset. Food was important to her but so were people.

This prolific, undauntable woman returned to Toronto three more times over the years, in each case to promote a book. During that time, we kept in touch by letter, occasionally by phone and frequently by email. In 1994, I talked with her at CBC's downtown headquarters about her latest book, *Baking with Julia*. I'd closed my notebook and put down my pen when Child turned her lovely round face to me. "So Marion, how's your love life?" she asked, knowing I was single from previous chats. I mumbled something about things being bleak. "How's yours?" I piped up, knowing she was now a widow. "I had a beau but he died," came the matter-of-fact reply. She saw I was stuck for words and saved the day by adding, "At my age, it happens."

In 1999, I went to Cambridge, Mass., to visit family. Child immediately invited me for breakfast at her beautiful Victorian home near Harvard Square. You can imagine how magical it was to sit in her cozy, sunny kitchen decked with copper pans eating creamy scrambled eggs and sipping strong coffee made by her own fair hand. Four years ago, that kitchen was transferred intact to the Smithsonian Institution when Child moved, as she had long planned, to an assisted-living home not far from Santa Barbara in California. I knew my friend wasn't recovering well from knee replacement surgery almost two years ago. In fact, there were at least 20 emails from Hersh to this effect. Still, Child and I continued to discuss food, including the best way to make Tarte Tatin for which she recently sent two recipes clipped from newspapers.

I received an email in May saying how much she enjoyed lunch in the garden under the apricot, fig and avocado trees. Also, that she hoped our paths would soon cross. So it was a shock to hear she'd died in her sleep on August 13, news I received while on holiday in England. When I returned, there were calls from media who wanted to interview me but several chef friends just wanted to talk.

"I watched her make those Pears in Puff Pastry at George Brown," said Joanne Yolles, pastry chef at Pangaea. "I made it the next day and have been using her recipe ever since." Donna Dooher, co-owner of Mildred Pierce Restaurant and The Cookworks, keeps Child's biography beside her bed. "She loved people and knew cooking is the best way of showing your love," says Dooher. "She was very unpretentious and brought joy to cooking."

I cherish these words from Hersh, who included them in a beautifully poignant message sent to those on Child's email list just after her death. "Julia said that 'When you die, you're dead and that's the end. There isn't anything else.' But I know in my heart that she was happily surprised to be wrong. And I am sure she is eating an In-N-Out burger with Paul on the beach surrounded by friends and family and Escoffier, who is undoubtedly intrigued with the burger."

Child once said, "Cooking is the best work because you can eat the results." I'll think of that when I prepare, then savour her unequalled Cheese Souffle, Food Processor Pastry, Salade Nicoise and Shrimp Sautéed with Lemon, Garlic and Herbs.

I'll also relish the advice she offered young people when I interviewed her a couple of years ago by phone. "They should get into the food business. They'll join a wonderful group of friends and be part of one big family." Then she added, "After all, Marion, that's how I met you."

There will never be another Julia Child. She was one of a kind. Charismatic, funny, clever, a class act and the epitome of the Jewish word "mensch."

Dear Julia, as a fellow atheist, I hope you're wrong about death. As a fellow foodie, I pray the burger you're eating on that beach is medium to medium-rare and has a large, dry martini on the rocks to wash it down.

❧

BREAKFAST AT JULIA'S

✳ CAMBRIDGE, MASS.—HERE'S HOW THE croissants intended for breakfast with Julia Child turned into buns.

The day before our memorable meal, I had scoured Cambridge on foot with the help of a map and advice from my savvy friend Jim Dodge—a talented pastry chef and cookbook author who is currently director of food services at the Museum of Fine Arts in Boston.

After agreeing that croissants from a Boston bakery called Iggy's (to be correct, Iggy's Bread of the World) would fit the bill, Dodge offered to order them for me since he dealt with that establishment regularly.

Here was the plan: The croissants would be delivered to the front desk of my hotel between 8 and 8:10 A.M. the next day, ensuring enough time for me to arrive, goodies in hand, chez Child for breakfast at 9 A.M. The next day, 8:10 A.M. arrived and I was at the hotel's front desk. The croissants were not. By 8:20, I was biting my nails. A phone call to Dodge informed me the driver was stuck in traffic but only five minutes away. By 8:30, I decided I could not wait any longer

Star photographer Richard Lautens was dispatched to get the car. I decided to wait on the sidewalk and scan the horizon for an Iggy's delivery van. Minutes later, a vehicle bearing that name drove down the side street beside our hotel. I ran like the wind, flung open the van's door and began to babble, "I'm Marion Kane. Where are my croissants—the ones for Julia Child?" The perplexed, dark-haired, olive-skinned young man at the wheel either spoke no English or was in a state of shock at the sight of a frantic woman who was, by now, rummaging through the brown bags containing baked goods piled on the seat beside him

He managed to mumble a few words that sounded like, "Miss, I don't know…." But 'twas in vain. I had discovered a bag with stickers on it bearing my hotel's name. Inside, it appeared, was an assortment of buns and rolls but no croissants. "These will have to do," I reasoned. In hindsight, I was incapable of reason at this point as, glancing at my watch, I realized it was 8:45 A.M. Sheer panic had set in. Clutching the large bag of buns to my chest, I slammed the van door shut and ran back to the front of the hotel where a nervous and confused Lautens was looking for me. "We'll have to take these," I gasped, opening the car door. "Let's go."

I was both jittery and elated at the prospect of breakfast chez Julia Child as we drove along her quiet, leafy street a few blocks from bustling Harvard Square. But as soon as my favourite foodie, main mentor and, by now, firm friend appeared at the door (on it was a small black-and-white plaque bearing the name of Child's beloved husband Paul who died in 1994) and welcomed me with a big bear hug, I knew all would be well. "It's so good to see you again," said Child sweetly and looking directly at me.

Moments later, our coats hanging on hooks in the hall, we were invited into the large kitchen and those buns, graciously received with a "Thank you—that's so nice," were already out of their paper bag and in the oven.

"Paul and I moved here in 1956," said Child in answer to my question about her lovely, lived-in, spacious home. "It was built in the 1880s and was once owned by a famous philosopher called Josiah Royce. We bought it for the kitchen." Scanning the colourful, cozy room before me, I could see why. Covering one kitchen wall was an array of hanging pots and pans, most of them gleaming copper. "I got those in France," Child explained. "I don't use them much; they're lined with tin and have to be re-done. These days, they're lined with stainless steel, which is better, but they cost a fortune."

As we chatted, Child, slightly stooped ("I used to be 6 foot 2 but I've shrunk a bit,") and dressed casually in beige slacks, a burgundy man's cardigan and patterned shirt, was slowly moving about the room getting together ingredients for scrambled eggs. In the middle of the kitchen table sat an oversized, cauldron-shaped, antique silver sugar bowl; beside it was a small white pitcher of cream. At each place was a big tumbler filled with orange juice. A Braun coffee maker gurgled in the background as the room filled with the luscious aroma of brewing coffee.

By now, Child had broken six eggs into a bowl and was standing over the stove heating a generous slice of butter in her "non-stick Wearever skillet." The large commercial gas range was, she told me, "a Garland. I've had it since 1945." As she poured the beaten eggs, seasoned with only salt and pepper, into the pan and began stirring them with a white plastic spatula, I realized this was my chance to watch first-hand as Child made scrambled eggs the way I'd once tried—with amazing success—from a recipe in her indispensable book, *The Way to Cook.* "The trick is to keep the heat low, only to have about an inch of eggs in the pan, to stir slowly so you make a soft custard and to reserve a little bit of raw scrambled egg to add at the end," Child explained, as she proceeded to do just that. Then, as if on cue, wielding that spatula, our host exclaimed, "And then a little extra butter for company!"

My offer to pour coffee was graciously accepted. And as we proceeded to savour those wondrously creamy eggs along with the warmed rye buns smeared with butter, the conversation flowed.

Here are some choice tidbits from that magnificent morning meal:

- ON HER HEALTH: "I don't feel myself slowing down. I just got back last night from a two-and-a-half-week media tour across the country. My only problem is my leg; I do exercises for it."
- ON ROMANCE: "There's not much happening at this age but if you know any nubile men my age, lead them on!"
- ON COOKBOOKS: "I just keep a few in the kitchen: most of mine and the new *Joy of Cooking* plus some reference books. I have more books upstairs but I gave most of my collection—thousands of books—to the Schlesinger Library at Radcliffe College."
- ON HER MISSION: "I would like people to take cooking as a serious hobby: learning the basics of how to use and sharpen a knife, cut quickly and easily, how to sauté. It's all very simple—just a matter of practice."
- ON RECIPES: "There are as many ways to make a dish like coq au vin as there are cooks. I'd like to free people from slavish dependency on recipes to the freedom of knowing the basics."
- ON NUTRITION: "A few years ago, people were so afraid of their food. Things seem to have calmed down a bit. People were using their emotions, not their heads. I believe in moderation—a bit of everything—and no snacking."
- ON JETLAG: "I don't have a problem with it. I just set my watch to the new time and keep on going."

- ON GENETICALLY MODIFIED FOODS: "I think it's all fascinating. There's no one-minute answer. The technology's here. If they can give us a better tomato, I'm for it."
- ON IRRADIATION: "We need it because we can't afford to have tainted meat. It should be carefully studied and regulated."
- ON FILMING A TV SERIES IN HER KITCHEN: "It was wonderful. We were all together so much, it was like a big family. All the camera crew are cooks now. Anyway, this is a big house—I rent out the third floor—and I love having people around."
- ON FAME: "If you're off TV for a year, you're dead—so don't get a swelled head. Celebrity's part of the business. If you can't stand the heat, get out of the kitchen."
- ON ENTERTAINING: "I love to entertain. It's always casual. If I meet new people, I like to have them over here and show them this is a nest of simple folk."

When I returned to the hotel a couple of hours later, a young woman called me over to the front desk. "This note arrived for you with a package." On it was written, "8:30 A.M. Your croissants are late due to problems with proofing." I didn't have the heart or stomach to eat or even look at those pesky, proof-challenged pastries. "Please give them to the nearest hostel," was my defeated reply.

Here's the recipe for those famous eggs, as enjoyed by me at Child's kitchen table, from *The Way to Cook* by Julia Child, with her introduction.

Julia's Scrambled Eggs

Perfect scrambled eggs are tender and creamy, really a kind of broken custard. The only secret is to do them slowly over low heat, so that the eggs coagulate into soft curds. You don't want the eggs too deep in the pan or they will take too long to cook, and if there is too shallow a layer they will cook too quickly. A one-inch layer is easy to handle and a non-stick pan is certainly my choice: the 10-inch (25 cm) size does nicely for 6 to 8 eggs. Plain scrambled eggs are lovely for breakfast but chopped green herbs are always an attractive addition, especially parsley, chives or tarragon; add them along with the seasonings as you beat the eggs before scrambling them.

8 eggs
Salt and freshly ground pepper
1 tbsp (15 mL) or more unsalted
   butter
1 tbsp (15 mL) or more heavy cream
   (optional)

3 to 4 tbsp (45 to 60 mL)
   chopped fresh herbs: parsley, or
   parsley and chives, chervil,
   tarragon or dill (optional)

1. Break eggs into medium bowl, adding salt and pepper to taste; beat just to blend yolks and whites. Set frying pan over moderately low heat; add enough butter to film bottom and sides. Pour in all but 2 tbsp (30 mL) of beaten eggs. Slowly scrape bottom of pan from edges toward centre with spatula, continuing slowly as eggs gradually coagulate. It will take them a minute or so to start thickening; don't rush them.

2. In 2 to 3 minutes, eggs will have thickened into a lumpy custard; cook a few seconds more if they are too soft for your taste. Fold in reserved beaten egg. Adjust seasoning; fold in butter, cream and herbs, if using.

3. Serve at once on warm (not hot) plates. Accompany with, for instance, bacon or sausage or ham, broiled tomatoes and buttered toast wedges.

MAKES 4 TO 6 SERVINGS.

Cheese Soufflé

There are versions of this sweet and simple dish—a Child trademark—in almost all of her many cookbooks including my favourite: The Way to Cook. With a tossed salad and hunks of crusty baguette, it makes a lovely light lunch or supper. I didn't bother making a collar for the baking dish, which makes for an elegant presentation, but it looked and tasted great. You'll need a 6-cup (1.5 L) soufflé dish or straight-sided baking dish.

About 1 tbsp (15 mL) softened
    unsalted butter
2 tbsp (30 mL) finely, freshly grated
    parmesan cheese
2½ tbsp (37 mL) unsalted butter
3 tbsp (45 mL) all-purpose flour
1 cup (250 mL) hot milk
¼ tsp (1 mL) paprika

A pinch of grated nutmeg
½ tsp (2 mL) salt
Pinch of ground white pepper
4 egg yolks
5 egg whites
1 cup (250 mL) coarsely grated
    gruyere cheese

1. Preheat oven to 400°F (200°C).

2. Grease bottom and sides of baking dish with softened butter. Sprinkle on grated parmesan, turning dish so cheese adheres to its sides and bottom.

3. In medium saucepan, melt 2½ tbsp (37 mL) butter over medium-low heat. Add flour and cook, whisking, until mixture foams, about 2 minutes. Remove from heat. Whisk in hot milk. Return to heat, bring to boil, reduce heat and simmer 1 to 2 minutes or until thickened. Remove from heat; stir in paprika, nutmeg, salt and pepper, Stir in egg yolks, one at a time, until combined.

4. Using manual or hand-held electric mixer, in medium glass bowl, beat egg whites until stiff and glossy. Whisk about a quarter of them into sauce in saucepan, then delicately fold in remainder alternately with grated gruyere. Carefully turn mixture into prepared baking dish.

5. Reduce oven temperature to 375°F (190°C). Bake soufflé 25 to 30 minutes or until puffed and nicely browned. It will fall slightly as it cools. To serve, hold serving spoon and fork upright and back-to-back in middle of soufflé and pull it apart.

MAKES 4 SERVINGS.

EATING WITH MRS. LATTE

✳ New York—It has to be her.

The slim young woman with porcelain skin, fine, chiselled features, neatly bobbed hair and trademark knit cardigan is surely Amanda Hesser. And as she walks toward my table at Blue Hill—the chic, subterranean restaurant just steps from Washington Square that she chose for our interview—I clearly recognize my dinner date.

Hesser, not only resembles the whimsical sketches that ran with her clever food column for almost two years in the *New York Times Magazine*, she's also the spitting image of the wide-eyed cook holding a roast chicken that illustrates the cover of her second, book, *Cooking for Mr. Latte*.

While I enjoy my glass of Pinot Noir and she sips a dry sherry, we both opt for the mouthwatering $65 (u.s.) six-course tasting menu. Daintily knocking back a shot of warm asparagus soup inundated with tiny chunks of apple, Hesser—arguably America's most up-and-coming food writer—tells how the book came to be. "Thirty-seven of the chapters are columns I wrote for the magazine about our relationship," she explains, referring to the Mr. Latte of its title, a 40-year-old writer for the *New Yorker* called Tad Friend and the man she married last September. "But 14 of them never appeared in it," she quickly adds.

"My mother was a deep influence," she says with a shy smile. "She cooked pot roast, chicken a la king—she had a crockpot phase. Even when she worked, she didn't compromise. We always had a proper meal. There was no microwave—often dinner was at 9:30 p.m." But Hesser's passion for food and cooking didn't surface until she left home to study finance at a small college outside Boston. "It seemed practical," she explains, "but I was unhappy and really bored."

So it was off to Europe where she spent three years as an apprentice in all manner of kitchens and worked on a book with well-known foodie Anne Willan at the latter's chateau in Burgundy. Back on home turf, there were demanding stints cooking at a bakery and restaurant in Cambridge, Mass., while she studied culinary history at Radcliffe College."

When Hesser arrived in New York in 1997, she had the grounding to pursue her career of choice. "I felt I had to learn a lot about cooking to be a food writer," she says. She began writing feature articles and co-writing a wine column called "Pairings" for the *New York Times* Wednesday food section. But it was the usually personal, often quirky and always passionate food diary she penned until last fall in the *New York Times Magazine* that endeared her to many, including me.

"I love to cook," she says, stopping in mid-bite. "I love being at home—in my kitchen where it's quiet and peaceful." Sharing that food with others is added pleasure.

"I love eating well," she continues, "and eating well alone has its place but that's not the way I want to spend my life." The main reason she wrote the book was "to explore the relationships people have with food and each other."

It begins with her and Friend's first date and concludes with their wedding. In between, there are lively chapters on dining alone, eating out with fellow foodies and dinner at the in-laws'. Accompanying recipes run the gamut from her mother-in-law's Ginger Duck to chef Barber's Smoked Trout Salad with Quail Eggs. She talks affectionately about Friend, who has a down-to-earth approach to things culinary. The couple regularly host dinner parties at the brownstone apartment they own in Brooklyn Heights.

They've devised a system for such soirees. "He shops, buys flowers and sets the table," Hesser continues. "I cook; I dim the lights. He pours drinks and lights the candles. Afterwards, we clean up together and re-hash the events of the evening. We keep a dinner party diary and both write in it." And she offers some advice, "When you're giving a dinner party, you must remove yourself from the pressure to impress," says she. "People are happy to be there. They want to have fun, laughs, good conversation. That won't happen if you put too much emphasis on the food." She adds, "If your best dish is meatloaf, make that. Be who you are."

When Mr. Latte served these two simple dishes to Hesser the first time he cooked for her, he instinctively knew that credo. By the way, Friend got his nickname by ordering a latte after dinner on their first date—a dining no-no that instantly endeared him to his wife-to-be.

Chicken Roasted with Sour Cream, Lemon Juice and Mango Chutney

I slightly adapted this recipe from Cooking for Mr. Latte. *He served it with the purée below and couscous. Use more or less curry powder, according to taste.*

4 about 1¹/₂ lb (750 g) boneless, skinless chicken breast halves
Salt and freshly ground black pepper
¹/₂ cup (125 mL) mayonnaise
¹/₂ cup (125 mL) sour cream
2 tbsp (30 mL) Major Grey mango chutney
1 to 2 tsp (5 to 10 mL) curry powder
Juice of 1 lemon

1. Preheat oven to 400°F (200°C).
2. Place chicken breasts in earthenware or glass baking dish just large enough to hold them in single layer. Sprinkle lightly with salt and pepper.
3. In bowl, whisk together remaining ingredients until smooth or use food processor to eliminate chunks in chutney. Pour over chicken. Bake about 20 to 25 minutes, or until chicken is cooked through. (Place under broiler for about 1 minute to brown top, if desired.) Slice on diagonal; spoon sauce on top.

MAKES 4 SERVINGS.

Purée of Peas and Watercress

This tasty, bright green side dish also goes well with fish.

4 cups (1 L) frozen peas
2 bunches watercress, washed,
   trimmed of all but top 2 to
   3 inches (5 to 8 cm)
4 tbsp (60 mL) unsalted butter,
   cut in pieces

½ tsp (1 mL) freshly ground black
   pepper
¾ tsp (4 mL) sea salt, or to taste

Fill large saucepan with water; bring to boil. Add peas. When water returns to boil, turn off heat. Add watercress. Cover. Let sit about 5 minutes or until watercress is wilted. Drain, reserving some of cooking liquid; transfer to food processor. Add butter, pepper and salt. Purée until smooth, adding a little cooking liquid if desired. Taste; adjust seasoning.

MAKES 4 SIDE-DISH SERVINGS.

CELEBRATING CHEF BOCUSE

❋ "I FEEL SORRY FOR ANYONE EATING OUT in Toronto tonight," quipped one chef. His peers chuckled in agreement.

It was a mid-week evening and here, in the noisy atrium of George Brown's downtown campus—home to the college's faculty of hospitality and tourism—many of our city's top chefs had abandoned their kitchens for a celebration in honour of a famous guest: French chef Paul Bocuse.

When I arrived, at around 8 P.M., he had just left. But the room was still sizzling. The mood was happy, the excitement palpable. No doubt, the plentiful libations—a choice offering of Ontario's finest wines—and an amazing array of cocktail nibblies contributed to the lively vibe. But it's the people who make a good party and this gathering was a rare chance for those who spend long hours preparing meals for others to share great food, gossip and camaraderie with friends and peers.

A cheerful Keith Froggett of Scaramouche looked pleased as punch as he and his team served up rabbit rillettes smeared on tiny garlic toasts garnished with spiced prunes. Nearby, Four Seasons executive chef Lynn Crawford, recently back from a stint in New York, yucked it up with buddies she hadn't seen for a couple of years as she dished out little lobster ravioli in a luscious vanilla-spiked sauce.

This scintillating soiree—and the rest of Bocuse's three-day visit here—came about when Cuisinart, a company Bocuse endorses, approached the college. "Bocuse is the godfather of chefs," says John Higgins, the hospitality department's capable co-ordinator of new initiatives, who had a key role in arranging events in his mentor's honour. "He's got tradition, longevity," Higgins adds. "He was the first chef to make it big."

The next afternoon, I return to George Brown in plenty of time to meet Bocuse who is due later that day to give the final verdict on a student cooking competition and to be the star guest at a gala dinner, preparations for which are in full swing.

Niels Kjeldsen, corporate chef for the pub division of Prime Restaurants, and John Cordeaux, executive chef at the Fairmont Royal York, are cruising two spacious, main floor kitchens, clipboards in hand, checking out the work of five students. All are in their 20s. All are standing over a chopping board or hot stove. All are totally engrossed in the task at hand. Working with the same ingredients, the challenge is to create a meal that will display their skills in the prescribed five hours.

Kjeldsen and Cordeaux muse about their judging criteria. "The key is creativity," Kjeldsen notes. "And at the end of the day, the food has to taste good. If the carrots are a bit misshapen, it's not the end of the world." Cordeaux feels "the key to competitive work is planning, technique and organization." Both are big Bocuse fans. "He's a bit of an icon," Kjeldsen notes. "He's part of the Old Guard, a mentor and third-generation chef who's done more for professional cooking than anyone I know. Bocuse isn't a TV chef. He's a real chef with three Michelin stars." Cordeaux cites Bocuse's signature dish: Truffle Soup en Croute, adding, "The man has so much class and dignity."

I decide to check out dinner preparations on the floor above. Here, a culinary "who's who" of local chefs has assembled, all raring to go with his/her part of the five-course meal, to hear Higgins give a rundown of the evening's game plan and a well-received pep talk. Michael Smith of Food Network fame, in charge of the appetizer—Maple-Cured Salmon with Celery Root Brandade—is all smiles. Soup is a Chestnut Veloute, the work of Jamie Kennedy. He's standing next to his longtime friend Michael Stadtlander who's made dessert: Sweet White Winter Dream. It will follow Roasted Venison with Chanterelle Cabbage Roll, Potato Tuile and Truffle Sauce prepared by another Bocuse admirer, Mark McEwan. As I run back downstairs, I get the word: Bocuse is in the house.

Smiling and nattily dressed in his chef's whites complete with medals, he looks every bit the culinary guru. At 77, he's founder of the prestigious Bocuse d'Or chefs' competition. He owns seven restaurants in his native Lyon and three at Disneyworld and is the author of seven cookbooks. Meanwhile, this feisty man finds time to jet around the world promoting products.

"What is the key to good food, Mr. Bocuse?" I ask nervously in mangled French shortly after he declares a beaming Jamila Rawlins the student contest winner. "Good product, seasoning and the right cooking," he replies without missing a beat.

Here is my rendition of a classic French country dish for which Bocuse is known.

Chicken in Vinegar (Poulet au Vinaigre)

I like to use chicken legs, cut into thighs and drumsticks. Use fresh, not canned, tomatoes; the latter are too acidic. Add cured black olives at the end, if desired. Serve with mashed or roasted potatoes, a green salad and crusty bread.

About 3½ lb (1.75 kg) chicken parts
Salt and pepper
1 tbsp (15 mL) olive oil
2 tbsp (30 mL) unsalted butter
8 cloves garlic, halved
¾ cup (175 mL) good quality red wine vinegar

3 ripe medium tomatoes, cored, seeded, chopped
¾ cup (175 mL) chicken stock, preferably homemade
¼ cup (50 mL) fresh parsley, chopped

1. Sprinkle chicken with salt and pepper.

2. Add olive oil and 1 tbsp (15 mL) of butter to large, deep skillet or dutch oven. Heat until very hot but not smoking. Add chicken (do not crowd) and cook, in two batches, over high heat, turning once, until browned all over, about 5 minutes per side. (Adjust heat if necessary so chicken is very brown but does not burn.) Transfer to plate.

3. Drain and discard all but about 1 tsp (5 mL) of fat from skillet. Add garlic; cook over low heat about 5 minutes. Gradually add vinegar. Bring to boil; cook over medium-low heat, scraping browned bits from skillet, until reduced by about half, about 5 minutes. Stir in tomatoes. Add browned chicken. Bring to boil over high heat. Reduce heat to low; simmer, covered, about 20 to 25 min. or until chicken is cooked through. Transfer chicken to warmed platter.

4. Add stock to skillet. Bring sauce to boil. Cook over medium-low heat until reduced, about 10 minutes. Whisk in remaining butter; cook briefly until melted. Add more salt, pepper and parsley. Pour over chicken.

MAKES 4 TO 6 SERVINGS.

THE INIMITABLE MR. TRILLIN

"The most remarkable thing about my mother is that for 30 years she served the family nothing but leftovers. The original meal has never been found." – Calvin Trillin

※ New York—It's late one night and Ruthie is alarmed.

"What's going on in there?" she yells in response to loud belly laughs coming from me in the adjacent bedroom of our home. "I'm reading a book by Calvin Trillin," I reply breathlessly. It's the chapter called "Barbecue and Home" in that brilliantly funny American writer's latest offering: *Feeding a Yen.* Here's the sentence in the slim collection of food-themed essays that made me howl out loud: "I am on record as saying that in Kansas City going to a white barbecue joint is like going to a gentile internist: everything might turn out all right, but you're not playing the percentages."

A week later, Ruthie and I are at the front door of Trillin's Victorian row house in the heart of Greenwich Village. I'm excited and nervous about meeting the famous author of 22 books—four of them filled with funny, first-person stories about food—whose impressive bio includes being a long-time contributor to the *Nation* and *Time* and 40 years writing for the *New Yorker.* Today's plan, discussed by email, is for me to interview him over lunch at nearby Shopsin's, a favourite eatery of his and the subject of another chapter in *Feeding a Yen.*

I'm looking forward to meeting Kenny Shopsin, colourfully portrayed in the book's quote from *Time Out New York* as "the foul-mouthed middle-aged chef and owner" who is "a culinary genius if, for no other reason, than he figured out how to fit all his ingredients into such a tiny restaurant." Sadly, this encounter is not to be. On the bright side, my interviewee turns out to be charming and quietly upbeat about our initial glitch.

"Shopsin's is closed on Mondays. Come in and we'll talk about where to eat," says the trim, short Trillin leading us up narrow stairs to the third floor flat where he's lived since the late 1960s. "We've added on to the place over the years," he explains motioning to a free-standing staircase leading to an upper level.

The midday sun fills this large, inviting open space with its high ceilings and ivory walls. A low, cream-coloured couch is the focal point of the comfy living room. There's a long, dark wood dining table surrounded by chairs. The adjacent kitchen has high-end appliances and is spotlessly clean.

Trillin is a secular Jew who grew up in Kansas City, Missouri. After graduating from Yale, he came to New York to write for *Time* and has lived here ever since. It was in this home that he and his wife Alice raised two daughters, Abigail and Sarah, now 35 and 32 respectively. Tragically, Alice, who was Trillin's beloved muse and soulmate, died while being treated for congestive heart failure on the evening of September 11, 2001. But with work, family and a fierce curiosity as strengths and solace, this man still has a wicked sense of humour.

When I ask about some exotic sculptures tastefully arranged on one wall, Trillin tells me they're "from Java. We bought them in London." Being a good Canadian, I ask, "London, England?" He doesn't miss a beat. "I believe there's a very small Javanese population in London, Ontario."

I quickly direct the conversation back to lunch. Soon we're off to Pearl Oyster Bar, a little New England seafood restaurant on nearby Cornelia St. owned by chef Rebecca Charles. I can't wait to try the lobster roll immortalized in *Feeding a Yen*. Soon, there's an amazing spread before us. Trillin and Ruthie have bonded. She's twigged to his jokes, enjoying their deadpan delivery, and is appreciating crispy fried oysters with silky tartar sauce, sublime clam chowder and luscious Caesar Salad. She's having a hard time battling my fork as I take stabs at the lobster roll: succulent chunks of that crustacean bathed in herb-laced mayo that tumble off the top and sides of a halved baguette. Happily, she's not a fan of the salt-crusted shrimp of which Trillin and I are making short work.

Trillin claims food writing is "a sideline." He enjoys biking around Chinatown where he sleuths out dumplings, scallion pancakes and the hearty, rice-based soup called *congee*. "I took some to a friend who's not well the other day," he notes. "It's wonderful if you're sick." Fancy restaurants are not his thing. "Around the entrée, I say, 'It's admirable and all that but I'm not having a good time.'"

Feeding a Yen grew out of the many travel features he's penned. "I've always written about 'vernacular food' that's particular to a place," he says. "The book is about foods I've particularly liked or have trouble getting." These qualify for inclusion in his "Register of Frustration and Deprivation." On it are Lunenburg Sausage and Lunenburg Pudding, meat products impossible to find, he claims, outside the part of Nova Scotia where he has long owned a summer home.

We're bidding Trillin farewell—but first he draws Ruthie a map of our return route. It goes past Shopsin's and on to Russ & Daughters: a Jewish deli and Lower East Side landmark featured in the bagel chapter of his book. Apparently, we should also check out the *knishes* at Yonah Shimmel's and try Kossar's for *bialys*. Not to mention a few of Trillin's local haunts: a restaurant called Home, one named Mexicana Mama, ice cream from Cones, 'Ino's for panini and risotto at Risotteria. As we leave, I ask Trillin how he stays so slim. "I take Miss Piggy's advice," he replies. "Never eat more than you can lift."

Fish tacos occupy another chapter of his book and are high on his "Register of Frustration and Deprivation." Maybe this recipe will help.

Fish Tacos

Corn tortillas are hard to find; I substituted flour tortillas. Grilled fish can be used instead of deep-fried.

¼ cup (50 mL) each ketchup, mayonnaise and sour cream
Salt and pepper to taste
1 cup (250 mL) all-purpose flour
1 tsp (5 mL) sea salt
½ tsp (2 mL) ground pepper
1 cup (250 mL) dark beer, at room temperature
1¾ lb (875 g) skinless, boneless fish fillets (halibut or other firm-fleshed white fish), cut in about 24 strips

2 limes, halved
Vegetable oil for deep-frying
12 small 7-inch (18 cm) flour tortillas
1½ cups (375 mL) finely shredded cabbage or iceberg lettuce
2 large tomatoes, chopped
Hot pepper sauce, optional

1. In bowl, stir together ketchup, mayonnaise and sour cream. Add salt and pepper to taste.

2. In another bowl, combine flour, salt and pepper. Add beer; whisk until smooth.

3. Sprinkle fish with salt and pepper; squeeze juice of 1 lime over strips. Let batter and fish stand 15 minutes; add fish to batter.

4. Preheat oven to 350°F (180°C).

5. Stack tortillas; wrap in foil. Bake about 5 minutes or until warm.

6. In medium skillet or wok, add oil to depth of 1 inch (2.5 cm). Attach deep-fry thermometer to side. Heat oil to 350°F (180°C). Slide 4 fish strips into oil. Fry until golden, about 3 minutes. Transfer to paper towel. Repeat with remaining fish.

7. Fill each tortilla with 2 fish strips. Top with mayo mixture, lettuce, tomatoes, juice from remaining lime and hot pepper sauce.

MAKES 6 SERVINGS.

GREEN CUISINE QUEEN

✳ LIKE FAMOUS FORMER FLOWER CHILDREN Emmy Lou Harris, Joan Baez and Alice Waters, Deborah Madison is doing a great job of aging gracefully.

A chef who made her name cooking innovative vegetarian fare at the famous Greens restaurant during California's hippie heyday, Madison looks 21st century chic when I meet her recently for a cappuccino in Kensington Market. She's wearing a knee-length black skirt with fringed hem and a tailored beige linen jacket thrown elegantly over her shoulders. Her ear-length gray hair is stylishly streaked with silver. Her carefully applied lipstick is fashionable burgundy. And, in spite of a hectic schedule and a steamy hot day, she's as cool as your proverbial cucumber.

Madison is enchanted with this feisty Toronto neighbourhood: a place I chose as it echoes the theme, Canadian-style, of her sixth cookbook *Local Flavors: Cooking and Eating from America's Farmers' Markets*. Picking up a jar of chipotle salsa at Perola's—the wondrously cluttered little shop on Augusta Ave. packed with an array of Mexican, South and Central American wares—Madison urges me to try some in quesadillas. Next, she points out a bottle of "really special little wild chiles"—a delectable pickle she recently ate in Mexico. Guava paste, which comes in a package, is, she notes enthusiastically, "nice and moist—great with salted cheese."

She tells me about her life later that day over dinner at Avalon. Here, chef/owner Chris McDonald, who is a huge fan, has designed and prepared an immaculate tasting menu of 11 mini-courses accompanied by five carefully matched wines. Madison grew up not far from San Francisco. "My mother rebelled against traditional Jewish cooking," she explains, "and spent money on art and music lessons. Our food was not memorable—plenty of iceberg lettuce with Wish-Bone dressing." At the University of California in Davis, she studied sociology and city planning. Then she went to Harvard where she played violin in the orchestra and worked as a research assistant in psychology. Madison began cooking "as a job" in 1969 when, back on home turf, she joined a Buddhist community in San Francisco. "I taught myself to cook from Julia Child and Elizabeth David," she recalls with a smile as we nibble on tiny corn blini draped with house-smoked salmon.

She developed a meatless repertoire that would please "people from different backgrounds—food with the quality of familiarity that everyone could enjoy at shared meals."

Ten years later, her professional cooking career reached a peak when she became chef at Greens, a vegetarian restaurant owned by the San Francisco Zen Center, to which she belonged. Located at Fort Mason—a military site dating back to World War II—the 120-seat eatery is still popular. By this time, Madison had spent a year working with top pastry chef Lindsey Shere at Chez Panisse, the landmark restaurant still located in Berkeley and owned by her friend and fellow culinary icon Alice Waters. Greens opened, she says, "to rave reviews." Though the chef and her menu were vegetarian, not all the diners were. "People didn't come because there was no meat," she adds. "You didn't notice it. The food was bright and delicious. There were no sprout garnishes, no orange slices, no macramé, no plants, no vegetarian clichés."

The place quickly became known for Madison creations like Black Bean Chili, Wilted Spinach Salad and the Marinated Mesquite Grilled Tofu Sandwich. But after four years, she was burned out. "We were doing 350 covers at lunch," she continues. "It was wild, a zoo." In addition to designing menus, cooking and supervising an inexperienced kitchen crew, Madison recalls, "doing the books, clean-up and even mopping floors."

These days, Madison's main concern is our food supply. "It's important to know where your food comes from," she says emphatically. "What's its history? Who raised it if it's an animal? Who grew it if it's a plant?" Hence her emphasis on buying from local growers at farmers' markets. "I don't buy meat at a supermarket," she insists. "God knows what it is and where it comes from. People are justified in being squeamish." She cites the cattle business and factory farming as being "wrong on so many levels. They're an ecological disaster as well as producing questionable food." She urges consumers to "seek alternatives. Find free-range chickens and buy meat raised locally and naturally in small herds."

As we savour one of three tiny desserts—aromatic Charentais Melon with a Midor Lemon Gelee and Hibiscus Soup—Madison sums up her credo:

"Buy local. If it's organic, so much the better. Eat what grows near you—for taste, nutrition, food security, everything that matters."

I bought Ontario-grown, organic veggies at my local health food store for this super dish from *Local Flavors*—a yummy sidekick for free-range roast chicken laced with fresh herbs and lemon juice.

Roasted Peppers and Tomatoes Baked with Herbs and Capers

Use red, yellow and orange peppers in this timely dish that's even better made a day ahead. Go easy on the salt as both capers and olives are salty.

4 large bell peppers
1³/₄ lb (875 g) ripe tomatoes, 6 or 7 medium
½ cup (125 mL) fresh parsley leaves, finely chopped
¼ cup (50 mL) fresh basil leaves, finely chopped

1 large clove garlic, minced
2 tbsp (30 mL) capers, rinsed
12 pitted black olives, preferably nicoise
¼ cup (50 mL) olive oil
Salt and freshly ground black pepper to taste

1. To roast peppers, place under broiler or on medium-high barbecue and cook, turning at intervals, until skin is blistered and charred, about 10 minutes. Place in bowl. Cover with plate; let steam about 15 minutes. Peel off skin; discard along with seeds. Cut peppers in strips.

2. Score 'x' on stem end of tomatoes. Drop into saucepan of boiling water for about 10 seconds or until skins loosen. Remove skins. Halve tomatoes crosswise. Squeeze out seeds; discard. Cut tomato flesh in strips.

3. Preheat oven to 400°F (200°C).

4. In bowl, combine parsley, basil, garlic, capers, olives and 3 tbsp (45 mL) of oil.

5. Brush remaining oil over bottom of baking dish. Place half of peppers and tomatoes in dish. Sprinkle with salt and pepper. Spoon on half of caper mixture. Arrange remaining peppers and tomatoes on top. Sprinkle on more salt and pepper. Spoon on remaining caper mixture. Cover with lid or foil. Bake about 20 minutes, or until bubbling.

MAKES 4 TO 6 SERVINGS.

PRIZE FRIES

❀ WHEN PAM ANDERSON SAID SHE WANTED to talk French fries, I went into a feeding frenzy.

After all, this is a topic dear to my heart and beloved by my tastebuds. An action-packed day of peripatetic noshing yielded a pared down list of top spots around town to savour the best thing to happen to a potato. Making their fries fresh to order using the double-fry method is key to the success of places like Bistro 990, Harbord Fish & Chips, Le Select Bistro, several Swiss Chalets including the one on Yonge north of Elm St., and Mildred Pierce Restaurant.

It was at that gorgeous, west-end dining spot, where fries are a specialty, that Anderson and I agreed to meet for lunch one recent afternoon. While she munched on a burger and I relished their aromatically spiced rendition of India's curry-filled crepe dosa, we shared a heaping helping of golden fries and digested the culinary subject du jour. "I could eat French fries at least once a week," says Anderson between bites. "I grew up in the South," she continues, "where they were mostly inferior and originally used as a mop to remove flavours from oil used for other kinds of frying."

She admits the French fry recipe she perfected for her latest cookbook, *CookSmart,* wasn't her invention. It's based on one attributed to famous French chef Joel Robuchon that she found in U.S. food writer Jeffrey Steingarten's book *The Man Who Ate Everything.* "I was testing French fries at the time," she explains, "and discovered that Robuchon's technique of adding the potatoes to cold oil then walking away from them is a great way for home cooks to duplicate what restaurants do. They blanch the potatoes in oil first, then fry them a second time." Most recipes for fries, she notes, use a lot of oil. In her method, which uses less, they only absorb about 1 tbsp (15 mL) per serving. Draining them on a wire rack and adding salt while they're still hot are, she says, restaurant techniques easily adopted by home cooks.

Anderson, a former caterer with no formal training who calls herself "a cook who happens to write," was born near Birmingham, Alabama, and grew up in Panama City, Florida. After moving to Connecticut in the late 1980s with her husband David and their two small children, she found herself working as a recipe tester for the new, high-end *Cook's* magazine, the test kitchen for which was near her home. After three years, she decided to take a sabbatical. The magazine folded in 1990, then started up again as *Cook's Illustrated* in 1993, when Anderson returned to work as a freelance writer for its savvy founder and editor Chris Kimball. She soon became food editor and eventually executive editor.

"I love to deconstruct a dish," says Anderson, "tinkering with a recipe and exploring the best and smartest way to make it." This approach, which often involves testing a recipe 50 times, was a terrific fit for the magazine in which in-depth articles aim to perfect the dish in question. This attitude also led Anderson to write her first her cookbook: *The Perfect Recipe*, published in 1998. In 1999, she left *Cook's Illustrated* and began her second book *How to Cook without a Book*, which was published a year later. It showcases another side of the author. "On the one hand," says Anderson, "I'm a perfectionist who wants to get the best results possible. On the other, I'm a cook who likes to improvise and just wants to get dinner on the table."

Anderson enjoyed the challenge of devising a Caesar Salad without raw eggs. She discovered mayo is the ideal replacement and that regular olive oil, not extra virgin—"Its taste is too prominent"—works best. "I identify with the average cook," says Anderson. "I have to feed a family, to entertain whether I feel like it or not." Her goal is simple. "I want to demystify the cooking process," she explains, "so people will sit down and share a meal with family, colleagues, friends and strangers because I believe good things almost always happen when you sit down and share a meal."

Here's Anderson's excellent recipe that mimics the ultimate, twice-fried French fry made by certain restaurants, a few fast food outlets and some choice chip wagons, followed by her superb Caesar Salad. Both are from *CookSmart*.

French Fries

Anderson recommends white all-purpose potatoes; Yukon Gold also work well. Use a skillet with fairly high sides to avoid spattering. You can move the potatoes around for the first 10 to 15 minutes of cooking but don't disturb for the next 10 to 15 minutes.

2½ cups (625 mL) peanut oil
2 lb (1 kg) about 4 medium
   potatoes, peeled, cut in sticks
   about ⅜-inch (5 mm) thick

1. Pour oil into 12-inch (30 cm) skillet. Add potatoes in single layer with some sitting on top and oil almost covering them. Turn heat to medium-low; cook until potatoes form golden shell, occasionally jiggling skillet, about 25 to 30 minutes.

2. Increase heat to medium-high; cook, turning with tongs at intervals about 8 minutes, until browned all over. With tongs, transfer to wire rack set over cookie sheet. Sprinkle with salt. Serve at once.

MAKES ABOUT 4 SERVINGS.

Caesar Salad

You won't miss the raw egg in this superb salad. Anchovy fans can add ½ teaspoon (2 mL) anchovy paste to dressing. Tear romaine leaves in pieces, if desired. Anderson reckons three romaine hearts yield 10 cups (2.5 L). You must use freshly grated parmesan, preferably Parmigiano Reggiano.

CROUTONS
4 cloves garlic
¼ cup (50 mL) olive oil
2 cups (500 mL) ¾-inch (2-cm)
 bread cubes cut from baguette
 or Italian loaf
Large pinch of salt

SALAD
10 generous cups (2.5 L) inner leaves
 of romaine lettuce
2 tbsp (30 mL) lemon juice
2½ tbsp (37 mL) mayonnaise
¼ tsp (1 mL) worcestershire sauce
5 tbsp (75 mL) olive oil
¼ tsp (1 mL) salt
Freshly ground black pepper to taste
¼ cup (50 mL) freshly grated
 parmesan cheese plus extra for
 sprinkling

1. For croutons: In food processor or blender, process garlic briefly until minced. With motor running, pour oil through feeder tube; process about 30 seconds. Strain though fine sieve. Reserve oil and half of strained garlic for dressing; discard or save remainder for other use.

2. In bowl, toss bread cubes with salt and garlic-infused oil.

3. Heat large skillet over medium heat. When hot, add bread cubes; cook, turning often, until crisp and golden, 3 to 7 minutes.

4. For salad: Place romaine leaves in large serving bowl.

5. In small bowl, whisk together lemon juice, mayonnaise, worcestershire sauce and reserved garlic.

6. Drizzle romaine leaves with olive oil, sprinkle with salt and pepper. Toss to coat. Add dressing; toss to coat. Add parmesan; toss again. Sprinkle on croutons and a little more parmesan.

MAKES 6 TO 8 SERVINGS.

THIS JILL'S JUMPIN'

※ JILL DUPLEIX'S COOKING CREDO COULDN'T be more timely: Keep it simple.

The titles of her cookbooks, which include *Favourite Foods, Simple Food* and *Very Simple Food*, say it all. And, as we chat over lunch at Pangaea restaurant during a hectic North American tour to promote her terrific new offering, she talks about her no-nonsense, but passionate, approach to food.

Dupleix's love of fresh ingredients prepared at their peak with a minimum of fuss was instilled growing up on a sheep farm in South Australia. "We were a typical happy, easygoing, busy family," she begins. "Riding horses, up fruit trees. My parents were both a bit obsessed with food." She cites an example, aware it might make vegetarians wince. "My father once fed a lamb a mixture of red wine, garlic and rosemary before he slaughtered it," she explains, adding cheerfully, "It had a happy last month." Lamb, she notes, is still her favourite food. It also inspired a popular recipe in *Very Simple Food* called Slashed Roast Lamb. "You stuff the slashes with a gooey mixture of bread-crumbs, lemon rind, capers, garlic and anchovies," she says, illustrating that step with her hands, "then roast it slowly for a long time. When you slice the meat right across the slashes, it falls in fingers onto the plate."

Dupleix goes for "bold flavours" and concedes, "there's nothing subtle about my cooking." Improvisation is her forte and was the impetus for a favourite dish in *Simple Food* called Crash Hot Potatoes. "I went to the fridge one day and found some unpeeled whole boiled potatoes," she begins. "I put them on a baking sheet, got out the potato masher and smashed each one, then drizzled on olive oil, fennel seeds, fresh thyme and rosemary." After 20 to 30 minutes in a very hot oven, "they were unbelievably crisp on the outside and mushy on the inside."

When the vivacious Dupleix talks about food, you can see and taste it. This ability, along with the fact that her recipes produce fabulous results, explains her popularity in England where she moved from Sydney three years ago with her restaurant critic husband Terry Durack. Happily ensconced in London's trendy Notting Hill—"It's very Julia Roberts," she notes jauntily—the couple have no children. "We've been mad foodies from the '70s on," Dupleix says. "With no kids, we're allowed to be completely selfish."

Picking up a slice each of grilled eggplant, purple tomato and bocconcini from her salad, she lays them between hunks of sourdough bread, then tucks in. "I love eating with my hands," she notes with relish. "I can turn anything into a sandwich." She's also pretty good at transforming a few choice ingredients into a delicious meal. "I can read a recipe on the Tube in the morning," she explains, "and cook it that night."

She calls herself "a home cook, not a chef," who has no formal training but studied cooking in Italy, China, Australia and France. She's learned "by making mistakes," and emphasizes the social aspect of preparing and sharing food. "I don't want to be stuck in the kitchen. I like being with people."

Her approach is down to earth. "I try to get away with less time, less fat, less work," she says, adding, "More eating and drinking." Many of Dupleix's trademark dishes are the result of trial and error. She cites her famous Jump-in-the-Pan Chicken from *Very Simple Food*. In this case, she once tried tearing the pounded raw chicken into pieces instead of slicing it and loved the crispy, flavourful results. She found shaking the skillet during cooking was a nifty technique. "It's really just a sauté," she says, noting that "*sauter* means 'to jump' in French. A chef doesn't just stir; he jiggles, tosses and really works the pan." The addition of lemon juice and white wine, she adds, magically makes a yummy sauce.

This brilliant recipe, which I adapted slightly, makes a super quick meal for family or guests.

Jump-in-the-Pan Chicken

Serve with noodles, mashed potatoes or rice and a green salad.

Three 5 oz (150 g) each boneless, skinless single chicken breasts
2 tbsp (30 mL) all-purpose flour
½ tsp (2 mL) salt
¼ tsp (1 mL) freshly ground black pepper
2 tbsp (30 mL) olive oil

1 tbsp (15 mL) unsalted butter
1 clove garlic, crushed
2 tbsp (30 mL) capers, well rinsed
½ cup (125 mL) dry white wine
1 tbsp (15 mL) fresh lemon juice
2 tbsp (30 mL) flat-leaf parsley, coarsely chopped

1. Place chicken breasts between two sheets of plastic wrap or waxed paper; flatten as much as possible without breaking, using a meat pounder or rolling pin. Tear chicken into ragged pieces with fingers.

2. Combine flour, salt and pepper on large plate. Add chicken. Toss to coat.

3. In large heavy skillet, heat olive oil and butter over high heat. Add chicken, scattering pieces so they don't clump together. Shake skillet at intervals, tilting slightly so chicken jumps and turns over. Cook about 4 minutes or until nicely browned. Add garlic, capers and wine. Cook, shaking skillet, until there is only a little wine left, about 1 minute. Add lemon juice and parsley. Cook, shaking pan, until sauce is slightly thickened, about 30 seconds more.

MAKES ABOUT 4 SERVINGS.

A TOAST TO TOAST

"It is impossible not to love someone who makes toast for you. People's failings, even major ones such as when they make you wear short trousers to school, fall into insignificance as your teeth break through the rough, toasted crust and sink into the doughy cushion of white bread underneath."

– From *Toast* by Nigel Slater.

✳ LONDON—AMONG LITERARY GENRES, FOOD MEMOIRS ARE HOT. Take the hugely popular *Kitchen Confidential* in which New York chef, globe-trotting TV food show host and proud bad boy, Anthony Bourdain, dishes up a wondrously earthy, behind-the-scenes look at the underbelly of the restaurant biz. Or the tell-tale, tell-all tome *California Dish*: the controversial offering from American chef Jeremiah Tower who voraciously chews up and spits out several of his culinary peers, including Alice Waters, famous owner of Berkeley's Chez Panisse. And the less gossipy *Toast*, a bittersweet, first-person, coming-of-age story told poignantly by brilliant British food writer Nigel Slater.

While visiting my mother here this summer, I seized the chance to chat with the *Observer* food columnist and cookbook author about how *Toast* evolved from "My Life on a Plate," a feature article he wrote for that paper a couple of years ago and "the first personal bit of writing" he'd ever done.

Slater chose our lunch spot: the unpretentious little French restaurant in otherwise posh Knightsbridge that's a favourite of his, and now mine, called Racine. As I nibbled on a luscious, buttery starter of Soft Roes and Sorrel on Toast (the connection with his book's title is pure accident), this slim, shy man dressed in black jeans and a black shirt explained how his eat-and-tell autobiography, which took two difficult years to write, came to be. "The article was supposed to be about food of my childhood," he begins, "but once you start, slowly, slowly you remember things. It opens a world you've forgotten." Writing it, and then the book, was cathartic. "It closed a chapter in my life that was unresolved and that I'd put off dealing with."

Slater was the youngest child in what he calls "a second generation middle class family." His life growing up in Wolverhampton, an industrial town in the Midlands "Black Country" not far from Birmingham, was lonely and often sad. "It was very much a childhood of living in fear," he says without self-pity. "I was scared of my father—the person I needed for comfort, to be there for me." This was especially so after his mother's untimely death when he was nine. The sibling of two much older brothers, he was the only one still at home. Soon after, his strict father, who could be physically violent, married a woman whom Slater bluntly describes as "an old-fashioned charlady" who had come to their house to clean and cook.

Enter food—eating and cooking it became a refuge for young Slater. Its intensely evocative descriptions are his forte. It is the glue that holds his often heartbreaking, sometimes funny and occasionally dark tale together. Ironically, the gentle, genteel, asthmatic mother whom Slater loved was a terrible cook. She burned the toast and made watery rice pudding. Her annual Christmas cake, he writes, "always sank in the middle. The embarrassing hollow, sometimes as deep as your fist, having to be filled with marzipan."

The abrasive stepmother he resented and rejected "smoked, cursed and even wore curlers in her hair" but could work magic in the kitchen. She was skilled at baking. "Joan's lemon meringue pie was one of the most glorious things I had ever put in my mouth," he writes, "the most airy pastry imaginable and a billowing hat of thick, teeth-juddering sweet meringue." Slater's mouthwatering descriptions of old-fashioned sweets will be deliciously nostalgic for those with British roots. Among them: Walnut Whip (his favourite candy); Butterscotch Angel Delight (he lists the dubious ingredients of this packaged dessert), sherry trifle, tapioca pudding and treacle tart.

There are disturbing moments like the time an uncle fondles the young boy. "I've looked at pictures of him recently and he looks quite camp," Slater tells me with a smile. "It never went any further than that." His intent was to tell the truth, even if it wasn't pretty. "So many foodie memoirs are a nice holiday read," he notes. "They're by people who've gone to France, don't have to work and are always walking round the market picking up darling little cheeses."

Lemon Surprise Pudding

A yummy version of the classic self-saucing dessert from Slater's Real Cooking. *Serve warm or cold.*

½ cup (125 mL) unsalted butter, at room temperature
¾ cup (175 mL) fruit (superfine) sugar
Grated rind of 2 lemons

Juice of 3 lemons
4 large eggs, separated
½ cup (125 mL) all-purpose flour
2 cups (500 mL) milk

1. Preheat oven to 350°F (180°C). Grease 8-inch (20 cm) square glass baking dish.

2. In bowl, using electric mixer, cream butter with sugar until pale and fluffy. Beat in lemon rind and juice. (Mixture will curdle.) Beat in egg yolks one at a time. Gently beat in flour, then milk. (Batter will be thin.)

3. In another bowl, using clean beaters, beat egg whites until stiff. Stir one-quarter into batter. Gently fold in remaining whites. Pour into prepared baking dish. Set dish in roasting pan. Add enough water to come halfway up sides of baking dish.

4. Bake 30 to 35 minutes, or until there is firm sponge on top and thick custard underneath.

MAKES 6 SERVINGS.

Sticky Toffee Pudding

This sublime pudding is from British foodie Delia Smith's Christmas. *If you like, serve with half-and-half cream, vanilla ice cream or yogurt. It can be baked ahead and frozen; just thaw, reheat and make the sauce at serving time.*

PUDDING

1¼ cups (300 mL) pitted dates, chopped (6 oz/175 g)

¾ cup (175 mL) boiling water

1 tbsp (15 mL) strong brewed coffee

½ tsp (2 mL) vanilla extract

¾ tsp (4 mL) baking soda

⅓ cup (75 mL) unsalted butter, at room temperature

¾ cup (175 mL) fruit (superfine) sugar

2 eggs

1 cup (250 mL) self-raising flour

SAUCE

¾ cup (175 mL) packed dark brown sugar

½ cup (125 mL) unsalted butter, softened

⅓ cup (75 mL) whipping cream

2 tbsp (30 mL) chopped pecans

1. Preheat oven to 350°F (180 C).

2. For pudding: In bowl, combine dates and boiling water; let stand 10 minutes. Add coffee, vanilla and baking soda; stir to combine.

3. In large bowl, cream butter and sugar with electric mixer until light. Beat in eggs, one at a time, until smooth. Lightly fold in flour; fold in date mixture. Batter will be runny. Pour into lightly buttered 8-inch (20 cm) square baking pan. Bake about 25 minutes, or until pudding springs back when lightly touched.

4. Cool 5 minutes. Run knife around edges. With fork or skewer poke holes all over top of pudding.

5. For sauce: In small saucepan, combine dark brown sugar, butter, cream and pecans. Heat over medium heat, stirring, until butter has melted and sugar has dissolved. Pour slowly over pudding, allowing sauce to soak into pudding evenly. Place pudding under preheated broiler about 6 inches (15 cm) from heat; broil about 8 minutes or until top is browned and slightly crunchy.

6. Serve warm with vanilla ice cream, custard, softly whipped cream or Yogurt Cream (page 119).

MAKES ABOUT 8 SERVINGS.

THAT DOMESTIC GODDESS

✻ SHE'S BEAUTIFUL, BRAINY, BUXOM—and she can cook.

In Britain, where she was voted Third Most Beautiful Woman in the World in a recent survey, Nigella Lawson's gorgeous face is, I'm told, currently plastered all over the walls of the London Underground. And now the woman who has the chutzpah and sense of irony to call the second of her cookbooks, *How to Be a Domestic Goddess,* is hot on this continent.

Earlier this year, an article in *Gourmet* magazine featured a photo of the sultry, raven-haired foodie wearing a tight twin set, under the headline: "England's It Girl." And last month, an article on her in the *New York Times Magazine* bore the succinct title: Hot Dish. The main impetus for all this is "Nigella Bites": Lawson's slick, sometimes sexy and rarely dull TV cooking show, which is filmed in her chi-chi, rather untidy home in Shepherd's Bush.

It was to promote the show, which includes me among its large following, along with its companion cookbook, *Nigella Bites,* that Lawson was due to visit Toronto as part of a media tour. When the trip was cancelled, I decided to interview her by phone.

She began by explaining that the death of her husband John Diamond— after a lengthy battle with cancer—was the main reason she'd decided not to travel. "Of course, September 11 had something to do with my decision," she said in her breathy, upper-class voice, as usual pronouncing her r's as soft w's. "But mainly I felt my children had just lost their father and it didn't seem right to leave them to promote my book."

Next, I asked about her famous pea soup recipe: a favourite "not-for-food-snobs" prescription that she demonstrated on popular British food writer Nigel Slater's TV show and because of which he affectionately dubbed her "queen of the frozen pea." I had tried to make it using the rather vague instructions in Lawson's first cookbook *How to Eat*—with disappointing results. The flavour was bland, the texture grainy. Lawson, whose fast-paced, happy-go-lucky cooking style gives the impression that preparing everything from Thai Seafood Curry to Turkish Delight Syllabub is a breeze, seemed genuinely perturbed. "Could it be the kind of peas you used? Maybe you should use a blender instead of the food processor."

A clever journalist who got into food writing almost by accident when an editor at the *Spectator* offered her a weekly gig reviewing restaurants in the mid-1980s, Lawson has a degree in languages. But the woman who seems to have it all readily reveals her flaws.

She has called herself "slatternly"—certainly, the chaotic state of her bulging freezer, which she refers to as "the deep-fweeze," is confirmation—and confesses that, at 5 foot 7 and age 40, she, who enthusiastically gnaws on fried chicken and wolfs down chocolate cake on her show, has worried about her weight. "I have my insecure moments and moods when I feel fat," she says. "But I love food and don't aspire to be skinny. I preach moderation. People who are slim eat a bit of everything." Lawson, whose well-known father, Nigel Lawson, was Chancellor of the Exchequer under Margaret Thatcher, attributes her affinity for things culinary to her Jewish roots, saying: "I come from a very greedy, food-conscious family. Food was central to our existence."

These days, she makes simple meals for her two children, Bruno and Cosima. "They like noodles, especially pasta carbonara," Lawson says. "My son likes salad, my daughter doesn't and they both eat broccoli—but only with soy sauce. I've stopped asking them what they want. Giving them choice is a disaster. I can't be a short-order cook."

She's comfortable with fame, saying, "It never occurred to me to disguise myself when I go out. It's not a huge problem." Then, her voice trailing off, "I guess I don't give off that vibe of needing to be recognized."

As we end our chat, Lawson offers a hesitant apology: "I'm sorry about the soup."

Keeping in mind that her recipes are best used as guidelines, here's my tested—and, I think, improved—version of a dish she whipped up with typical speed and nonchalance on a recent show.

Pasta with Chicken, Raisins and Pine Nuts

Lawson found the original recipe—a Friday night dish from Italy in The Book of Jewish Food *by Claudia Roden. Use a sturdy pasta. Toast pine nuts in a dry skillet, shaking, over medium-low heat until golden brown, about 5 minutes.*

1 cup (250 mL) raisins
½ cup (125 mL) Madeira or good quality fruit juice
4 lb (2 kg) or larger roasting chicken
1 tbsp (15 mL) olive oil
½ tsp (2 mL) each salt and freshly ground pepper
Juice of 1 lemon
1 cup (250 mL) chicken stock
1 lb (500 g) dried pasta
2 tbsp (30 mL) fresh rosemary leaves, finely chopped, or 1 tsp (5 mL) dried

2 tbsp (30 mL) fresh sage leaves, finely chopped or 1 tsp (5 mL) dried sage
¾ cup (175 mL) sundried tomatoes (packed in oil), thinly sliced
Salt and freshly ground black pepper to taste
1 cup (250 mL) toasted pine nuts
Freshly grated parmesan cheese
Chopped fresh parsley

1. Preheat oven to 400°F (200°C).

2. In small bowl, combine raisins and Madeira or juice.

3. Roast chicken as is or butterfly: Remove backbone by slicing down each side of it with poultry shears. Crack breastbone by pressing down on it to flatten. Place chicken on rack in roasting pan, breast side up. Brush with olive oil; sprinkle with salt, pepper and lemon juice. Roast in oven 30 minutes; pour stock around chicken. Roast 20 to 30 minutes more or until cooked through. Transfer to platter. Pour pan juices into small saucepan.

4. Just before chicken is ready, cook pasta in plenty of boiling, salted water until al dente. Drain. Add to large, warmed bowl.

5. Add raisins with liquid, rosemary, sage and sundried tomatoes to pan juices. Bring to a boil, reduce heat to low and simmer, uncovered, 10 minutes or until slightly thickened. Add salt and pepper. Keep warm.

6. Tear chicken meat and skin into bite-sized pieces. Add to pasta with raisin mixture and toasted pine nuts. Toss. Taste; adjust seasoning. Top with parmesan and serve more on side. Garnish with parsley.

MAKES 8 GENEROUS SERVINGS.

AN AMERICAN IN PARIS

✳ FOR ME, IT'S BECOME A RITE OF SPRING.

Attending the annual James Beard Foundation Awards in New York is especially good for body and soul.

For four days, I savoured the hustle and bustle of the Upper West Side neighbourhood where I was staying, warmed by glorious sunny days muted by a soothing breeze.

I relished my morning ritual: sipping full-bodied coffee from a big paper cup as I watched the endless stream of people, dogs and traffic from a sidewalk bench. Feeling at home and welcome, I was gripped by the city's energy, which, all the more since 9/11, urges one and all to seize the day. And as always, Manhattan is the place to check out what's cooking on the cutting edge. I got a taste of that during a magnificent, four-course dinner for media types prepared by 10 top U.S. chefs at the JBF Journalism Awards handed out two evenings before the main event.

Who would have thought Red Snapper Parfait with Carrot Orange Mousse, Saffron Ice and Pistachio Sticks would be a surprising contrast of sour, sweet and salty that really worked?

Or that Roast Filet of Beef coated in black olive tapenade laced with huitlacoche—a prized corn fungus used in Mexican cuisine—and encased in a crisp phyllo purse would be divine?

From humble to haute, the Big Apple is a hot spot for culinary innovation. So it was apropos I should interview one of America's foremost foodies there. It was the day after the awards gala that I met Patricia Wells for a mid-morning rendezvous at the place of her choice. Owned by Eli Zabar, E.A.T. is a no-nonsense Upper East Side dining institution known for its rib-hugging breakfast, lunch and take-out fare. Over coffee and hunks of multi-grain bread smeared with strawberry jam, we began by discussing the previous night.

"I know. I didn't win," Wells says cheerfully of her nomination in the International Book Award category—a prize that went to Madhur JaVrey for her latest tome. "That's okay," she continues, "I've won twice—for *Simply French* and *At Home in Provence*." Wells grew up in a suburb of Milwaukee,

Wisconsin, with an Italian mother and German father, feeling "that there should always be good food around." From a young age, she knew she wanted to be a journalist. After gaining those credentials, she worked for four years as art critic for the *Washington Post*. "I found it boring," she recalls. "I wanted to talk to people instead of going to galleries." Cooking had long been a hobby and, after moving to New York in 1976, she began writing about food for the *New York Times*. The next year, she married her second husband Walter Wells, a journalist for the *International Herald Tribune*. Soon after, he landed a job in Paris.

For 22 years, the two have divided their time between an apartment on the Left Bank and their farmhouse near Avignon in Provence. Between trips to places like Morocco, India, Japan and the United States, Wells teaches cooking classes. Her food philosophy is sweet and simple. "I want to get people into the kitchen," she explains, "and make them realize that good food—a nice gratin or a great apple tart—is not complicated." Sometimes, translating chefs' recipes into doable dishes for home cooks—a Wells specialty—is no mean feat. "The recipes in *Simply French* are the most complicated," she notes, referring to the book she co-wrote with chef Joel Robuchon. "I had to give up on his royale of foie gras," she says. "It needed a hi-tech steam oven to make the custard—and on a couple of his soups."

According to Wells, food in France has not taken a turn for the worse as some media have reported. "There is an increase in fast and frozen food," she concedes, "but ingredients are constantly getting better. There's a greater choice, greater variety. You can eat at McDonald's, at home or in a restaurant—it's a choice." At a dinner party the following evening, the conversation turned to other Wells cookbooks, which have a major following among hardcore foodies. Quickly, a theme emerged. Top marks went to two potato dishes—Gratin Dauphinois Mme Cartet and Gratin Dauphinois Madame Laracine in her bestselling *Bistro Cooking*. Those who'd dipped into *The Paris Cookbook* deemed many dishes worth the effort, especially David Van Laer's Potatoes Anna.

Wells readily admits she loves the lowly spud. Here's a recipe featuring it that I adapted from *Simply French*.

Potatoes Chanteduc

The potatoes can be sliced by hand, but a mandoline does the job more easily. You can use an earthenware dish instead of a glass one, but don't use a metal pan as it will react with the tomatoes.

2 tbsp (30 mL) olive oil
1 large onion, halved and thinly sliced
3 cloves garlic, finely chopped
5 medium tomatoes cored, seeded and chopped
1 tbsp (15 mL) chopped fresh thyme leaves

1 tsp (2 mL) granulated sugar
Salt and freshly ground black pepper
3 lb (1.5 kg) Yukon Gold potatoes (about 10), peeled and thinly sliced
1/2 cup (125 mL) finely chopped fresh Italian parsley
2 cups (500 mL) chicken stock, preferably homemade

1. Preheat oven to 400°F (200°C).

2. In large frying pan, heat 1 tbsp (15 mL) of the oil over medium heat; cook onions, stirring occasionally, until soft, about 5 minutes. Stir in garlic; cook 1 minute. Stir in tomatoes, thyme, sugar and pinch each salt and pepper. Reduce heat to low; cook until thickened, stirring occasionally, about 15 minutes.

3. In bowl, stir together one-quarter of potatoes, remaining olive oil and parsley. Set aside.

4. Place tomato mixture and remaining potatoes in 9 x 13-inch (23 x 33-cm) glass baking dish. Add 1/2 tsp (2 mL) salt and pepper to taste; stir to combine. Smooth top. Pour on stock. Arrange reserved potatoes in a single layer on top, overlapping them slightly. Cover dish with foil. Bake for 1 hour. Remove foil. Bake 30 minutes longer or until browned on top and potatoes are tender.

MAKES 6 TO 8 SERVINGS.

THE BEER-CAN MAN

✵ STEVEN RAICHLEN IS A SMOOTH TALKER.

But he doesn't have to sell me on the dish that inspired his cookbook *Beer-Can Chicken*. I tried and immediately became a convert to this bizarre but brilliant recipe when it caught my eye four years ago in this lively American food writer's grilling compendium *The Barbecue! Bible*. Even before that, I had become a Raichlen fan from dipping into several of his other cookbooks, most written during what he calls his "tropical," "vegetarian" and "low-fat" phases.

So when he showed up at my house, two chickens and a six-pack of beer in hand, to demonstrate his latest culinary coup, I was game for a lesson in grilling.

As we came to grips with what he calls "live fire," it soon became apparent this man is a mine of culinary information, a natural born teacher and, in spite of that day's excruciating heat, a bundle of energy. In a nutshell, what began as Beer-Can Barbecue 101 turned into an afternoon of old-fashioned fun.

As agreed, I had fired up my trusty charcoal kettle barbecue on my back deck. Raichlen was impressed. "Those coals are going to be perfect," he noted encouragingly as he checked out the still red-hot charcoal I had ignited half an hour earlier. Then he complimented me for my use of "real hardwood charcoal, not briquettes." Proud of myself, I followed him back into the kitchen to begin poultry preparation.

With no-nonsense speed, Raichlen rattled off ingredients and their amounts for his All-Purpose Barbecue Rub. Using my hands, I dutifully mixed them together in a bowl to create a rich brown, crumb-like mixture. On his advice, I rubbed olive oil—"Any vegetable oil is fine" he noted casually—all over the bird's skin. Then I patted the rub mixture into the cavities and all over the outside of each bird.

Impaling the chickens on their respective beer cans was more daunting and, to put it bluntly, a tad weird. Raichlen came to the rescue and deftly inserted an open can of Labatt's Blue in each upright chicken, having poured half the contents of each over some mesquite wood chips I'd emptied into a large bowl. "Canadian canned beer is a lot better than ours," he noted, referring to his American roots, adding that a top quality beer isn't necessary for this dish. "God intended for this recipe to happen," he continued, adjusting the second bird on its Labatt's Blue perch. "He/she made the cavity of a chicken just wide enough and deep enough to fit a beer can inside."

Then it was back outside to check the coals. "They're almost ready," he proclaimed cheerfully. "They should be glowing red and beginning to be covered with white ash."

Some minutes later, he readied the barbecue by shoving the glowing coals to each side, placing a foil drip pan in between and scattering the soaked mesquite chips over each mound of coals. He then planted the legs of each upright chicken firmly on the grill and closed the lid, leaving the vent holes open. Flashing me a big grin, Raichlen suggested we crack open a couple of those remaining "cold ones" and wait for the fire to work its fowl magic.

"What we're doing here is smoke-roasting—the true meaning of barbecue," he began, settling in for a cozy chat. "We've created an outdoor smoker oven—our own barbecue pit." Meanwhile, our senses were regaled by the sight and aromas of this wondrous cooking method. "We're smelling the smoke," he continued, "listening for a crackle from the nice browning and the chicken fat dripping down."

He explained how he got bitten, a few years ago, by the barbecue bug.

"My barbecue phase began with a voice from God," he proclaimed with just a hint of irony. "It was an epiphany summed up by the words 'Follow the fire.'" He was sitting outdoors at his home in Miami, where he and his wife live for much of the year, at the time. "I thought: Grilling is the oldest, most universal cooking method. The idea was breathtaking in its simplicity." He decided then and there to write a definitive book on the topic. "I figured there must be a barbecue trail around the world," he explained. "I wrote the book proposal for it in half a morning." The publisher loved it. Raichlen spent the next three years visiting 25 countries on five continents in search of great grilling and another year writing *The Barbecue! Bible*, which came out in 1998.

He discovered Beer-Can Chicken in the mid-'90s at the International Festival Barbecue Contest in Memphis. This quirky culinary technique was invented, he reckons, "by some bubba who drank too much beer." The Indian-inspired Beer-Can Tandoori Chicken, Duckling a l'Orange made with orange soda pop, Beer-Can Turkey, which uses an oversized can of lager, and Sake Chicken laced with Japanese flavours like wasabi, sesame oil and teriyaki are just a few unusual variations on the theme in his book.

Here's how to prepare chicken the way Raichlen and I did that day. They were juicy, crisp-skinned and infused with delicate, smoky flavour. I salvaged the contents of the drip pan by chilling, then removing the top layer of fat, to come up with a rich sauce.

All-Purpose Barbecue Rub

1/4 cup (50 mL) sea or kosher salt
1/4 cup (50 mL) dark brown sugar
1/4 cup (50 mL) paprika
2 tbsp (30 mL) freshly ground
    black pepper

1. In bowl, combine all ingredients. (For this, hands work best.)
2. Stored in airtight container in dark, cool place, it keeps at least 6 months.

MAKES ABOUT 3/4 CUP (175 mL).

Basic Beer-Can Chicken

10-oz (355 mL) can beer
3½ to 4 lb (1.75 to 2 kg) chicken
2 tbsp (30 mL) All-Purpose
  Barbecue Rub (recipe previous page)
2 tsp (10 mL) vegetable oil

1. Prepare gas or charcoal barbecue for indirect grilling; preheat to medium. If using charcoal, place large drip pan in centre of coals. If using gas, place soaked wood chips in smoker box; preheat on high until you see smoke, then reduce heat to medium. If using charcoal, toss soaked wood chips on to medium-hot coals.

2. Meanwhile, open beer can. In bowl, add half of beer to mesquite or other wood chips; let soak until barbecue is ready or reserve for other use.

3. Remove giblets from chicken cavity; reserve for stock or other use. Using hands, pat 1 tsp (5 mL) of All-Purpose Barbecue Rub inside body cavity of chicken, then about ½ tsp (2 mL) inside neck cavity at other end.

4. With hands, smear vegetable oil over outside of chicken. Pat on 1 tbsp (15 mL) of rub. Spoon remaining rub through hole in top of beer can. (Don't worry if beer foams up.)

5. Hold chicken upright, with opening of body cavity facing down. Lower on to beer can so it fits neatly into chicken cavity. Pull chicken legs forward to form tripod so bird stands upright and beer can forms rear leg of tripod. Tuck wing tips behind chicken's back.

6. Stand chicken upright in middle of medium-hot grill over drip pan. Cover grill, leaving vents open. Cook chicken until skin is dark golden brown and very crisp and juices run clear when pierced or meat thermo-meter inserted in thickest part of thigh reads 180°F (82°C), about 1¼ hours. If chicken threatens to burn, cover loosely with foil.

7. Let chicken rest about 5 minutes before carving. Carefully remove from beer can.

MAKES 4 SERVINGS.

~ Chapter Three ~

FEEDING BODY AND SOUL

✳ WE ALL HAVE TO EAT. MOST PEOPLE PREPARE some of their own meals. Many of us are passionate about food and cooking. All of which explains why I love being a food writer: It so easily connects me with individuals of every age, colour, social status, shape and size. I've written about where and what Toronto taxi drivers like to eat—a story that led me to burger joints, an African take-out, South Asian eateries and a Jewish deli. I once checked our city's cops' top spots to nosh and, for another article, visited favourite haunts of local truckers. In a different vein, I talked to chefs who man high-end kitchens atop downtown skyscrapers for CEOs, and penned a feature about those who prepare the fare at local spas and health clubs. Food is the great equalizer and, from my experience, there's no better way to lift one's spirits or create a bond than sharing it with others.

During the many years I've been a newspaper food editor and columnist, it's the average folk I meet on a daily basis—as I shop for food, grab a bite in a small ethnic eatery or check out food finds gleaned by word of mouth—who've most often engaged my interest, sparked my imagination and provided fodder for my work. Sure, I could easily do my job sitting at a desk in the newsroom or home office answering calls from publicists who peddle this or that product, beg me to interview a cookbook author and hype corporate-sponsored food events. I've written about those things and, chosen selectively, they can yield perfectly good, even lively articles that both educate and enter-tain. However, one of the roles I cherish most has always been to tell the stories of those I call "the invisible people."

When it comes to food, these are often the underprivileged have-nots who, instead of perusing the pages of *Gourmet* for the latest way to incorpo-rate zucchini blossoms into a party appetizer, make regular trips to the local food bank and wonder how to incite their children to drink powdered milk.

In this vein, I discovered a Toronto priest who began operating a drop-in for our city's homeless in his small, east-end church. His truly Christian mis-sion—to help those on the margins of society by encouraging them to be part of his centre's daily operation—mushroomed. Soon, there was a popu-lar hot lunch prepared and served by those who frequent the place. Then a bakery was started up in the church basement producing high-quality organic bread, based on a famous French version of sourdough that quickly became a hit in food shops around town. I was so happy to tell my readers this uplift-ing story. It illustrates how heartless our society is and how unfair a social system that relegates a chunk of the population to degrading poverty. Yet the tale shows what a unique bond cooking and eating communally can forge. How sharing and preparing food can feed and heal body and soul.

My article about handsome, talented British TV chef Jamie Oliver's London restaurant, Fifteen, is more proof. Having burst onto the scene in the late 1990s with his distinctive lisp, contagious enthusiasm and fierce passion for cooking, Oliver used the millions earned from his TV cooking shows, cookbooks and product endorsements to finance a pet project based on his desire to give back. His restaurant Fifteen, which opened in the shabby/chic central east London neighbourhood of Hoxton in late 2002, is a non-profit business where underprivileged youth train to become chefs, 15 of them at a time—hence the name. This noble goal turned out to be fraught with pit-falls. Oliver, with the energy and idealism of youth, soon had his plate full and his nerves sorely frayed trying to make this happen. He even began to doubt himself, wondering if his hopes and dreams had been naïve. As I write, the saga is still ongoing, but there have been positive signs as a handful of young chefs graduate from Fifteen each year and move on to important placements in their profession.

It's the human drama and, secondarily, the always mesmerizing topic of food that drew me to this story. The feedback I've had from readers tells me they feel the same.

The drama was of a much more harrowing, tragic kind when it came to my interview with Michael Lomonaco, who had been the stellar executive chef of Windows on the World for several years when two hijacked planes flew into the World Trade Centre on September 11, 2001. Windows on the World was the landmark dining room with a spectacular location on the top two floors of one of the Twin Towers. By an almost unbelievable quirk of fate, Lomonaco's life was saved that fateful morning when, arriving early for work, he decided to buy a pair of eyeglasses in the building's main floor mall instead of taking the elevator up to his restaurant.

I interviewed a still emotional but stoic Lomonaco about his experience in May of the following year during the annual James Beard Foundation Awards in New York.

Seated in a huge ballroom at the Marriott Marquis in the heart of Times Square where preparations were in full swing for that night's gala event, we talked quietly about his many friends and colleagues who were lost in the tragedy. But the main thrust of our conversation was how he and a group of like-minded New York chefs were giving hope to others by spearheading a project to raise money for victims' families. Never forgetting those who are gone, Lomonaco has moved on. He now happily and successfully owns and operates a Latin American restaurant called Noche in mid-town Manhattan—another example of how feeding others can nurture and heal.

HER HEART'S IN GREEKTOWN

❊ It began as your basic interview.

I had arranged to meet Sue Zindros during the mid-afternoon lull at Mezes, the Greektown restaurant she's owned and operated for 10 years, to discuss her contribution to an excellent new cookbook called *Tasting Diversity*. Little did I know that her dramatic story would soon unfold, complete with unexpected twists and turns, like a Greek tragedy—but with a happy ending.

My first hint of things to come is the answer to my question about her first name, which appears in the book as Anastasia. "That is my real name," she replies softly, carefully enunciating each word with the slightest trace of a Greek accent. "My family used the diminutive Anastasoula, which became Soula for short. But being a young immigrant child, I didn't want to have those names so I started using Stacy, Anna and then Sue." These days, that's what most people call her but Zindros has come a long way from that timid girl who was ashamed of her roots.

She was six years old when her family emigrated here from the Greek island of Rhodes.

"We came to a large city from a village of 600 people," she explains. "My parents were farmers. They were uneducated, had few skills and didn't have 'city manners.' They didn't know how to dress or behave a certain way. They were too busy trying to survive."

In her father's case, this meant working long hours as a dishwasher at the Westbury Hotel on Yonge St. in the heart of downtown Toronto. "He saw drugs, the 60s revolution," she continues. "His view of Canadians was that men were all alcoholics and women prostitutes." In contrast, "the roles had been very clear in his village. The women stayed home, helped on the farm and raised the children while the men worked to support them."

Her father, who died last year, was extremely strict with all three daughters and, she adds, "never believed a woman could be self-sufficient or independent. If you left control of the family, you would become a drunk, promiscuous female."

Growing up, Zindros was not allowed to go out or even play sports at school. "He didn't want me to integrate into Canadian life or get a university education," she says. "He wanted me to get married young, have children and do the village thing." It's taken time but she has come to understand and to forgive. "My family came out of World War II," she notes. "They had been an occupied people and had lived in fear." Still, as an immigrant child, it made life difficult. "My parents couldn't speak the language," she recalls. "They couldn't teach me how to be polite. In class, instead of asking the teacher, 'Please may I go the washroom,' I would just say, 'I want to pee.'" But she had inner resources. "I picked up how to be a Canadian by watching," she recalls. "I felt like an outsider to both the Greek and Canadian cultures. I didn't know where I fit." At 21, she fulfilled family expectations when she married George Zindros. The couple had two children: daughter Vasha and son James.

But things took a dramatic turn one fateful night in July 1992. George had gone for a bite to eat with his chef and a couple of friends at a nearby restaurant after closing time at his Danforth eatery, Mezes of Rhodes. When a fight broke out at the next table, he was stabbed to death for no apparent reason.

It may have been fate that drew Zindros to attend the U. of T. as a part-time student in the B.A. program a couple of years before this happened. While studying classics and literature, she began to use what she calls her "analytical mind" to comprehend some profound truths about herself and the world around her. "Learning excited me," she says with obvious pleasure. "It's in the genes of being Greek. I felt plugged in." She cites one professor who "didn't tell you what to think. He led you there," and whose teaching spoke to her. "He was a lover of Hellenism," she adds. "It had to come from outside for me to think how great Greeks are. Subjects like philosophy, literature and psychology all began with Greeks like Socrates, Hippocrates, *Oedipus Rex*." The self-confidence that grew from this was empowering.

"I started exploring the outside world," Zindros recalls, fixing her eyes on me. "I could forget the victim who has no freedom and is controlled by her family." She harnessed her anger and used it to move on. "I said, 'Okay, you've been put down, put in categories, told you're not good enough. Now what are you going to do about it?' I realized it was in my control. So the survival of Sue began."

With the sudden death of her husband, Zindros needed every survival skill she could muster. She owned a restaurant that was floundering in a time of recession, she attended painful, prolonged murder trials both here and in Greece, and had two young children to raise. "I believe life prepares you," she says quietly, "and I was being prepared for being a widow and standing on my own feet." She had "never written a cheque, paid bills or owned a credit card" when her husband died. She has battled depression and still has the constant stress of running a busy restaurant seven days a week. But today, she credits "friends, family and neighbours"—in particular her sisters Christine and Eleni who work in the kitchen at Mezes—for much of her success.

Here is Zindros's delicious dish from *Tasting Diversity*.

Avgolemono Soup

Zindros makes the stock by boiling a whole chicken and adds one diced, cooked breast to the soup. I just simmered chicken bones (feet are even better) with an onion, carrot and herbs, partially covered, for about 2 hours. Don't use bottled lemon juice. I used two eggs instead of one and loved the thicker consistency.

8 cups (2 L) homemade chicken stock
½ cup (125 mL) long-grain white or arborio rice
Juice of 2 lemons, about ½ cup (125 mL)

Salt and freshly ground black pepper to taste
2 eggs
½ cup (125 mL) chopped fresh parsley

1. Add stock, rice and half of lemon juice to large saucepan. Bring to boil; reduce heat to low and simmer, covered, about 20 minutes or until rice is tender. Add salt and pepper.

2. In bowl, beat eggs lightly. Whisk in remaining lemon juice until combined. Add a ladle of hot stock from saucepan, whisking until combined. Return mixture to saucepan, stirring. Cook briefly until heated through. Don't let mixture boil. Serve garnished with parsley.

MAKES ABOUT 6 SERVINGS.

NOT THE SAME OLD GRIND

✳ IT'S A SUNNY MID-MORNING IN THE heart of downtown Toronto.

Five of us are gathered around at a table at the jazzy little Yonge/Richmond location of Miofrio! each sipping Fruforio: a surprisingly tasty, froth-topped latte drizzled with strawberry purée and streaked with chocolate and caramel syrup.

Four of us are Canadian and, after a long, hard winter, look a tad pasty-faced. However, Rafael Terraza Raymundo, a South American coffee grower, has the healthy, swarthy complexion of a man who works outdoors in a kinder, gentler climate. Even though he speaks no English and arrived by plane a mere hour ago, this wiry young man is cheerful and calm. Watching each of us intently as we speak, he occasionally makes eye contact and flashes a broad smile. Raymundo, is a member of ASOBAGRI: a co-op of coffee growers in west central Guatemala's Huehuetenango region. He is here to promote the product that is his passion: Fair Trade coffee. That's the specialty of Normand Roy, an international Fair Trade coffee expert from Montreal who has worked as a marketing manager for coffee co-ops in South America, including Raymundo's, and is today acting as translator.

Fair Trade coffee is the bread and butter of Ian Cameron, the fifth member of our group. Ninety percent of the beans sold to places like Miofrio! by his company Cameron's Coffee—a micro-roaster in Port Perry—is Fair Trade. And if his luscious Guatemalan and Bolivian javas are any indication, he knows more than beans about coffee.

Likewise for the bright, articulate Roy who, translating as he goes, tells me what Fair Trade means to Raymundo. As the owner of four hectares of land in one of the best coffee-growing regions in the world, Raymundo says he and others in the 800-member ASOBAGRI produce coffee that's "strictly hard bean which means it grows at more than 1,300 metres above sea level. The higher the coffee grows, the better. Our region is very mountainous and we produce top quality beans." Growing coffee is, he continues, "a delicate balance between hot and cold that involves a chain of steps: meticulously tending seedlings, transplanting them to a covered area, then to a field—all of which takes four to five years of labour-intensive care." Raymundo and others in his co-op do this within Fair Trade constraints. Biodiversity is a priority. "We teach members to be environmentally friendly," he says. "We grow organically and want to stop pollution of the region. We use byproducts such as pulp as compost and the 'honey water' used in processing as fertilizer."

Fair Trade means fair wages: "We run our co-op democratically and take care of the standard of living of our members," he continues, "especially in the context of the coffee crisis." Roy elaborates. "Coffee is one of the most traded commodities in the world after oil." He notes, "It is produced by over 25 million people internationally, most of whom live below the poverty line within one of the world's richest industries." They are often exploited, he explains, "because almost 100 percent of coffee comes from Third World countries, many of which are ex-colonies." Today, much more coffee is produced globally than is consumed. This glut has landed many coffee growers, especially in Latin America, in dire straits. Roy sums it up: "Coffee is the flagship of Fair Trade." He says, "Fair Trade's goal is to get better conditions for small producers around the world."

Here's my recipe for biscotti—the perfect accompaniment to a cup of Fair Trade coffee—that's easily the best I've tried. Toast almonds over low heat in dry skillet 3 to 4 minutes or until golden brown. I bake cookies on Silpat or other silicone baking sheet liner.

Cranberry Almond Biscotti

½ cup (125 mL) unsalted butter,
 at room temperature
¾ cup (175 mL) granulated sugar
1 tbsp (15 mL) finely grated orange
 rind
½ tsp (2 mL) vanilla extract
2 eggs
2 cups (500 mL) all-purpose flour
1½ tsp (7 mL) baking powder

¼ tsp (1 mL) salt
2 oz (60 g) white chocolate, chopped
¾ cup (75 mL) dried cranberries
1 cup (250 mL) coarsely chopped
 almonds, toasted

WHITE CHOCOLATE DIP
8 oz (250 g) white chocolate, finely
 chopped

1. Preheat oven to 325°F (160°C). Grease and lightly dust large baking sheet with flour. (Or use silicone liner.)

2. In large bowl, using electric mixer, beat together butter, sugar, orange rind and vanilla until light and fluffy. Add eggs, one at a time, beating well after each addition.

3. Into another bowl, sift together flour, baking powder and salt. Beat into butter mixture a ½ cup (125 mL) at a time. Stir in white chocolate, cranberries and almonds. Cover dough; chill, about 30 minutes.

4. Turn on to lightly floured surface; cut in half. Form each half into flat log about 12 x 3 inches (30 x 8 cm). Arrange logs at least 3 inches (8 cm) apart on prepared baking sheet. Bake in centre of oven until golden, about 30 minutes. Place baking sheet on wire rack; cool 5 minutes.

5. Transfer logs to cutting board. Using long serrated knife, cut crosswise into ¾-inch (2-cm) thick slices. Stand slices upright on baking sheet. Bake in centre of oven 20 minutes or until well browned. Transfer to wire rack; cool completely.

6. To dip, place white chocolate in heatproof bowl. Place over saucepan of simmering water until half-melted. Remove bowl from saucepan, stir and let stand until remaining chocolate melts. Stir until smooth. Spoon some chocolate over half of a biscotti. Using butter knife, scrape excess chocolate off biscotti back into bowl. Place on waxed paper-lined baking sheet. Repeat with remaining biscotti and chocolate. Store in airtight container at room temperature.

MAKES ABOUT 32.

OLIVER'S NEW TWIST

"Oliver should be knighted for effort, energy, financial risk-taking and genuine empathy." – Fay Maschler, restaurant critic

※ LONDON—'TIS THE SEASON TO GIVE THANKS: a sentiment near and dear to the heart of British chef Jamie Oliver.

And his latest project—a non-profit restaurant called Fifteen that opened here last fall to rave reviews—is this seemingly unstoppable, talented young man's innovative way of putting his money where his mouth is.

After a meteoric rise to fame and fortune Oliver is the reigning hottie host of TV cooking shows on both sides of the Atlantic, author of bestselling cookbooks and high-profile promoter for the U.K. grocery chain Sainsbury's. But now, the blonde, boyish celebrity chef whom some mock as "Mockney" and many consider overexposed, has shelved all other endeavours to focus his considerable energy on a more serious, socially conscious goal: giving back to the profession that is his passion and being a mentor to underprivileged, budding cooks.

The concept seems sweet and simple. Working with a team of professional chefs and in tandem with a charity called Cheeky Chops, he trains and then hires 15 unemployed young people with little or no cooking experience to be chefs at Fifteen. The plan is to do this on an annual basis and to help successful trainees find good employment elsewhere once their year is up. Other staff are paid as in a regular restaurant. Oliver does not take a salary from the business and has personally invested more than 2 million pounds in it so far.

But, as my mother and I sit glued to Channel 4 on my first night here watching *Jamie's Kitchen*—a five-part documentary about how Oliver's noble, but arguably naïve, plan tempestuously unfolds amid tears, laughter and some broken crockery—it's also clear his sweet and simple concept has turned out to be anything but. The intriguing film dramatically shows how several of the 15 trainees, who range in age from 16 to 24 and were selected from thousands who applied, couldn't stand the heat of the kitchen. In fact, only eight survived the year. Financial and emotional problems at home, long hours of gruelling work, a lack of self-discipline and romantic notions of what chefs do caused those drop-outs to bite the dust.

Meanwhile, we see another side of Oliver: the fair but firm—and occasionally downright tough—teacher who can't fathom why anyone would waste the chance to cook for a living when it's handed to them on a platter.

So, naturally, ensconced with my mother at her Primrose Hill home for a two-week stay, I'm curious to check out what's cooking with Oliver and his raggle-taggle kitchen crew.

It took numerous calls to two publicists and one agent well in advance for me to secure a late lunch reservation at Fifteen—widely considered this city's hottest restaurant.

Disappointed that Oliver won't be there—he's taking a much-needed summer vacation with wife Jules and two young daughters Poppy and Daisy—mum, her friend Lily and I head out to Hoxton one sunny afternoon, elated at our prized outing. What ensues closely resembles an episode of *Jamie's Kitchen*. Things are up, down, good and bad—but never dull.

Fifteen's subterranean dining room, brightly lit and jazzily decorated with plenty of hot pink, flashes of neon, exposed brick and vinyl chairs, is abuzz. We're abuzz too after tucking into giant pre-meal gin and tonics in the lively bar-cum-bistro upstairs. Mixed drinks, we're told cheerfully, are always doubles. Cheerful is the operative word once we reach our table. Our handsome waiter is all smiles and, happily, attitude has no place at this trendy spot where the likes of Tony Blair are wont to dine.

The meal kicks off with Fifteen's most famous starter: Scallop Crudo, described on the menu as "kinda sashimi." This Asian-inspired take on ceviche bathes raw scallops in yuzu lime juice then crowns them with juicy cherries and olive oil, all topped with crispy shreds of deep-fried ginger and fresh coconut. Yum! Things take a dive with veggie Fritto Misto: a chewy mixture of dry, battered and deep-fried veggies and fish. A salad of spicy arugula with fresh figs and buffalo mozzarella is a delicious, bold-flavoured Oliver trademark. But Fresh Pea Risotto inundated with pancetta and mint is much too salty. It takes three lines of the menu to describe what is basically roast pork served on a bed of beans—an underwhelming dish. However, things look up with desserts of Wobbly Panna Cotta with Grilled Peaches and Vanilla Ice Cream with Hazelnut Brittle. As mum polishes off the latter and licks her spoon, it's agreed—they're both divine.

After lunch, I chat with sweet-faced Elisa Roche, 25, a trainee who's made the grade and is just finishing her shift. She admits working 80 hours a week is no picnic. "I don't have much of a social life," she adds, "but Jamie told us this was a hard career." After high school, Roche found herself on the island of Martinique cooking in a small café. Thinking back, most of her part-time jobs also involved food: "I waitressed," she begins, "worked in a kebab bar, fish and chip shop, making salads in a pub." Fifteen has changed her life. "Jamie gave me a chance to get a career when I felt I had no chance," she says affectionately. "Throughout the year, he's gone from the coolest boss to a friend I can call. He even helped with my rent arrears." Hanging out with her mentor can also be lots of fun. "Last weekend, a group of us went with Jamie to Prince Charles's Highgrove estate," she says, noting that the two men are friends. "We picked vegetables there in the rain and served them up that week as Royal Salad."

Back in Toronto, Oliver phones from his restaurant's kitchen for a friendly chat. He concedes the place is ridiculously busy. "We get 3 to 5,000 calls a day," he notes. "We've blown up three telephone systems." He explains his new project hasn't been a piece of cake. "Running restaurants is a big deal," he explains. "It's frustrating. You can't wrap it up and put a bow on it. You're only as good as your last plate." Then there's the matter of money. "The restaurant's not yet profitable. It's finding its feet," he continues, adding, "We've just had a problem with pilfering. But it's not the students. They're the people I trust most." The latter aren't the only ones being educated. "I've learned a lot about people," Oliver explains. "They're all individuals. Each learns and reacts in his or her own way. You can't teach them until their home life is happy and stable." And, in spite of the stress, he's enjoying the role of mentor. "You have to be patient and firm," he notes, then cites his best asset: "I'm a positive person."

Ricotta Lemon Parmesan Tortellini in Sage Butter

From Jamie Oliver's The Return of the Naked Chef.

PASTA DOUGH
3½ cups (875 mL) all-purpose flour
5 eggs

FILLING
14 oz (400 g) container ricotta cheese
⅓ cup (75 mL) each freshly grated
romano, and parmesan cheese

Finely grated rind, juice of 2 lemons
Salt and freshly ground pepper
¼ cup (50 mL) unsalted butter
Handful fresh sage, coarsely chopped
Freshly grated parmesan

1. To make pasta dough by hand, place flour in a large bowl and form a well in centre. Break eggs into well. Using a fork, break up eggs slightly and bring flour in from sides. When it begins to form a ball, turn out on to clean work surface and knead 3 minutes, until smooth and elastic. (If using a food processor, combine flour and eggs and pulse until mixture forms a ball. Turn out on to clean work surface and knead 2 minutes.)

2. Wrap dough in plastic wrap and refrigerate at least 1 hour.

3. In bowl, combine ricotta, romano and parmesan cheeses. Add lemon rind and most of the juice, salt and pepper. Set aside.

4. On a clean, dry work surface liberally dusted with flour, roll out dough as thin as possible using pasta machine or rolling pin. Cut into sheets 4 inches (10 cm) wide and 15 inches (38 cm) long.

5. Place one sheet pasta on clean work surface. Cut out 3 or 4-inch (8 or 10 cm) circles using cookie cutter or top of glass jar. Put 1 level tbsp (15 mL) filling just off centre of each circle. Using fingers, moisten edges with water. Fold in half, sealing edges and pressing out air. Bring end points towards each other and overlap about ½ inch (1 cm). Pinch to seal. Place tortellini in single layer on baking sheet and cover with a tea towel.

6. Cook tortellini in boiling salted water 4 to 5 minutes. Drain.

7. Melt butter in large skillet over medium heat. Add sage; cook, stirring, until crisp and butter is foaming but not brown. Add tortellini; toss to heat through. Sprinkle with remaining lemon juice and parmesan.

MAKES 4 TO 6 SERVINGS.

Baked Fruit

You can't get more sweet and simple than this super way Oliver devised to cook tender fruit like plums, peaches, strawberries, etc. I usually add a little marsala or Madeira along with a few spoonfuls of good fruit juice at the end of cooking. Serve with vanilla ice cream, crème fraîche or Yogurt Cream (page 119).

1 vanilla pod, cut in pieces
1 cup (250 mL) granulated sugar
4 lb (2 kg) fresh tender fruit
    (e.g., plums, peaches, nectarines,
    figs, strawberries, bananas, etc.)

1. Preheat oven to 425°F (220°C).
2. In food processor, whir vanilla pod and sugar until combined.
3. Place fruit in single layer on baking sheet. Sprinkle with about ½ cup (125 mL) vanilla sugar. (Store leftover vanilla sugar in airtight container.)
4. Bake 10 to 15 minutes or until fruit is soft but still holds its shape.

MAKES **8** TO 10 SERVINGS.

WINDOWS ON THE POST 9/11 WORLD

✳ New York—Michael Lomonaco is a mensch.

I first noticed him at a sumptuous Italian buffet laid out by some of this city's top chefs for a group of food writers gathered here almost 10 years ago. Flashing his handsome, winning smile as he ladled creamy risotto on to diners' plates, he stood out as a warm, articulate, down-to-earth man who also happens to be a chef of outstanding talent. Our most recent encounter was a mid-afternoon interview at the Marriott Marquis in Times Square.

Seated in a back row of one of that hotel's ballrooms lined with chairs, we chatted as Lisa Ling, co-host of ABC's "The View," practiced her gig as master of ceremonies for the 12th Annual James Beard Foundation Awards due to take place there a few hours later. He requested we meet in this odd location as he had plans to watch a short video about September 11 scheduled to be screened during that evening's ceremony.

Lomonaco came late to his calling as a chef. "My first choice was to be an actor," he explains over the booms and squeaks of technicians testing mikes. "I studied drama and worked in acting until I was 27." Growing up in Brooklyn's lively Italian community, a love of food had always been part of life and he had long had an interest in cooking. He decided to take a two-year course near home at City University, where he's now a visiting prof, got his chef's papers and has worked in restaurants ever since.

Lomonaco claims his first job at an "Old World Italian restaurant in Brooklyn" was invaluable training. "I knew the food," he recalls, "but not how to produce it for hundreds of diners a night." That soon became second nature. "Restaurant chefs must master organization, planning and timing," he explains. "It's what every good grandmother cook knows applied in a highly organized, well-timed production."

By the late 1980s, Lomonaco had landed a job as sous-chef at the famous 21' Club in mid-town Manhattan. During nine years there, he worked his way up to executive chef and was responsible for injecting new energy into that dining institution. "It was a power-broker place where politicians and the business community came to eat," he notes, adding modestly, "Some people say I revitalized the restaurant. Certainly, I sought to lift a sagging food culture to more contemporary taste."

During that period, Lomonaco hosted a popular TV show called *Michael's Place* that aired on the Food Network for three years. He quickly became known as a star chef who relishes a challenge. So when Windows on the World, the landmark dining spot on the 106th and 107th floors of the World Trade Centre, re-opened under new owners after closing for three years as a result of the 1993 bombing, he got a call. "My mandate as chef/director at Windows was clear," he explains. "It was to transform it from a restaurant with a view to a restaurant and a view."

He overhauled a menu "that did not reflect the current state of gastronomy" by focusing on "pristine ingredients—in particular local organic produce from the Hudson Valley, the Greater New York area, Connecticut and Pennsylvania," prepared with "precision and simplicity." Lomonaco cites his and owner David Emil's mission statement: "From Windows on the World, you could see America and we wanted to reflect back the food traditions of America."

With uncanny timing, this is the moment at which Lomonaco receives the sign that his video is about to begin. As the lights dim, he presses my arm and whispers, "Excuse me for a few minutes. I need to watch this." Complete with solemn music, the film shows how a group of Manhattan chefs and restaurateurs, with Lomonaco at the helm, banded together after 9/11. In the days following the disaster, they pooled their considerable resources to get food to firemen, police and other rescue workers. Soon after, they established Windows of Hope, a charitable relief fund to assist victims' families.

"I felt empty and very much alone," says Lomonaco, looking pale and shaken as he sits around a table with his cohorts. "Our passionate business was all of a sudden infused with compassion," he continues. "As an industry, we will never forget." The lights come back on and I see him brush a tear from his eye. He turns to me and resumes talking. "We've raised $18 million (U.S.) for the families of victims who worked in the foodservice business," he explains. There were 102 in all, 79 of whom worked at Windows.

That Lomonaco was not among them is a miracle. That fateful day, he arrived at the World Trade Centre, as usual, at 8:15 A.M., but, on the way to the elevator, decided to purchase eyeglasses at an optometrist's on the concourse level. "It saved my life," he says quietly. "They evacuated the building half-an-hour later. I saw it all unfold from the street."

He knew all his colleagues who died, to some degree. "More than 30 of them were from the kitchen," he says sadly. "I was very close to my pastry chef Norberto who I'd worked with for 14 years," a reference to Norberto Hernandez who was photographed jumping to his death. He finds strength in cooking. "Like my 79 friends who lost their lives," he says, "it's a privilege and what we love to do. I'm completely conscious of my blessing to be here and of continuing the work we were all doing together."

Roasted Vegetable Ragout

I took liberties with Lomonaco's recipe for Vegetable Gratin to come up with this. Feel free to vary amounts and types of veggies. Add a rinsed, drained can of chick peas, lentils or favourite beans for a super main course. Omit the tomatoes and you've got a basic recipe for roasted vegetables to serve as is or toss with a vinaigrette and chopped fresh herbs. Make your veggie chunks large.

¹/₃ cup (75 mL) olive oil
1 tsp (2 mL) salt
³/₄ tsp (4 mL) freshly ground black pepper
4 cups (1 L) Yukon Gold and/or sweet potato chunks
4 cups (1 L) butternut or buttercup squash chunks
3 cups (750 mL) cauliflower florets
3 cups (750 mL) thickly sliced portobello mushrooms
2 large red or yellow bell peppers, seeded, cut in chunks

1 large red onion, cut in wedges
2 large zucchini, cut in chunks
1 head garlic, separated into cloves
6 large sprigs fresh rosemary
Salt and freshly ground pepper to taste
1 cup (250 mL) vegetable or chicken stock
28 oz (796 mL) can whole tomatoes, chopped OR can diced tomatoes in juice
³/₄ cup (175 mL) chopped fresh herbs (e.g. basil, coriander parsley)

1. Preheat oven to 425°F (220C).

2. In a large saucepan, cover potatoes with cold salted water and bring to a boil. Reduce heat to low; simmer about 3 minutes or until they begin to soften. Drain.

3. In a large bowl, combine olive oil, salt and pepper. Add potatoes, squash, cauliflower, mushrooms, peppers, onion, zucchini and garlic cloves; toss to coat. Transfer to large rimmed baking sheet(s) and arrange in a single layer. Place sprigs of rosemary on top. Roast in centre of oven, stirring occasionally, about 50 minutes, or until vegetables are browned and tender. Remove rosemary. Add salt and pepper.

4. Transfer to a large earthenware or glass baking dish. Stir in stock and tomatoes. Return to oven and cook about 20 minutes or until heated through. Sprinkle with chopped fresh herbs.

MAKES 8 TO 10 SIDE DISH SERVINGS.

ALICE IN LOTUSLAND

✳ My first conversation with Alice Waters a few weeks ago ended abruptly when her cell phone cut out.

At the time, she was travelling by train to Newhaven, Connecticut, to visit her daughter Fanny who is a first-year arts student at Yale. Waters had just finished explaining the other reason for her trip: the project she recently cooked up with the president of that university—"to change the food in the college dining halls and to help change the way people there think of food." To that end, she agreed to give lectures twice a year on "the sustainability of our food supply."

Trains come up again when Waters continues our chat by land phone a few days later from her home in Berkeley, California. "I'm terrified about what's happening to our food," she says in a soft voice that communicates steely determination. "We're going over the cliff," she continues. "We have to stop the train. The way to do that is by not fuelling it." And Waters, has been putting her money, time and effort where her mouth is to fulfill this mission since opening her famous Berkeley restaurant Chez Panisse more than 30 years ago.

At that time, she and a couple of friends served what she calls "French country food" from a simple, fixed price menu in a small, 50-seat dining room. Waters, who has a degree in French Cultural Studies and a Montessori teaching diploma, attributes the success that followed to equal parts luck and good intentions. "We learned from trial and error," she says. "We were fortunate. There were a lot of people interested in doing it right." Today, she heads up a thriving, three-restaurant business that employs 30 chefs and about 80 others. "We're a family with too many children," she notes with a chuckle.

The original Chez Panisse serves a single fixed-price, three-, four- or five-course meal by reservation only. Upstairs, Chez Panisse Café is home to more casual fare with an open kitchen and wood-burning pizza oven. A couple of miles away, Café Fanny is a compact, stand-up café that serves only breakfast and lunch. All three restaurants are famous for their daily-changing menus that emphasize locally grown, seasonal, organic produce gleaned from a network of hand-picked suppliers.

A full-time forager searches out ingredients that meet Waters' high standards. "Finding new sources is an ongoing project," she explains. "We're constantly evaluating and looking for farmers who are committed to good quality and have integrity about what they're doing."

Her philosophy is serious but simple. "My obsession," she says, "is trying to get people to understand the consequences of the food they eat." In practical terms, this means making informed choices. "If you choose to buy from people who grow organically," she explains, "it supports a whole system of values. These farmers are taking care of our land for the future." On the other hand, she adds, "Those in agro-biz, who have a whole other set of values, are destroying the topsoil and natural resources at such a rapid pace, I can't imagine the world in 50 years."

Waters is adamant it will take a groundswell of support for those using benign farming methods to stop the degradation of our planet. "We must give our money to organic producers who come to farmers' markets," she insists but concedes this isn't always easy.

"Everything in our culture goes against it," she continues. "There are huge advertising and fast food budgets. The voices of ecologists and conservationists go largely unheard."

Unfortunately, she notes, it often takes a crisis "like mad cow disease or some other scare" for people to take heed.

For her part, Waters "has never been so vocal," devoting her considerable energy and using her stellar reputation to promote a slew of causes. She is on the board of Slow Food u.s.a., which advocates sustainable agriculture, home cooking and a respect for the best ingredients. Her Chez Panisse Foundation supports children's educational programs that connect gardening, cooking and the table. She helped write the mission statement for the Chefs' Collaborative: a network of cooking professionals who advocate "sustainable cuisine." She is also on the board of the Edible Schoolyard, an innovative program she initiated in Berkeley public schools to develop a curriculum that teaches the value of land stewardship, nourishment and communication.

It makes one wonder how and when Waters finds time to work on cookbooks. "I've produced all eight Chez Panisse cookbooks," she explains, "but, except for *Chez Panisse Fruit*, most were written by chefs at my restaurant."

Each chapter of *Chez Panisse Fruit* is devoted to a different fruit. In typical Waters style, she discusses heirloom varieties, seasonality and the purest, freshest ways to prepare each one. "I like to eat fruit raw," she notes. "A perfect fig, blood orange or wild strawberry is wonderful on its own." She loves old-fashioned fruit jellies, candied citrus peel and her book's prescription for mulberry ice cream.

Here are two recipes from the "fig" chapter of *Chez Panisse Fruit*. Fresh California figs (sadly, organic ones are almost impossible to find) are in season all summer.

Bacon-Wrapped Figs

A tasty appetizer served hot off the grill with salad or as a sidekick for grilled meat.

8 ripe fresh black mission figs
8 slices bacon

Remove stem ends from figs. Wrap each in a slice of bacon; secure with toothpick. Grill on medium-hot barbecue or under broiler about 8 minutes, turning halfway through cooking with tongs, until bacon is browned and slightly crisp.

MAKES 8.

Plum Galette

A fantastic, easy-to-make pie that's the perfect way to enjoy those intensely tart purple prune plums that are in season during late summer. Don't use any other kind—prune plums have the tang you need. And don't even try to make this when prune plums are out of season—you'll be disappointed. There's only one crust, and folding the dough over the fruit before baking gives a rustic effect that's visually stunning. I got the idea of sprinkling a mixture of almonds, flour and sugar under the fruit from ace chef Jacques Pepin; it stops the juice from making the crust soggy. I like to make pastry in the food processor; you can also do it by hand using a wire pastry blender.

PASTRY

1½ cups (375 mL) unbleached
    all-purpose flour
¼ tsp (2 mL) salt
1 tbsp (15 mL) granulated sugar
¾ cup (175 mL) cold unsalted butter,
    cut in chunks
⅓ cup (75 mL) ice water

ALMOND LAYER

⅓ cup (75 mL) finely chopped
    almonds

3 tbsp (45 mL) granulated sugar
3 tbsp (45 mL) unbleached all-
    purpose flour

PLUM LAYER

1½ lb (750 g) purple prune plums
(20 to 24), pitted, quartered
¼ cup (50 mL) granulated sugar
3 tbsp (45 mL) peach, apricot or
    apple jelly, melted

1. For pastry: Combine flour, salt and sugar in bowl of food processor. Add butter. Pulse a few times until mixture resembles coarse crumbs. Add water through feeder tube, pulsing, until mixture forms a ball. Transfer dough to bowl. Gather into ball; cover in plastic wrap. Chill in fridge for at least 30 minutes.

2. For almond layer: Add all ingredients to food processor. Process until mixture resembles coarse crumbs.

3. Preheat oven to 400°F (200°C).

4. Bring dough to room temperature. On floured surface, roll into circle about 14 inches (35 cm) in diameter. Drape over rolling pin and transfer to baking sheet. (I like a round pizza pan with holes in it for better browning.)

5. Sprinkle almond mixture over dough to within 1 to 2 inches (2.5 to 5 cm) of pastry edge.

6. For plum layer: arrange plums, slightly overlapping, in concentric circles on top of almond mixture, again leaving a bare border around the
edge. If you have any plums left over, use them to fill in any gaps. Sprinkle
plums with sugar, reserving about 1 tbsp (15 mL). Carefully fold edges of
dough over plums, pleating as you go, to form rustic tart.

7. Brush dough border with water and sprinkle it with remaining 1 tbsp
(15 mL) of sugar. Bake about 40 minutes or until crust is golden brown
and plums bubbly. Cool on wire rack.

8. Melt jelly in microwave or over medium heat in small saucepan.
Drizzle over plums. Serve with vanilla ice cream, thickened yogurt, crème
fraîche or try the following recipe for Yogurt Cream.

MAKES 10 TO 12 SERVINGS.

Yogurt Cream

Lovely with any fruit dessert. I use low-fat yogurt, preferably MC Dairy.

1½ cups (375 mL) plain yogurt
1 to 2 tsp (5 to 10 mL) maple syrup
1 to 2 tsp (5 to 10 mL) vanilla extract

Drain yogurt in paper-lined coffee filter, or sieve set over a cup about
1 hour, or longer for thicker cream. Stir in maple syrup and vanilla.

MAKES ABOUT 1 CUP (250 mL).

SANCTUARY

✳ It's a sad irony.

Here at Sanctuary, within the shadow of the posh Manulife Centre and a stone's throw from chi-chi emporiums like Holt Renfrew, Chanel and Prada is a refuge—both physical and spiritual—for our city's dispossessed. Located in a church formerly called Central Gospel Hall at 25 Charles St. E., a few steps from Yonge St. just south of Bloor, this humble haven is a busy downtown drop-in for Toronto's homeless. And on the subzero morning I arrive, the welcome is as warm as the room.

The latter is thanks to an electric fireplace burning gently at one end where assorted visitors are sitting—or, in one case, sleeping—on three well-worn, slightly tattered, overstuffed couches. Others gather at long wooden tables. Some drink coffee from a couple of urns, others sit in small groups talking while one elderly man, still wearing his hat and coat, reads a book. When I ask to speak to Greg Paul, who founded this place 11 years ago, his wife Karen has to point him out. Dressed in a checkered wool jacket and jeans, he's chatting with two young men as he hands them pairs of socks. Along with sleeping bags, these are the Sanctuary's most requested item.

Greg invites me to sit down near the fire where he is having one of many relaxed conversations I notice him engaged in during my two-hour visit. He introduces me to Andre Durant, who found himself on the street after coming here from Guyana, as "my friend." Durant calls his "a rough life—survival of the fittest" and is one of many who know they can drop by here for the Wednesday lunch, Thursday dinner and Saturday morning breakfast. Greg is a minister of the Brethren Church. "People here call me a pastor," he says, speaking softly. "But Sanctuary is a non-denominational community of faith."

He also tells me he's the singer and keyboard player for rhythm and blues band Red Rain and a "suburban Toronto boy" who used to work as a carpenter doing historical renovations.

These days, he and Karen, who has been on staff for three years, devote their time to Sanctuary's charitable mission. It includes offering food, clothes and drop-in services on-site as well as outreach for people on the street. "We want to create a dignified environment," Greg explains, "that holds out hope for marginalized people that they can have meaningful and respectful relationships in their lives." He sees those who come to Sanctuary as "a cross-section of the street and at-risk population." He reckons half have no home; the rest live in rooming houses or hostels. "Most of those are actually homeless," he adds. This mild-mannered man admits it makes him angry. "As a society, we've traded economics for justice. Philosophically, we've criminalized poverty."

As for my main reason for being here—to check out lunch—Greg points out that meals here "aren't about feeding the most people as efficiently as possible." He sees food as the perfect way to share: "There's no more potent symbol of community and fellowship than sitting around a table eating."

It is now almost noon and, as the crowd in the main room grows, lunch is coming together.

Overseeing the group of half a dozen volunteers is burly, shy Donald Sturrock, a former regular who was hired last month as kitchen manager. He uses tongs to transfer Italian sausages from stockpots in which they were boiled to roasting pans for finishing in the oven. Meanwhile, two helpers mound washed lettuce in giant bowls, then top them with chopped green onion and tomatoes while another empties frozen mixed veggies into steaming saucepans. Once cooked, they are wheeled out on trolleys with bottles of salad dressing and more oversized bowls filled with crisp chunks of roasted potatoes.

As the group of about 80 appreciative diners pass platters, Sturrock and I sit down with them and tuck in. "I cooked my first Christmas dinner when I was 11," he begins, explaining that he grew up in Etobicoke with a single mother and four siblings. "Everything was good," he adds, "but there were lumps in the gravy." Stints at McDonald's, in the kitchen at summer camp and making pizzas and subs for a year honed his cooking skills. A few years ago, Sturrock's wife died and he "fell on hard times." While living at Seaton House, a friend brought him to Sanctuary "to be the fourth hand at bridge."

The place lived up to its name. "I felt really comfortable," he says, smiling. "You can sit down, relax, talk. There's a feeling of warmth and sharing." The following week, he met Greg. "Our friendship bloomed from that moment," he adds. "He just listened."

One Saturday, he offered to help cook. "I gradually did it more and more," he says with enthusiasm. "Karen gave me more and more responsibility.

Now, she has complete trust in my judgment in the kitchen."

Sturrock feels his key skill is "taking nothing to make something out of it," and is especially proud of his soups. He credits Sanctuary with bringing him out of his shell. "A year ago, I couldn't have talked to you like this. I had no communication skills," he notes. "It's love. Once you're part of this church, it's family."

Here's the recipe for Donald Sturrock's devilled eggs.

Devilled Eggs

Sturrock made seven dozen of these for lunch and he doesn't use a recipe. I followed Julia Child's method of hard-boiling eggs from The Way to Cook *and kept Sturrock's special touches: Thousand Island dressing and a little sugar.*

24 large eggs
¹/₃ cup (75 mL) mayonnaise
¹/₃ cup (75 mL) Thousand Island
   dressing
1 to 2 tsp (5 to 10 mL) granulated
   sugar
¹/₄ cup (50 mL) chopped fresh parsley

Pinch cayenne pepper, or to taste
Salt and freshly ground black pepper
   to taste

GARNISH
24 stuffed olives, halved
Paprika

1. Prick hole in large end of each egg with push-pin. Place eggs in large saucepan; add cold water to cover by 1 inch (2.5 cm). Bring to boil; remove from heat. Cover; let sit exactly 17 minutes. With slotted spoon, transfer eggs to large bowl of cold water containing ice cubes. (Do not discard cooking water.) Let sit 2 minutes. Return cooking water to boil. Add eggs; boil 10 seconds. With slotted spoon, return to iced water, cracking shells in several places. Let sit 15 to 20 min. Crack eggs all over by gently tapping. Peel under thin stream of cold water, starting at large end.

2. Slice each egg in half horizontally. Scoop out yolks. Add to food processor with remaining ingredients except garnish; purée until smooth. Using pastry bag or spoon, fill whites with yolk mixture. Garnish with olives; dust with paprika.

MAKES 48.

AMAZING BRAISE

✳ HANG AROUND WITH JEFF CRUMP AND LIFE IS NEVER DULL.

I should know. My first encounter with this resourceful young man was in March when I shared a lively table with him and several of this city's finest chefs at Grano Restaurant. Our dinner, which included Chestnut Crepe with Rainbow Trout, Lamb Two Ways and Old Cheddar with Truffled Honey, featured at least one Ontario ingredient per course.

In the midst of a freak April blizzard, I barely made it to our second rendezvous at the location of his choice: a hockey rink in a west-end Toronto park where he was checking out pizza baked in the communal ovens.

And last week, I found myself driving to the town of Fergus where he is currently the chef at Xavier's, a picturesque restaurant that opened four months ago in a former foundry.

Crump is a fresh-faced police officer's son from London, Ont., who is blessed with a curious mind, loads of energy and plenty of talent. "My dad didn't want me to become a chef," he says as we chat at one of Xavier's sunny window tables overlooking a waterfall while I munch on yummy pulled pork, wholegrain bread and sweet butter, all made by Crump. But when he abandoned plans to be an accountant and enrolled at the Stratford Chefs School, his family came around. "They realized that, as a chef, I'd never be out of a job." So far, he never has. What's more, that career has allowed him to enjoy both his passion for cooking and his wanderlust.

When Lumiere opened in Vancouver in 1996, he cooked there with owner Rob Feenie of Food Network fame and former Toronto chef of note, Ned Bell. For four months, he was an apprentice at the famous Chez Panisse in Berkeley where he "started by peeling onions and graduated to making soup." During his pal Bell's short-lived, recent stint at the new Niagara winery Peninsula Ridge, Crump shared the kitchen for an equally brief time as his sous-chef. Earlier this year, he spent a month in Thailand with his wife Julie Johnson, a former chef and now holistic healer.

His longest stay in one spot was three years as a saucier at Agora restaurant in the Art Gallery of Ontario. "That's because I was working with Anne (Yarymowich)," he explains. "She's my mentor." Yarymowich was one of the chefs at Grano that night in March. She and several of her peers were there to share a great meal but also to support what has become Crump's main mission: promoting "slow food."

He first got interested in this increasingly popular concept at Chez Panisse where owner Alice Waters is an impassioned advocate. "I believe standardization of taste is ruining the food we eat," he says adamantly when asked why he founded an Ontario branch of the Slow Food movement, which has more than 70,000 members in 45 countries, last summer.

"Industrialization and giant food companies have created this," he continues. "Slow Food is defending the authentic pleasures of the table."

Only 12 stalwarts attended Slow Food Ontario's first meeting. But, with several events under its belt, the group is rapidly gathering steam. Their message is positive and not intimidating. "I'd like people to really cook dinner once a week," Crump proposes. "I want them to shop at farmers' markets whenever possible and to buy local food—in season." He urges us to find out where food comes from. "People need to think more about what they're eating," he says passionately. "If possible, to put a face to the person who grew it or made it."

Crump isn't a fan of convenience products but is no food snob. "I decided to make macaroni and cheese for a staff meal one night at Peninsula Ridge," explains this down-to-earth chef. "One of the apprentices wanted to go out and buy Kraft Dinner. Instead, I used macaroni and a Mornay sauce with double-smoked bacon. It was easy to make and tasted awesome."

Often, Crump notes, the simplest foods are best. He cites a lunch prepared by a Mennonite woman for a Slow Food Ontario event near St. Jacobs earlier this year. "She made the butter, pickles, bread, tomato and apple juice," he says with relish. "We had scalloped potatoes, pork sausage and roast pork—all made with ingredients from local farms. The dessert was 'egg cheese' with maple syrup. It tasted like warm ice cream." He is convinced "if people start to eat really delicious food, they'll spend more time shopping, cooking and eating." Meanwhile, he'll pursue his goal "to be part of something important. I'm not out to change the world. I just want to hold the torch and not let it go out."

Here's a delicious "slow" dish from Crump. Make it on a cool evening to enjoy reheated with baby new potatoes and a watercress salad with orange segments and shaved fennel in a simple vinaigrette laced with juice from the oranges.

Braised Pork with Olives

Use cured kalamata or nicoise olives, not canned.

3 lb (1.5 kg) boneless pork shoulder butt roast

1 tsp (5 mL) salt

1/2 tsp (2 mL) freshly ground black pepper

3 tbsp (45 mL) vegetable oil

2 medium onions, diced

1 large carrot, peeled, diced

1 celery stalk, diced

19 oz (540 mL) can tomatoes, undrained

2 cups (500 mL) chicken stock or water

4 cloves garlic, chopped

1 tbsp (15 mL) fresh thyme leaves

1 tsp (5 mL) fennel seeds

1/2 cup (125 mL) coarsely chopped pitted black olives

1/4 cup (50 mL) chopped fresh Italian parsley

1. Preheat oven to 325°F (160°C).

2. Sprinkle pork with salt and pepper. In large skillet, heat oil over medium-high heat. Add pork; cook, turning, until browned on all sides, about 10 minutes. Transfer to large dutch oven or oven-proof saucepan with lid. Reduce heat to medium. Add onions, carrot and celery to skillet; cook, stirring occasionally, until soft and golden brown, about 9 minutes. Stir in tomatoes, stock, garlic, thyme and fennel seeds, scraping browned bits from bottom of skillet. Increase heat to high; bring to boil. Pour over pork dutch oven. Cover and bake, turning pork halfway, about 3 hours or until very tender. Transfer pork to serving platter; cover loosely with foil.

3. Skim fat from sauce. Transfer sauce to blender; purée. (Strain through fine sieve, if desired.) In saucepan, bring to boil. Reduce heat to medium; cook until reduced and thickened, about 10 minutes. Stir in olives and parsley. Serve with sliced pork.

MAKES 6 TO 8 SERVINGS.

THE STAFF OF LIFE

"Give a man a fish and you feed him for a day. Teach a man to fish and you feed him for a lifetime." – Chinese proverb.

✳ IT'S A FRIGID, BLEAK, MID-WINTER MORNING and my mood is a match for the weather. But, as I walk through the doors of St. John the Compassionate Mission on Broadview Ave. just north of Queen, a soothing warmth quickly envelops me, body and soul.

Near the entrance to this humble church is a tiny kitchen. It's a hub of activity filled with the aroma of that day's lunch: a giant pot of turkey stew simmering away on the small stove. Stirring it slowly is a young man wearing a black chef's beret who's adept at making creative use of donated ingredients dropped off each morning by Second Harvest.

I make my way into the high-ceilinged, homey church itself. It's filled with the gentle buzz of conversation from about 50 people seated at long tables set with cups, plates, teapots, sliced cake and scones.

A smiling, bearded man invites me to join them. He is Father Roberto (Ubertino) who has been director of this Orthodox mission since it began 17 years ago. Somebody motions me to an empty chair. There's no formal introduction, no announcement of a journalist in their midst—just a roomful of folks about to share simple food, a few words and an uplifting community of spirit.

The soft-spoken South Asian man next to me explains the colourful mural painted across one wall. Not quite finished, it's by an artist who frequents the mission and tells the Bible story of the loaves and fishes. In it, Father Roberto and several others in this room are whimsically portrayed as biblical figures. Lunch prep is now in full swing and Father Roberto leads me down narrow stairs to the basement bakery.

Baking is finished for the day but a man called Jim is tending a vat of dough for the next day's bread in one of several spotless rooms sparsely furnished with ovens, a large table, walk-in fridge, big trolleys and a couple of freezers. On the walls hang a few religious icons. Then it's up to a quieter, second-floor room where Father Roberto tells me about St. John's Bakery, which started 17 years ago and now produces loaves so delicious my daughter Ruthie insists theirs be our new house bread.

He speaks with quiet enthusiasm about his pet project. "First, the bakery's goal is to be a profitable business," he's at pains to point out. "Right now, it breaks even but, if the bread doesn't turn out, it's a catastrophe. For those who work here, it's a real job, not play." He's referring to several part-time employees—people with problems, some of them homeless, many sent via workfare—and a couple of full-time managers. All are paid.

Most ingredients are organic and purchased from local Mennonite farmers. The product, he notes, is "high-end," adding with a half-smile, "We sell to the rich to help the poor."

It all began with small batches of cookies and muffins. Then, with the help of a European baker who came to the mission after falling on hard times, bread became its forte.

Ten years ago, Father Roberto and a couple of others went to Brittany in France to work with a religious community whose specialty is a kind of sourdough similar to the famous "pain Poilane" currently flown in from Paris and sold at Holt Renfrew. They gradually perfected it and currently produce more than two dozen variations on that theme.

Then there's what Father Roberto calls the bakery's "human side."

Key is his fervent belief in the importance of work, that each person has a gift and that self-confidence is a fundamental need. He rejects the culture of poverty. Many come to him with "a diagnosis. I'm a schizophrenic or I'm depressed" and a belief "that my resource is my handicap." His response is powerful and refreshing. "My attitude is not: What can I give you but what can I take from you?" He explains, "This could mean folding tea towels each day, as one woman does. Or making lunch for the mission like that young man in the kitchen preparing turkey stew."

Rejecting the idea of charity, he quotes Mother Maria, an orthodox Russian nun and a saint in his church who died in Auschwitz after helping others escape the Nazis: "Unless a hungry person feels they matter to you personally, they will not be able to forgive you for what you've given them."

Here's a Lemon Pound Cake similar to one served at the mission.

Lemon Pound Cake

From the cookbook The Real Dish, *a fundraiser for Sistering, a drop-in centre for homeless women.*

½ cup (125 mL) unsalted butter, at
 room temperature
1 cup (250 mL) granulated sugar
2 eggs
1 tbsp (15 mL) grated lemon rind
1½ cups (375 mL) all-purpose flour

1 tsp (5 mL) baking powder
½ tsp (2 mL) salt
½ cup (125 mL) milk

SYRUP
¼ cup (50 mL) granulated sugar
Juice of 1 lemon, about ¼ cup (50 mL)

1. Preheat oven to 350°F (180°C).

2. In bowl, using electric mixer, beat together butter and sugar until light and creamy. Beat in eggs, one at a time. Beat in lemon rind.

3. In another bowl, combine flour, baking powder and salt. Beat into butter mixture alternately with milk, making three additions of flour mixture and two of milk, just until mixed. Pour into buttered 8 x 4-inch (20 x 10 cm) loaf pan. Bake in middle of oven 45 to 50 minutes, or until tester comes out clean.

4. Just before loaf is done, cook sugar in lemon juice in small saucepan over medium heat, stirring, until dissolved.

5. While loaf is hot and still in pan, prick all over with fork or cake tester. Slowly pour on hot syrup, allowing it to soak in. Turn out onto wire rack before slicing.

MAKES ABOUT 12 SERVINGS.

WHY I LOVE THE 'Y'

❋ I TEND TO GUSH WHEN TALKING ABOUT THE DOWNTOWN Y.
In fact, words like "uplifting" and "a microcosm of our city" have actually passed my lips when raving to friends, family and perfect strangers about the wondrous establishment that has practically become my second home. After all, I'm wont to ask rhetorically, where else can you hang out with people of every age, shape, colour and sexual persuasion under the watchful eye of cheerful, bright-eyed staff while indulging in a wholesome activity guaranteed to elevate one's mood?

So naturally, I relished the recent opportunity to enjoy almost an entire day savouring three of the Y's disparate offerings. It began with an interesting interview, was followed by great eats and wound up with the delicious release of endorphins.

It's late morning and I'm chatting with Cesar Sevcik, a graduate of the Y's Enterprise Self-Employment Assistance Program, in the sunny cafeteria of YMCA headquarters at 42 Charles St. E. As the lovely aroma of that day's lunch specials—chicken and vegetable curries—wafts our way, he informs me that both spice-scented dishes are "very tasty." Having just finished a six-week stint helping those who operate this welcoming eatery on a consulting basis, he should know.

For the past three years, Sevcik—a handsome, soft-spoken young man born and raised in Venezuela whose last name comes from his father's Czech heritage—has used his considerable experience as a chef along with know-how gained from the Y's one-year course, to build his own small business called Artichoke Catering. Beaming, Sevcik tells me he loves his life as "a special occasion personal chef." His company has no kitchen, he explains. "My specialty is dinner parties in clients' homes. I'm a chef who's on call, like a family doctor."

Sevcik, who graduated from "hotel school" in Caracas and arrived in Toronto five years ago, comes by his mélange of cooking styles honestly. His resume includes several years with Club Med cooking at resorts in the Caribbean, Brazil and France. He worked as a caterer with a French chef in Columbus, Ohio, where he also ran a kosher dining room for students, and spent about three years in France's Burgundy region cooking in hotels and restaurants.

He attributes much of his current success to the assistance he got from the Y. "They helped me not to feel I'm alone in the middle of nowhere," he says, smiling sweetly. "They were my bridge to the community." Small wonder he wants to give something back by participating in that organization's sixth annual fundraiser Taste of the Community. He and a stellar roster of local chefs, caterers and winemakers—that includes Ruth's Chris Steakhouse, Jamie Kennedy at the Museum, Dufflet Pastries, Cave Spring Cellars and President's Choice—will serve up a delectable moveable feast. Most of the proceeds from the $50-a-ticket event go to the YMCA's Food Service Training Program from which many of the participants have hired graduates.

At my next stop—a magnificent lunch served at a chef's table amid the hubbub of the Charles St. building's bustling, lower-level kitchen—I see that program in action. And I mean action. Today, the entire group of 18 students, dressed immaculately in chefs' whites, are in on the preparation of our group's four-course lunch.

Seated next to Jerry Kiviluoma, the program's director, I hear more about this 12-week course while munching on a tasty tempura shrimp served atop lemongrass-laced salmon mousse. "It's intended to help people develop the skills required to get entry-level jobs," he explains. "A few go to colleges like George Brown afterwards. For most, it helps them start their career." The majority of students, he adds, are referred by Toronto Social Services who pay their $2,000 fee. Others are subsidized by the Y.

The meal's entrée has now arrived: a luscious, crispy-skinned, citrus-spiked half Cornish hen stuffed with a duxelles of mushrooms and accompanied by perfectly steamed baby carrots and bok choy. "These students are here for eight hours a day," Kiviluoma continues. "From 8:00 A.M. until 1:30 P.M., it's hands-on in the kitchen. In the afternoon, they have food labs or workshops."

Lunch is over and, after a leisurely stroll down Yonge St. in the afternoon sun, I'm ready for my next Y boost to body and soul—an invigorating workout on the treadmill in that lively, convivial downtown gym.

Meanwhile, here's the recipe for a superb salad from Cesar Sevcik.

Warm Salad with Bacon, Pecans and Cherry Tomatoes

A mixture of romaine and leaf lettuce, which both have good body, work well in this. You can add a handful or two of baby greens for eye appeal. If using those yummy little grape tomatoes now widely available, leave them whole.

9 bacon slices, ½ lb (250 g)
½ cup (125 mL) pecans
2 tbsp (30 mL) chopped shallots or onion
¼ cup (50 mL) dry red wine
3 tbsp (45 mL) maple syrup
3 tbsp (45 mL) balsamic vinegar

1 cup (250 mL) halved cherry tomatoes
1 tbsp (15 mL) chopped fresh thyme leaves
Freshly ground pepper to taste
12 cups (3 L) torn lettuce

1. In large skillet, cook bacon over medium-high heat about 5 minutes, or until crisp. Transfer to paper towel with slotted spoon; chop coarsely.

2. In small skillet, toast pecans over low heat until browned, about 4 minutes. Transfer to cutting board; chop coarsely.

3. Add shallots to bacon fat in large skillet; cook over medium-low heat about 2 minutes, or until soft. Stir in wine, maple syrup and vinegar; cook about 3 minutes more, or until thickened. Remove from heat. Add tomatoes, thyme, bacon and pecans.

4. Place lettuce in large serving bowl. Pour on warm dressing; toss to coat. Sprinkle with pepper. Serve at once.

MAKES ABOUT 6 APPETIZER SERVINGS.

⌕ Chapter Four ⌕

STAR GRAZING

✳ CELEBRITY—SO WHAT? THAT'S USUALLY MY ATTITUDE.
As a newspaper journalist, I find it more rewarding to discover and write about ordinary people who have uplifting, original stories to tell rather than re-hash stuff about famous folk who have little or no justifiable claim to fame. On those occasions when I have interviewed celebs because of some food connection, it's often a major hassle. There are layers of publicists. Many so-called stars are prima donnas prone to showing up late, in a bad mood and with little or nothing of interest to impart. Over the years, I've found that the bigger the celebrity, the more this nonsense applies. That said, I made an exception to all of the above when it came to one of the major scoops of my career: the intimate lunch I shared with living legend Sophia Loren.

It was a cold, rainy February Wednesday in 1999 and Loren was in Toronto for a rare and brief visit to promote her just-published, coffee-table food memoir *Sophia Loren's Recipes and Memories*. It's a flimsy excuse for a cook-book although there are gorgeous photos, cute gossip about film colleagues like her favourite director Vittorio De Sica and several sweet stories about her family, in particular husband Carlo Ponti and Nonna Luisa, the grandmoth-er she adored and to whom she dedicates the glossy tome. But I did find a couple of good recipes that worked and hey, you don't turn down a chance to chat one-on-one with a star this big, especially when it's the only print interview Loren is giving as she's whisked through town amid a flurry of flashbulbs.

After spending a week watching all of Loren's movies, including the mem-orable *Two Women* for which her heart-wrenching performance won an Oscar, and reading Warren G. Harris's excellent biography cover-to-cover, I was ready for the big day. Needless to say, I had to pinch myself several times during the secret, multi-course lunch at Trattoria Giancarlo in Little Italy for which owner and chef Jenny Barato reproduced luscious little versions of dishes inspired by Loren's book.

My lunch partner loved the food and enthusiastically cleaned her plate each time.

Two personal details didn't make it to either of the articles I wrote about this interview, one of which appeared on the *Star's* front page, so here they are. Halfway through the meal, when both us were feeling quite relaxed, Loren put down her fork, looked me in the eye, smiled that inimitable wide smile and said, "I like you. You're like me. You have a passion for food." A course or two later, there was another moment I'll never forget. Again, there was a lull in the conversation. "You remind me of Simone Signoret," claimed my interviewee. "You have the same eyes." Giddy with this compliment, I headed for my local video store the next night to rent *Ship of Fools* and *Room at the Top*, then rushed to the Star's library for photos of that talented, husky-voiced French actress. And yes, there is a resemblance. I exited that landmark lunch on "cloud nine" but, thankfully, still had the presence of mind to have Loren sign my copy of her book.

In the case of Keith Richards, one of my favourite musicians, the celebrity autograph wound up scrawled across a feature article I wrote for the *Star's* "Food" section. It was the summer of 1994 and the Rolling Stones were in

Toronto to rehearse for their Voodoo Lounge tour and to make a video for their new single. They also wowed local fans with a couple of surprise concerts.

While chatting with colleague Peter Howell, our paper's rock critic at the time, I discovered a potential food story. It seems Richards has a predilection, to put it mildly, for shepherd's pie, a dish I recall fondly from my childhood hot school lunches in London, England.

I asked three chefs to create a version of this humble but clever British dish originally invented to recycle Sunday dinner. The result: a tasty, tongue-in-cheek tribute designed to come to Richards's gastronomical rescue and bearing the subtitle: "It's only shepherd's pie but he likes it." Apparently, the rakish rocker liked my article so much, he signed a copy handed to him by Howell, which I now have framed and hanging on my wall at home.

When Woody Harrelson hit town to promote his road trip documentary about the environment, *Go Further*, his publicist phoned to ask if I was interested in meeting the eccentric star and interviewing his personal chef. Naturally, my answer was a resounding yes. The next day, I watched the lovely Renee Underkoffler do her amazing stuff with raw food: a "cooking" style about which I'd been skeptical. Harrelson, whom I've admired ever since seeing that film classic *White Men Can't Jump*, finally showed up an hour late. He redeemed himself by being all smiles and showed his appreciation of Underkoffler's work by devouring her fresh fare with relish in mere minutes.

My interview with "Joe Dogs" Iannuzzi probably takes the cake for wildest and most wonderful of my career. Once a New York mobster and cook for the Gambino clan, Iannuzzi had turned state's witness on his Mafia brothers after a brutal beating. He used his time while under the witness protection plan to write a cookbook, a fantastic little recipe collection called *The Mafia Cookbook*. He would reliably and cheerfully call me at appointed times from places unknown. After several such conversations, we bonded. How can one not feel good towards a man with the best recipes going for Caponata and Arborio Rice Pudding? However, I drew the line at his proposal of coming to Toronto to take me out for dinner. I had grim visions of that being my last meal. However, I'm eternally grateful to him for one of the best articles I've written.

SCREEN CUISINE

✳ I HAD NO IDEA UNTIL IT HAPPENED that I would wind up crying during the last scene of *Big Night*. In fact, it only dawned on me how touchingly sweet is this simple little movie with a small cast of characters and minimal plot when the bittersweet emotion crept up on me at the very end.

One reason the movie grabbed me is its main theme—food—a subject readers know is dear to my heart. But, more important, *Big Night*—a story of two Italian immigrant brothers struggling to run a small restaurant in New York—is about the food/love connection and all that this universal topic can entail. Another theme is the elusive and, some might say, obsolete notion of the American Dream and how it can disappoint. But the film also grapples with complicated and profound aspects of the human condition like integrity, pride in one's work and honesty.

For anyone interested in food and cooking, the movie touches many nerves. The chef brother Primo (so named because he is the firstborn), wonderfully played by Tony Shalhoub (the taxi driver on the TV show "Wings"), is a talented purist who refuses to compromise his cooking to satisfy what he calls "philistine" diners, in spite of the urgings of his somewhat sleazy business manager and sibling Secondo, played by Stanley Tucci of television's "Murder One" fame. (A few local chefs—and you know who you are—will relate to this.) "To eat good food is to be close to God," says Primo, meaning every word of it. "If I sacrifice my work, it dies," he exclaims passionately during a fight with Secondo. And, describing a rival, much more successful eatery serving ersatz Italian food, he cries, "Rape of cuisine! It goes on in that restaurant every night."

Of course, there is romance (mostly in the shapely shape of Isabella Rossellini) and plenty of mouthwatering food scenes. Best of all, the film, directed by Stanley Tucci and Campbell Scott, shows that friendship, closeness to others and the sharing of good food lovingly prepared, can triumph over superficial values—in this case, fame and the almighty dollar.

Here is a recipe to give you a taste of good things to come:

Timpano

A large enamel bowl, 12 inches (30 cm) across and 4 inches (10 cm) deep, is perfect for this and can be purchased at many kitchen or hardware stores. We recommend buying or making extra tomato sauce to serve on the side. In summer, this would make a great picnic dish. It's also a stunning creation to serve on a buffet.

PASTA FROLLA PASTRY
3 ¾ cups (925 mL) all-purpose flour
2 tbsp (30 mL) granulated sugar
Pinch salt
½ cup (125 mL) cold unsalted butter
⅓ cup (75 mL) shortening or lard
1 egg
1 egg yolk
½ cup (125 mL) white wine

MEATBALLS
1 lb (500 g) lean ground beef
2 eggs
¼ cup (50 mL) breadcrumbs
¼ cup (50 mL) chopped fresh parsley
½ tsp (5 mL) salt
Pinch freshly ground black pepper
2 tbsp (30 mL) vegetable oil

TOMATO SAUCE
3 oz (75 g) pancetta or bacon, finely
   chopped
1 large onion, chopped
2 cloves garlic, minced
½ cup (125 mL) dry white wine
28 oz (796 mL) can tomatoes, chopped
10 oz (300 g) package dried porcini
   mushrooms, soaked in 1 cup
   (250 mL) boiling water 30 minutes

ASSEMBLY
1½ lb (750 g) dried penne
8 eggs
4 oz (125 g) shredded mozzarella
   cheese, about 1 cup (250 mL)
¼ cup (50 mL) parmesan cheese
2 tbsp (30 mL) dried basil
4 cloves garlic, minced
½ tsp (2 mL) hot pepper flakes
1 tsp (5 mL) salt
Freshly ground black pepper to taste
5 hard-boiled eggs, cut into quarters

1. For pastry: In large bowl, combine flour, sugar and salt. Using pastry blender, cut in butter and shortening or lard until mixture resembles coarse crumbs.

2. In small bowl, beat together egg and egg yolk and half the wine. Add to flour mixture, tossing with fork. Add remaining wine just until pastry begins to clump together. Bring together into ball. Wrap with plastic and refrigerate 1 hour.

3. Meanwhile, for meatballs: In bowl, combine beef, eggs, breadcrumbs, parsley, salt and pepper, mixing until well blended. Shape into walnut-sized balls.

4. Heat oil in large, heavy skillet over medium-high heat. Cook meatballs about 7 minutes, turning to brown on all sides, until no longer pink inside. Drain on paper towels.

5. For sauce: In same skillet, add pancetta or bacon, onion and garlic to any fat remaining in pan. Cook about 5 minutes, stirring and scraping up brown bits. When onions are tender, add wine. Cook until almost evaporated. Stir in tomatoes. Finely chop soaked mushrooms. Add to sauce along with soaking liquid strained through coffee filter. Bring to boil, reduce heat to medium and simmer briskly about 30 minutes or until very thick.

6. In large saucepan of boiling salted water, cook penne about 8 minutes or until tender. Drain.

7. In large bowl, combine tomato sauce, 8 eggs, mozzarella, parmesan, basil, garlic, hot pepper flakes, salt and pepper. Stir in penne, mixing thoroughly. Gently stir in meatballs.

8. On large, lightly floured work surface, roll out two-thirds pastry into a large, rough circle. Line oiled 12-cup (3 L) deep casserole dish with pastry. Pour in half of penne mixture. Place hard-boiled eggs evenly over pasta. Top with remaining penne mixture. Roll out remaining pastry to fit top. Lightly brush edge of bottom pastry with water. Place top pastry over and press edges to seal. Trim excess pastry.

9. Preheat oven to 375°F (190°C).

10. Place large, flat ovenproof plate over pastry. Weight with pie plate full of pie weights or equivalent. Let stand 30 minutes.

11. Place casserole in large roasting pan. Add hot water to come halfway up sides of pan. Bake, with weights, for three hours. Remove weights. Cool in water bath about 1 hour. Cool at least a half-hour more before cutting. Can be served warm or room temperature.

MAKES 12 TO 15 SERVINGS.

Caponata

An Italian version of ratatouille, this is usually served as a veggie side dish with grilled chicken or fish; it can also be served on pasta or as a topping for grilled rounds of French or Italian bread as an appetizer. This can be made a few days ahead; chopped black olives can be added. Fresh tomatoes are ideal; in winter, canned ones work well. You can omit the pine nuts, if desired. This recipe comes, I'm told, from the mother of Stanley Tucci (sleazy Secondo in Big Night).

1 large unpeeled eggplant, cut in
    1-inch (2.5 cm) cubes
⅓ cup (75 mL) olive oil
1 large onion, chopped
2 stalks celery, chopped
2 large ripe tomatoes, peeled, seeded
    and diced OR 28 oz (796 mL) can
    plum tomatoes, undrained

1 tbsp (15 mL) capers, rinsed and
    drained
1 tbsp (15 mL) pine nuts
1 tbsp (15 mL) granulated sugar
3 tbsp (45 mL) white wine vinegar
Salt and freshly ground pepper to
    taste

1. Place eggplant in colander, sprinkle with salt and let drain 30 minutes. Pat dry with paper towels.

2. In large skillet, heat half the oil over medium-high heat. Sauté eggplant until softened and lightly browned, about 10 minutes. You may have to add a little more oil if skillet becomes too dry. Transfer to medium saucepan with slotted spoon.

3. Add remaining oil to skillet; sauté onion and celery until softened, about 10 minutes. Add onion mixture to saucepan along with tomatoes, capers, pine nuts, sugar, vinegar, salt and pepper; stir together. Cover and simmer 45 minutes, stirring occasionally.

4. Taste and adjust seasonings just before serving warm or at room temperature.

MAKES 4 SERVINGS.

ARE YOU HUNGRY TONIGHT?

❋ FOR YOU, BARBECUED PORK, COLLARD GREENS and banana pudding may not be the foods of love. But these seemingly mundane, down-home dishes were, I've discovered, a surefire way to the heart of Elvis Presley —the swivel-hipped, curled-lipped King of rock 'n' roll, the husky-voiced hunk who was and is, for many, the heart-throb of all time.

What's more, having sampled the versions of these and others of the King's favourite foods, lovingly compiled in a fabulous book called *Are You Hungry Tonight?* by Brenda Arlene Butler, I can heartily recommend a luscious lunch or sensual supper incorporating the above foods as the perfect way for you and the love of your life to celebrate Valentine's Day.

But back to Elvis. Seems that the King (he was born in Tupelo, Miss., on Jan. 8, 1935, and died at Graceland on Aug. 16, 1977) was a real Southern boy when it came to his taste in food. Elvis liked his meals made the way Mama Gladys Presley used to cook them. He wanted his meat well-done, verging on burnt. He preferred his roasts (like the superb, aforementioned Mississippi pork roast, see recipe below) slow-cooked in a pan covered with tin foil until they were soft and juicy. His cooks (several of whom contributed recipes and tidbits to Butler's book) knew to lace his beloved string beans with salt pork, pepper and a soupcon of sugar, just the way he liked them. And, of course, those same cooks were at the ready, day or night, to fry up the favourite peanut butter and banana sandwich that became the King's signature dish.

But, according to those who were there, Elvis did dabble in some healthier fare. Alvena Roy, his cook from 1964 to 1969, told the press three years ago: "Elvis liked salads—in particular, juicy beefsteak tomatoes peeled by hand." Iceberg lettuce had to be shredded and served with a little pitcher of dressing consisting of sunflower oil, lemon juice or vinegar, salt, pepper and paprika.

As for breakfast, Roy reports that Presley was specific about what he liked. "You couldn't give him the white of the egg," she recalled. "You had to give him the yolk of the egg and make it look like a pancake." To be exact, you had to break four eggs, discard the whites, beat the yolks with cream and then fry the mixture in butter. He insisted the "pancake" be served with a half to one pound of crispy bacon.

The King, who was a big fan of meatloaf, gravy, ham or T-bone steak, also had some quirky eating habits. According to Roy, he liked his food chopped in pieces small enough to pick up with his fingers and often eschewed the conventional knife and fork.

Tidbits on the King's eating habits from *Are You Hungry Tonight?*:

- The fridges of his Graceland mansion in Memphis and at his home in Beverly Hills always contained fresh lean ground beef, hamburger buns, at least six cans of ready-to-bake biscuits, pickles, potatoes, onions, shredded coconut, fudge cookies, assorted fresh fruit, sauerkraut, mustard and peanut butter.
- His favourite soft drinks were Pepsi-Cola, Nesbitt's Orange and Shasta Black Cherry.
- Elvis hated fish and never ate it in any shape or form. He even asked Priscilla not to eat fish (even tuna) around him, claiming it gave a person "cat breath."
- The King was a confirmed snacker. Freshly made banana pudding and homemade brownies had to be on hand at all times.
- Elvis's taste rarely strayed from good ol' Southern fare, but he did enjoy some Oriental food. He frequented a Chinese restaurant on Highway 51 in Memphis and sampled Oriental dishes when filming *Blue Hawaii*.
- The Gridiron—an all-night diner in Memphis—was his favourite spot to eat burgers (well-done, of course).
- Another of his favourite haunts was Chenault's Restaurant in Memphis, famous among locals for biscuits and sorghum syrup (a sweet syrup made from grain).
- The King loved butter and foods cooked with it. Margarine, for him, was no substitute.

Here then—as my offering to sweethearts everywhere in celebration of Valentine's Day—are some of Elvis's favourite foods, adapted from *Are You Hungry Tonight?*

Mississippi Barbecued Pork

This is probably the closest you'll come to a homemade version of that wondrous Southern staple: barbecue pork. It's the way to anyone's heart, any time, anywhere.

3 lb (1.5 kg) boneless pork butt or
    shoulder butt roast
1 tsp (5 mL) vegetable oil
1 cup (250 mL) tomato sauce
1/4 cup (50 mL) cider vinegar
1/4 cup (50 mL) Worcestershire
    sauce

1/4 cup (50 mL) packed brown sugar
1/2 tsp (2 mL) each celery seed, chili
    powder
1/4 tsp (1 mL) each salt, pepper
Dash hot pepper sauce

1. Preheat oven to 325°F (160°C).

2. Randomly pierce surface of pork with sharp knife. In ovenproof dutch oven over medium-high heat, brown pork on all sides in oil. Pour off fat.

3. Combine remaining ingredients. Pour over pork and bring to boil. Cover and transfer to oven. Roast, basting several times, about 2 hours or until pork is fork tender. Let stand 10 minutes before slicing.

MAKES 6 SERVINGS.

Savory Collard Greens

Elvis gave a nod to nutrition when he regularly scarffed down a plateful of his favourite greens.

2 lb (1 kg) fresh collard greens,
    about 18 leaves
2 tbsp (30 mL) unsalted butter
1/2 lb (250 g) cooked ham, diced

2 tbsp (30 mL) chopped onion
1 tsp (5 mL) granulated sugar
1/4 tsp (1 mL) each salt, pepper

1. Thoroughly wash greens and shake dry. Cut out tough centre ribs. Stack several leaves at a time, roll into cylinders and slice into 1-inch (2.5 cm) wide strips. Set aside.

2. In large saucepan or dutch oven, heat butter over medium heat. Cook ham 3 to 5 minutes or until lightly browned. Add collards, 1/2 cup (125 mL) water, onion, sugar, salt and pepper. Simmer, covered, over medium-low heat 15 to 20 minutes or until collards are tender. Drain if necessary. Taste and adjust seasoning.

MAKES 6 SERVINGS.

Pecan Pie

This creamy, custardy version of that fabulous Southern sweet is the best I've tried.

4 eggs
⅓ cup (75 mL) packed brown sugar
1¼ cups (300 mL) corn syrup
¼ cup (50 mL) unsalted butter,
   melted

1¼ tsp (6 mL) vanilla extract
1 cup (250 mL) pecan halves
9-inch (23 cm) unbaked pie shell
1 cup (250 mL) whipping cream,
   whipped

1. Preheat oven to 375°F (190°C).
2. In bowl, beat eggs until foamy. Add brown sugar; mix well. Blend in corn syrup, butter and vanilla. Stir in pecans. Pour into pie shell. Bake 40 to 45 minutes or until centre is puffed and set (filling will jiggle slightly in centre). Cool on rack.
3. Serve with whipped cream.

MAKES 8 SERVINGS.

IT'S ONLY SHEPHERD'S PIE, BUT HE LIKES IT

"It's certainly unfair to say that the English lack both a cuisine and a sense of humor. Their cooking is a joke in itself." – Calvin Trillin, Foreword to *Great British Cooking* by Jane Garmey

❋ I, FOR ONE, TAKE UMBRAGE AT THIS CHEAP SHOT by the usually right-on and often witty Mr. Trillin. After all, not only is the United Kingdom the source of some of the world's best comedy (Peter Sellers, Monty Python, Absolutely Fabulous, and Ali G immediately leap to mind), it is also the birthplace of notable culinary creations like Spotted Dick (a no-nonsense steamed dessert that gets its name from the raisins and currants that inundate it), Summer Pudding (the best thing ever to happen to a fresh berry) and, of course, Shepherd's Pie.

Which, without missing a beat, brings us to the Rolling Stones. It brings us in particular to Keith Richards (quick apologies here to Mick lest he feel ignored and a note to him that we once ran his excellent recipe for shrimp curry). Richards, by all accounts, is a serious shepherd's pie fan. And I mean serious.

"Once a member of the crew ate his shepherd's pie and Keith threatened to cut him up and put his legs in a shepherd's pie," goes the quote from Richards's first wife, Anita Pallenberg, in *Keith Richards: The Biography* by Victor Bockris. "So he gets his shepherd's pie, miles of shepherd's pie everywhere. He's always got shepherd's pie and he doesn't have to worry about it."

At least, almost always.

Apparently, before the huge, no-holds-barred 1989 Stones concert at the SkyDome in Toronto, a replica of an English pub was set up backstage at which a pre-concert meal was served. But, as caterer Greg Howe told the *Star* last year: "Keith Richards arrived late. There were literally two spoonfuls of shepherd's pie left." Response from the pie-deprived Keef (as he is affectionately known) was short and not-so-sweet. "Where's the rest?" asked he. "Get some more of it or I don't go on." Not surprisingly, the matter was resolved tout de suite: "We did and he did," Howe recalls.

Keef isn't alone in being a devotee of shepherd's pie. I have fond memories of this British standby when it was a regular on the rotating hot lunch menu (usually the day after its more elegant kissing cousin, roast beef) when I was a schoolkid in Jolly Old. Served with a good slathering of thick brown gravy (its source, natch, that trusty box of Bisto) and your mandatory two veg, shepherd's pie was up there for me with Spam fritters and rice pudding.

It has also long been a fave of former Brit Geoffrey Pimblett, owner of the wonderfully quirky restaurant, Pimblett's, at 263 Gerrard St. E., which specializes in British food. "Shepherd's pie is, quite simply, good grub," Pimblett replies cheerfully when I ask for an opinion on our dish du jour. "I didn't put it on our dinner menu for a long time," he continues, "I thought it was a lunch sort of thing—not exotic enough for a dinner menu. But when I did, eight years ago, it became a big seller. These days, it's up there with fish and chips, and steak and kidney pie."

Pimblett, whose family ran a pie shop in Lancashire for many years, has done his research on this illustrious dish. "Traditionally, it was made from the leftover Sunday roast, a lot like Bubble and Squeak (a fry-up of meat and veg)," he explains. "And often, that roast would have been leg of lamb, although in one of Mrs. Beeton's books, she does make it with leftover beef."

Michael Bonacini, well-known Toronto chef and restaurateur also attributes his penchant for shepherd's pie to his British roots. "Shepherd's pie is comfort food," Bonacini says. "It reminds me of home. In fact, I don't think there's a household in the U.K. where it hasn't been served at some time." As a kid growing up in Pembrokeshire, Wales, Bonacini ate shepherd's pie prepared by his English mum (his dad hails from northern Italy) "at least once every two or three weeks." Bonacini recalls the best shepherd's pie he has ever eaten: "They served it at the pub in Wales near the chefs' school I attended. It was delicious—maybe from sitting in the steamer for two or three hours!" As for shepherd's pie on Jump's menu, Bonacini plans to add it to his repertoire this fall: "I'll make it with beef and lamb and call it Keith Richards Shepherd's Pie. After all, we have a Keith and a Richard working here."

Shepherd's Pie

An updated version that incorporates sweet potatoes into the top layer. Use 4 cups (1 L) chopped or ground leftover roast beef instead of ground beef, if desired. If you have any leftover gravy from a roast, stir it into the sauce.

2 lb (1 kg) lean ground beef
1 tbsp (15 mL) vegetable oil
2 carrots, peeled, diced
2 stalks celery, diced
1 large onion, diced
1½ cups (375 mL) canned tomatoes, puréed
1 cup (250 mL) beef stock
½ cup (125 mL) dry red wine, or additional stock
3 tbsp (45 mL) ketchup
2 tbsp (30 mL) worcestershire sauce

1 tsp (5 mL) dried thyme
½ tsp (2 mL) ground cinnamon
¾ tsp (4 mL) each salt and freshly ground pepper
1½ lb (750 g) baking potatoes, peeled and quartered
1½ lb (750 g) sweet potatoes, peeled and quartered
6 cloves garlic
½ cup (125 mL) milk, heated
1 cup (250 mL) frozen peas

1. Preheat oven to 375°F (190°C).

2. In large saucepan, cook beef over medium-high heat about 9 minutes, stirring to break it up, or until no longer pink. Transfer to bowl with juices.

3. In same saucepan, heat oil over medium-high heat; cook carrot, celery and onion about 8 minutes, stirring often, or until softened and browned. Stir in puréed tomatoes, stock, wine, ketchup, worcestershire sauce, thyme, cinnamon, salt, pepper and browned beef. Bring to a boil. Reduce heat to simmer and cook, uncovered, about 20 minutes or until vegetables are tender and sauce thickened.

4. Place potatoes, sweet potatoes and garlic in another large saucepan. Add cold water to cover. Bring to a boil. Reduce heat to medium-high; cook about 15 minutes or until potatoes are soft. Drain. Return to saucepan. Mash with hot milk. Season to taste with salt and pepper.

5. Stir peas into beef mixture. Season to taste with additional salt and pepper, if desired. Transfer to 9 x 13-inch (23 x 33-cm) square glass baking dish. Spread potatoes over top. Bake in oven about 15 minutes or until sauce is bubbly. Place under broiler 4 minutes or until golden brown.

MAKES 8 TO 10 SERVINGS.

BY COOK OR BY CROOK

"Remember the crowd I was feeding—any meal may be their last, so it better be a good one. Crime may not pay, but it sure gives you a hell of an appetite." – The Mafia Cookbook by Joseph (Joe Dogs) Iannuzzi

❋ JOSEPH (JOE DOGS) IANNUZZI ISN'T SURE which he liked better: being a crook or being a cook. And he's had plenty of practice at both. For more than 30 years, as a mobster and major player in the Gambino crime family, Iannuzzi worked out of Florida and New York, dealing directly with such high-level Mafia members as Joe Gallo, the Gambino family's consigliere, and Carmine "The Snake" Persico, infamous head of the rival Colombo crime family. His criminal activities ran the usual gamut: everything from loan-sharking to leg-breaking.

But, as the Gambinos' resident and well-respected chef, his specialties were of a different kind. They included Manicotti Marinara with Mint, Pasta Fagioli, Lemon Granita and Shrimp Scampi. These days, in hiding somewhere south of the border under the Federal Witness Protection Plan, Iannuzzi has plenty of time to think, cook and hone his latest pursuit—writing books.

The first Joe Dogs, *The Life and Crimes of a Mobster*, is the graphic, lively account of his life. *The Mafia Cookbook* is a wonderfully witty little tome packed with his and his cohorts' favourite (and, I must add, excellent) recipes, peppered with terrific anecdotes about where, when and to whom the meals were served.

—⁓—

"And now I'm stuck in the Witness Protection Program, being taken to dinner out in the middle of wahoo land by u.s. marshals in joints that advertise 'Italian Night' and then serving macaroni and ketchup instead of pasta. I guess it serves me right." – The Mafia Cookbook

Iannuzzi decided to turn informant for the FBI after his mentor, co-mobster and, as it turned out, nemesis, Tommy Agro, tried to kill him over some unpaid debts at Don's Italian Restaurant on Singer Island, Florida, in 1981.

He describes the incident in his cookbook thus: "Then I had a terrible accident. I kept walking into this baseball bat and this iron pipe. Some of my pals were trying to see if my head was harder than those two instruments. It was, barely."

He was the star witness at 11 major trials during the 1980s. "I put away 20 of the top Mafia in New York and Florida—although most of them wound up doing it to themselves—including Tommy Agro and a chief of police." Now, in hiding after an attempt on his life a year ago, he spends his time writing, cooking and talking about his former life as a Mafia cook/crook.

"I've liked cooking for as long as I can remember," Iannuzzi told me enthusiastically in his inimitable Brooklynese the first time he phoned from places unknown at an appointed time arranged by our mutual contact, his publisher. "I learned a lot from my mother, who's an excellent cook, and from other relatives," he continued.

Iannuzzi also had some professional training when, as he told me, "I worked for a chef at a restaurant in Cleveland, Ohio, where I learned to make really good soups and sauces. "They let me into the Mafia because I knew how to cook," he says. And he loves to wax eloquent about how the mob loved his cooking.

There was the time in Queens in 1976 when he made his famous Mandarin Pork Roast for a Colombo family group that included Thomas DiBella, the Colombo boss, and soldier Dominick (Little Dom) Cataldo. "Joey, I want you to know how much I enjoyed that meal," DiBella told Joe Dogs after dinner. "I know it was some kind of southern dish because Little Dom tells me you're from the south. So where exactly in South Brooklyn you from?"

"Most of the meals I cooked were at someone's apartment when we were on the lam," Iannuzzi told me during our second phone interview. Cooking for his colleagues kept him busy: "They eat while planning crimes and they eat after committing crimes, and when there are no crimes, they eat waiting for them to happen."

SOME TIDBITS FROM THE BOOK:

- ON TURNING INFORMANT: "The guys in my new club asked me to spy on the guys in my old club who had tried to kill me. I had no problem with that. Revenge, like my Cicoria Insalata (Dandelion Salad) is best eaten cold."
- INTRO TO A BOUILLABAISSE RECIPE: "A nice fish stew for someone who some day may sleep with the fishes."
- ON COOKING AT AN FBI SAFE HOUSE: "I decided to do up something special, just in case this was my last supper."
- A TIP FOR "WOULD-BE COMPARES": "If any guy wants to join your crew and tells you he's just out of the joint, take him to dinner. If he orders anything but steak or lobster, he's lying and probably a Fed."
- HIS DEDICATION: "This book is dedicated to my good friend and compare Tommy Agro. Without you, this book would not be possible. Rest in Pieces."

And, in case you're wondering if Joe Dogs' writings glorify his former lifestyle, he told me: "I got into the mob for the girls, the money and the red carpet, and I'm honest in my books about the bad guy I was. However, I hope my writing about it will show younger people not to get into a life of crime."

―⋙―

"They all ate like they were going to the chair. You don't have to eat that way with the recipes in this book. You just have to enjoy them. Because they've been tested on the worst of the worst and the best of the best. And they've all passed with flying colors." – The Mafia Cookbook

And now, some recipes from *The Mafia Cookbook*:

Veal Marsala

"The secret to this is the Grand Marnier," says Joe Dogs. You could substitute pounded chicken breasts for the veal.

⅓ cup (75 mL) all-purpose flour
Six veal scaloppini, about 1½ lb (750 g)
⅓ cup (75 mL) unsalted butter
6 cups (1.5 L) sliced mushrooms,
   about 1 lb (500 g)
¾ cup (175 mL) marsala wine

¼ cup (50 mL) Grand Marnier
2 tbsp (30 mL) lemon juice
¼ tsp (1 mL) white pepper
Salt to taste

1. Put flour in wide shallow dish. Dip veal in flour to coat, shaking off excess; set veal aside on waxed paper.

2. In large skillet over high heat, melt half the butter. Add mushrooms; cook 2 to 3 minutes, until lightly browned. Remove mushrooms and any juice. Reduce heat to medium. Add remaining butter to pan. When hot, add veal. (Do not crowd pan. If necessary cook in two batches.) Cook veal about 2 minutes a side. Remove from skillet.

3. Add marsala to skillet, scraping up brown bits from bottom. Stir in Grand Marnier. Remove skillet from heat, stand back and carefully, using a long match, light liquid. Keep skillet off heat until flame disappears.

4. Return veal and accumulated juices to skillet along with mushrooms. Stir in lemon juice and pepper; simmer 5 minutes. Add salt.

MAKES 6 SERVINGS.

Ricotta Rice Pudding

Arborio rice can be found at Italian food shops and bulk food stores. This makes a lot.

4 cups (1 L) ricotta cheese
1¾ cups (425 mL) granulated sugar
1 tbsp (15 mL) grated lemon rind or
   to taste
1 oz (30 g) semisweet chocolate,
   melted

6 cups (1.5 L) milk
1 cup (250 mL) arborio rice
3 eggs
1 tsp (5 mL) vanilla extract
1 tbsp (15 mL) cinnamon

1. Preheat oven to 325°F (160°C).
2. Using electric mixer, beat ricotta and 1 cup (250 mL) sugar together until creamy. Stir in lemon rind and chocolate.
3. In large saucepan, combine milk, rice and remaining sugar.
4. Bring to boil, uncovered over medium-low heat. Reduce heat; simmer, stirring frequently, 20 minutes. Remove from heat; cool 20 minutes.
5. In small bowl, whisk eggs with ¼ cup (50 mL) rice mixture until blended. Gradually whisk egg mixture into rice mixture in pan. Stir in vanilla.
6. Spread about half rice mixture into buttered and floured 12-inch (30 cm) round baking dish with sides about 3 inches (8 cm) high. Top with ricotta mixture, then remaining rice mixture.
7. Bake uncovered 1¼ hours, or until tester comes out nearly clean and centre is just set. Sprinkle with cinnamon. Serve warm or cold.

MAKES 12 TO 14 SERVINGS.

RAW, RAW, RAW!

❋ Renee Loux Underkoffler wipes one hand on her apron, shakes mine with a firm grip and flashes me a gorgeous grin. Tall, tanned and toned, she is living proof that "living foods"—her unusual diet of choice— can do a body good.

Underkoffler, 28, is standing at the kitchen counter in a spacious, sunny studio-cum-loft on the second floor of a big, old former warehouse adjacent to the vintage Canary Bar and Grill near Cherry Beach. With the help of a young male chef from Liaison College, neatly dressed in chef's whites and working away quietly by her side, she is cheerfully and effortlessly preparing a labour-intensive lunch comprised entirely of raw food. Complete with cocktail appetizers, it will be served here soon for 40 patrons of the Toronto International Film Festival. The meal is a "thank you" to these folks for their support. It's also to promote the new documentary *Go Further* directed by local filmmaker Ron Mann, which was launched at the fest to rave reviews. Its star is Underkoffler's friend and fellow environmentalist Woody Harrelson, who is due to show up today as guest of honour.

The two met six years ago in Maui where they both have homes. At the time, Underkoffler was chef at The Raw Experience, the restaurant she owned for three years. Harrelson, his wife Laura Louie and their two children live on the same side of the island. "Woody and I connected right away," Underkoffler says fondly. "We're kindred spirits—yoga, living foods, being on Maui, environmental orientation." She respects Harrelson for being committed to his beliefs. "He's a very intelligent, compassionate human being," she continues, adding, "A celebrity—but I relate to him as a friend. He has the whole world to choose from and chooses something that matters."

That something inspired the five-week road trip they and a small group of fellow travellers took in the spring of 2001 that became *Go Further's* theme. While Harrelson, Underkoffler and a couple of other stalwart souls biked more than 2,000 km down California's Pacific Coast, their pals rode in a hemp-fuelled bus. The group's ecological mission, dubbed the Simple Organic Living Tour, was to convince people, says Harrelson, "to live with a light footprint on this Earth." Foodwise, they advocate organic farming, a ban on genetically modified crops and a vegan diet of raw food.

Underkoffler, who has been a vegan (no meat, fish or dairy) since her teens and has eaten 95 percent raw food for the past 10 years, talks about this as she spreads paper-thin slices of zucchini on a large platter: the base for a yummy strata that will be our entrée. As we chat, she deftly adds more layers: a paste of macadamia nuts laced with lemon juice, olive oil and maple syrup; thinly sliced, marinated portobello mushrooms; a mixture of spinach, sorrel and corn marinated in olive oil and sea salt; then a sundried tomato tapenade that includes fresh tomatoes and plenty of fresh herbs. Last, she sprinkles a garnish of ground pine nuts mixed with garlic, lemon and olive oil on top.

Underkoffler relies on bold seasonings, marinating and dehydration to give vibrancy to her food. Her favoured ingredients are "ample amounts of fresh produce, seeds, nuts, spices, herbs, olives, avocados, nut butters, tahini, miso and umeboshi plum vinegar." She admits, "preparing food without fire is challenging at first" but is adamant about the benefits.

"Living foods, which aren't refined, processed or pasteurized, embody what I feel," she explains, adding that such foods, when raw, are "at their nutritional peak." There is debate among nutrition experts about her claim that "all nutrients—rich enzymes, vitamins and minerals—are very heat-sensitive and rapidly decline after 110/112°F (55/57°C)." In fact, Toronto dietitian and food writer Janice Daciuk has serious misgivings. "Limiting oneself to foods cooked or not cooked a certain way or to a specific group of foods," she notes, "only means less variety in the diet. Eating a variety of foods is one way to ensure you get all the nutrients you need." As far as that's concerned, I think the jury's out. However, as I nibble on a sushi roll—seaweed wrap filled with a lusciously herb-enhanced raw almond paste—I'm impressed with Underkoffler's way with taste and texture.

The guests, who have now arrived and munch appreciatively on assorted appetizers, seem to agree. When Harrelson makes his entrance, almost an hour late, it's clear he's also an unabashed fan. He grabs Underkoffler in a bear hug, then picks up a plate of food. In no time, a big wedge of strata and accompanying mound of salad disappear and he's on to a second helping. Between mouthfuls, he enthuses about his friend's "cooking", then admits he's fallen off the raw food wagon. "I'd like to say I eat strictly raw food," he tells me with a grin, "but I've been eating cooked food while I'm in Toronto—especially hemp ice cream."

Harrelson, explains that his wife eats "95 percent raw food," but adds, "My kids aren't strictly raw." Asked about his favourite food, he doesn't miss a beat: "Definitely Renee's Avocado Chocolate Mousse Pie."

Underkoffler, too, has a sweet tooth. "I love fine dark chocolate," she concedes shyly when asked if she misses any foods. "The beans are roasted but I make an exception in a case like this."

Underkoffler's cookbook *Living Cuisine: The Art and Spirit of Raw Food* is available in bookstores.

Here is a quick and easy raw pea purée that Underkoffler used as a topping for tortillas made of dehydrated corn as appetizers at our delicious lunch.

Green Pea Mole

Serve this good-looking, fresh-tasting purée the same day or it loses its vibrant colour. Mound on toast, crackers or wedges of corn tortilla and top with a grape, halved fresh fig or slice of other fruit as a cocktail appetizer. Also, a nice dip to serve with tortilla chips.

1½ cups (375 mL) fresh coriander
   leaves
2 cups (500 mL) fresh peas (or
   frozen peas, thawed)
1 tbsp (15 mL) finely grated lime rind

¼ cup (50 mL) fresh lime juice
1 to 2 tbsp (15 to 30 mL) extra virgin
   olive oil
Sea salt
Freshly ground black pepper

Process coriander in food processor until finely chopped. Add peas, lime rind and juice; pulse on and off until mixed but not smooth. Season to taste with olive oil, sea salt and black pepper. Squeeze extra lime juice over top to preserve brilliant green colour.

MAKES ABOUT 2 CUPS (500 mL).

MY LUNCH WITH LA LOREN

"Cooking is an act of love, a gift, a way of sharing with others the little secrets—piccoli segreti—that are simmering on the burners."

– Sophia Loren's Recipes & Memories by Sophia Loren

❊ "THIS WAS OUR 'BIG NIGHT,'" exclaimed an exhausted but elated Jenny Barato as we all sat down for a much-needed glass of wine while Sophia Loren and her four-person entourage sailed off toward College St. in a silver limo. "The difference is our star showed up!" added the jubilant Barato who, with husband Tony, son Jason and two other staff, had just prepared and served a luscious lunch for the legendary Loren and me at their small, elegantly low-key eatery.

At Trattoria Giancarlo, in the heart of Toronto's Little Italy, our star—Sophia Loren, in town to promote her cookbook, *Sophia Loren's Recipes & Memories*—not only arrived, she made everybody's day by gracing us with her gorgeous, dignified, friendly presence for almost two hours. During a leisurely midday meal—a rendezvous that was kept completely hush-hush until it became big news later that day—Loren and I shared wondrous food, lively conversation and a promise that, if she returns to Toronto, we'll do it all again. So what was Sophia Loren like, what did we eat and what was the gist of our lunchtime chat?

As she entered the hushed restaurant—located on an unobtrusive side street and, by now, electric with anticipation of her arrival—Loren, dignified and walking tall at almost 5 foot 9, looked stunning in high heels, a beige Armani suit, ivory turtleneck and chunky gold necklace with matching earrings. Even her oversized, trademark specs—a necessity, she explained, in order to see—didn't look out of place on that big-boned, beautiful face.

As for Loren's manner, she was warm, personable and "confident everything" you might expect from a movie star who has made close to 90 films during a 40-year career, many of which—especially my favourite, the Oscar-winner *Two Women*, 1961—are classics. But, seated next to her at a small, linen-covered table set with crusty bread and small bottles of olive oil and balsamic vinegar, it didn't take long for me to relax and forget all that. Soon, we were enjoying each other's company like regular folk getting acquainted over good food.

Loren began by requesting a glass of water—"not too cold please, it bothers my digestion."

Then, as each dainty portion of our meal—a sublime, seven-course menu of tiny dishes devised by Jenny Barato and inspired by Loren's cookbook—was served, the conversation began to flow. "I wrote another cookbook a long time ago, in the 1970s," Loren recalled as our first course of paper-thin, seared beef garnished with shaved parmesan was placed before us. "I have always loved cooking, Italian food, of course," she continued, wiping her plate vigorously with a hunk of bread, "Oh, this is so good. I love this truffle oil," she added, returning to her train of thought. "I used to cook for the cast and crew on my movie sets—usually for about 70 people."

Her repertoire, not surprisingly, featured staples of southern Italy where she grew up, in the small town of Pozzuoli not far from Naples—dishes inspired by her grandmother, Nonna Luisa, to whom *Sophia Loren's Recipes & Memories* is lovingly dedicated. This big, glossy tome is peppered with photos and anecdotes that accompany recipes associated with family, friends and famous co-stars like Cary Grant, Marcello Mastroianni and Richard Burton.

"During the war, and even after the war, we were very poor," Loren told me, digging into a mini-mound of creamy polenta topped with juicy, garlic-laced slices of wild mushrooms.

"We were often hungry. My grandmother cooked food that would fill the stomach. She used whatever little we had to make tasty meals: pasta e fagioli, simple pizza or a salad made with just a crumb of cheese." A wonderful cook who died at age 68, Loren's grandmother "used fantasy, creativity to make our food. I always watched her cook and often helped by shelling peas or picking the stones from the dried beans."

These days, with homes in Geneva and Los Angeles, Loren admits that she doesn't do much cooking. However, meals are important and she usually has a substantial lunch with husband Carlo Ponti and their younger son Edoardo, 25, a writer/film director who still lives at home. Their elder son Carlo Jr., 29, a music conductor, visits whenever he can.

Loren decided to write her newest cookbook when a friend advised her to compile "all the recipes I had collected in a drawer from family, friends and places I've visited over the years."

Giving me a look of sheer pleasure as she nibbled on a delicate nest of tagliatelle with a silky, rich lemon cream sauce, Loren explained, "I felt an ordinary collection of recipes would be a bit dry so my editor and I decided to add the pictures and anecdotes. It took seven or eight months in all." Next, having appreciatively devoured a small serving of lusciously creamy lobster risotto, Loren cleansed her palate with a few spoonfuls of refreshing blood orange sorbet and agreed with me that this was a meal to remember.

"I like you," she said with a wide grin. "You're like me—you have a passion for food. For a long time, women were too thin. I go to Armani fashion shows. About eight or nine years ago, the models were so thin, it was disgusting. Now, I notice they have breasts and nice bottoms. Even a woman can tell it's much prettier."

Loren, who has no intention of retiring, has a plan in the works to make a movie directed by Michelangelo Antonioni. "My work is my life," she said with conviction. As for that movie, you'll have to wait. "He (Antonioni) doesn't want me to talk about it yet." About *Recipes & Memories*, which Loren is more than happy to discuss, she explained, "The cookbook is my way of thanking my mother and grandmother."

Linguine with Salsa Sophia

One of Loren's favourite recipes. She likes to make the sauce using a mortar and pestle but admits that a food processor works as long as you don't overblend; the pesto (sauce) should have some texture. In season, you could use fresh basil instead of parsley.

2 cups (500 mL) Italian (flat-leaf)
   parsley leaves, about 1 bunch
1 small onion, chopped
3 cloves garlic
¼ cup (50 mL) pine nuts
3 to 4 anchovy fillets

10 to 12 black olives, pitted
2 tbsp (30 mL) capers, drained
⅓ cup (75 mL) extra virgin olive oil
1 lb (500 g) linguine or spaghetti
Freshly ground pepper or paprika

1. With large mortar and pestle, or in food processor, combine parsley, onion, garlic, pine nuts, anchovy fillets, olives and capers. Gradually pour in oil while continuing to pound or process, until mixture forms a thick paste-like sauce.

2. In large saucepan of boiling, salted water, cook pasta about 8 minutes or just until al dente. Drain.

3. Place lightly oiled skillet over medium heat. Add pasta and cook, tossing, for less than a minute, just until it is dry and begins to brown. Transfer to large, warmed serving bowl. Toss with sauce and dusting of pepper.

MAKES 4 TO 6 SERVINGS.

~ *Chapter Five* ~

NO TASTE LIKE HOME

✳ IT'S ALWAYS SURPRISING—and occasionally upsetting—when friends, acquaintances and other potential dinner party hosts admit they're nervous about inviting me over to break bread.

The reason, they explain, is that I must be such a good cook and used to such fine food that cooking for me is intimidating and cramps their style. I always reply that eating at other people's homes is a privilege and a treat for someone who happens to write about food for a living and spends much of her time in the kitchen laboriously testing and re-testing recipes for work. I also say, for those who haven't been to my home for a meal, that I'm an average to good cook whose repertoire is big on simple dishes like roast chicken, hearty stews, salads strewn with grilled meat or veggies and the odd crumble or pie for dessert.

Once convinced of this, they usually relax, lighten up and wind up serving me the most delicious dinners with a heaping helping of good laughs and lively conversation on the side. After all, the latter is the mainstay of any convivial gathering. It and performance anxiety don't mix.

I'm also a fan of the potluck meal: an old-fashioned format for home entertaining perfectly suited to today's fast-paced lifestyle that has become de rigueur on my social calendar and which can be much more glamorous than its name implies. When people are invited to a communal feast in which the work is shared, they inevitably bring a dish they've perfected. The result is almost always an amazing spread. This is also when I often succumb to a role I can't resist: that of recipe mooch. All it takes is a mouthful of food that elicits the question, "Where has this been all my life?"—or, occasionally, even a secondhand story about such a food—and I move into full-blown mooch mode.

Once it was a weird but wonderful concoction I discovered at a lively New Year's Eve party to which several guests had brought things to eat. Most of it was your basic cocktail nibblies, but this creation, delivered and served in a two-handled cooking pot, immediately intrigued me. Prepared by well-known author Austen Clarke, it was the national dish of his native Barbados called *souse*: a meat salad made with some pretty peculiar parts of the pig, including its feet, nose and ears, inundated with aromatic chopped cucumber and tossed in a tangy vinaigrette. Unlike the more squeamish guests, I couldn't get enough of it. A week later, I was at the home of Clarke's cousin Rose Paradis (he was out of the country and she stepped up proudly to the plate to share her recipe) watching her prepare *souse* along with its yummy, slightly sweet traditional sidekick: puddin'. Naturally, the story and recipe wound up in my column.

So did the fabulous specialty of Toronto's premier pierogi pro Bozena Srubarek. This was one of those word-of-mouth connections that turned out to be pure gold. My contact was Kazik Jedrzejczak who, in addition to having an almost unpronounceable last name, is one of my most impeccable sources when it comes to what's cooking on Toronto's Polish scene. After hearing of her way with dumplings, it took only one phone call to Srubarek and I didn't even have to ask. She immediately and warmly invited me to pierogi production central—the pristine basement of her suburban home—and, while sipping delicious, strong coffee, I watched as she did her magic: mixing dough, shaping it into rounds, then stuffing each pocket deftly with assorted fillings.

Friends, of course, aren't exempt from my sleuthing. My pal Marie Philibert, word has it, makes the best baked beans known to woman. Soon after hearing this rumour, I was on her doorstep to learn firsthand how to make the wondrously down-home dish her Quebecois family has been making for generations. The result: a recipe that's a keeper.

Shirley Lum, who operated her own Toronto biz for years leading folks on walking tours of Chinatown, was another impeccable source. After clambering over boxes in the small downtown apartment she moved into earlier that day, I stood beside her small gas stove as she whipped up a chicken vegetable stir-fry in the wok she'd just unpacked. When I followed her example and made this brilliant version of an Asian classic for my daughter Ruthie, it got the big thumbs-up. The secrets: briefly marinating the raw chicken in egg white and using three sauces—hoisin, soy and oyster—along with Chinese cooking wine in the sauce.

Even Ruthie's friends are mooch material. Lisa Voutt is the mother of her friend Justine. When word reached me that Voutt was a fantastic vegetarian cook who went to incredible lengths to source ingredients, I was on the phone. That weekend, I found myself in woolly wilds of northern suburbia buying Middle Eastern ingredients and eating spicy lentil soup. On the way back, we stopped at an Italian pasta-maker's to pick up superb homemade noodles plus delectable pesto and vodka sauce. Like many others before her, Voutt wound up—where else?—in my column.

BEST BAKED BEANS KNOWN TO WOMAN

❋ MARIE PHILIBERT'S SPEAKING VOICE SHOULD be declared a national treasure. Her precise enunciation, carefully chosen words and French-accented, sing-song lilt are music to the ears and beautifully betray her background growing up in the Gaspe region of Quebec.

Philibert, whose French-speaking friends call her by her real first name Liette, spoke only French in the small town of Matane where she was born and raised. It was here she obtained a college degree in literature and linguistics before moving to Quebec City to study for a degree in translation at Laval University. In 1975, she arrived in Toronto where she soon put her top-notch bilingual skills to use by working as a translator for the federal government. She translated "everything and anything—from English to French," she says, adding, "It's always toward the mother tongue unless you have one English and one French parent—equal context for each language—which is quite rare."

These days, she's a corporate advisor for Ontario, who co-ordinates projects and purchases translation services for the private sector on behalf of various ministries.

And as we sit in the living room of her neat, cozily elegant house, she tells me what food was like in the Philibert home. "My mother was an incredible cook," she begins, recalling how, as a child, she spent long hours sitting at the kitchen table doing homework, reading or chatting with her mom as she cooked. "I was brought up in the kitchen," Philibert says with obvious pleasure. "Quebecers live in the kitchen. It's always an 'eat-in' kitchen. In fact, that translates into French simply as 'une cuisine'—for us, they are all 'eat-in.'" Watching and just being there imbued her with a feel for cooking that she would explore later. "I learned the essentials—the smells, the flavours—and that cooking was simple," she explains. "I absorbed a lot without learning consciously. When I started to cook later, it came back to me."

The dishes her mother Antoinette, who died in 1975, prepared for Philibert, her sister and father, were typical of the region: "Tourtiere and all sorts of pies, pot roast, pork roast, roast chicken and incredible pea soup—

not the mushy stuff we often find here—with whole peas that hold their shape." For many years, her mother cooked on a wooden stove. "She could do something quick on one burner," Philibert says proudly, "have a pot with something simmering on another burner and something else baking in the oven—all within a short time."

The Gaspe staple *cipaille* (pronounced sea-pie) was also big in their home. "It's not seafood, as you might think," Philibert is quick to note. "It's a pie sailors could take with them and reheat—our version of the Cornish pasty. In fact, the more you reheat it, the better it is." This delicious creation is, she explains, "layers of cubed meat (originally, it would have been game)—beef, pork and chicken—mixed with onions, herbs (mainly savoury), lots of potatoes, carrots and a bit of finely diced turnip. This mixture is baked, covered, between layers of pastry—as many as your pan allows."

Fish was plentiful and popular. "The Matane river is famous for salmon," she says. This is where her late father, also a good cook, comes in. "He would go and watch the fishermen and buy their catch immediately. We would eat it the same day, poached, with lovely new potatoes." Her mother would bake the leftovers into a salmon pie—still a favourite dish of Philibert's. She hastens to mention her mother's wondrous *pot-au-feu*. "It's similar to the New England boiled dinner," she explains. "We used to have this in summer and fall when every possible fresh vegetable was available."

By now, I'm getting hungry just listening and it's time to broach the dish du jour: baked beans. Philibert, who is an avid cook and hones her considerable skills by reading cookbooks and surfing the Net, makes a terrific version of this delectable Quebecois staple known in French as *feves au lard*. "It's a survival dish," she says succinctly. "In the old days, the ingredients were always available—beans, onions, salt pork. It could always feed a family and it was nutritious." In typical scholarly mode, Philibert has checked the beans' Canadian pedigree. "I've read that baked beans were introduced in Quebec by American lumberjacks in the 19th century," she begins, "but Quebecers made their own adaptation of the Boston recipe. The history is a mix of French pioneers and the Americans."

Her mother often made them for the family when she was young but, she says, "By the time I grew up, they had become an *après-ski* dish served with good wholewheat bread," and quickly adds, "We always ate two servings." These days, she only makes them once a year because of a restriction on sugar in her diet. This recipe is similar to her mother's. "My main change is the beer," she says. "I saw it in a cookbook and thought it sounded like a good idea." I agree, having baked these beans with great success. They are healthful, satisfying, inexpensive—and clearly Canadian. So in keeping with our bilingual theme and, as Marie Philibert might say in her dulcet tones: *Bon appetit!*

Marie's Baked Beans

It's debatable whether discarding the soaking water is a good or bad idea. I did, with fine results. Philibert doesn't in the belief it contains nutrients. I used a 2-cup (500-mL) can of German beer because that's what was in my fridge. Philibert uses what she calls "regular beer"—your basic Canadian lager or ale. It comes in 2⅓ cup (355 mL) cans; just add part of another can, water or some of the bean soaking liquid to make up the amount. She leaves the onions whole. I halved them because I used a large pot. For a vegetarian version, simply omit the salt pork and add more salt if necessary after the beans are cooked. If you wish, bake these more slowly, about 7 hours at 250°F (120°C), checking occasionally to make sure the beans don't become dry.

3 cups (750 mL) dried white pea (navy) beans

2 cups (500 mL) can or bottle of beer

1 large or 2 medium tomatoes, chopped

¼ lb (125 g) salt pork, bacon or pancetta, sliced

5 small onions, halved

2 tbsp (30 mL) molasses

2 tbsp (30 mL) brown sugar

2 tbsp (30 mL) tomato paste or ketchup

½ tsp (2 mL) dried mustard

1 tsp (5 mL) salt

1. Rinse beans; place in large bowl. Add water to cover by about 2 inches (5 cm). Let soak at least 8 hours or overnight. Drain. Place in large saucepan; add beer. Bring to boil; reduce heat and simmer, partially covered, 30 minutes. Transfer to large bowl; stir in tomatoes.

2. Preheat oven to 300°F (150°C).

3. Place half of salt pork in large earthenware bean pot or other oven-proof baking dish with lid. Spoon in half of bean mixture in even layer. Arrange remaining salt pork on top; spoon in remaining bean mixture. Arrange onions on top.

4. In small bowl, combine molasses, brown sugar, tomato paste, mustard and salt. Drizzle evenly over onions and beans. Cover tightly with lid or aluminum foil. Bake 4 to 4½ hours or until beans are tender. (Check at intervals during baking, adding a little water if beans become dry.)

MAKES ABOUT 8 SERVINGS.

KAREN'S INCREDIBLE CARROT CAKE

※ INCREDIBLE CARROT CAKE. THE NAME SAYS IT ALL. Round and tall. An oversized dessert with presence and pizazz. A moist, dense, dark brown cake studded with plump raisins and crunchy toasted nuts. Its sweetness, laced with an aromatic hint of cinnamon, a perfect match for the lemony tang of gooey cream cheese icing that sticks deliciously to the roof of one's mouth.

I first tasted this sublime sweet almost two decades ago. And when my good buddy Karen Boulton brought it to a recent potluck gathering at my house, I was struck by just how incredible a mouthful of carrot cake can be. I wasn't alone. Everyone who ate it, including several calorie-conscious females, was of one mind: This was one delectable confection. The raves were graciously accepted. Its recipe was promised.

Born and raised in Winnipeg in a family of four children, Karen grew up with an appreciation of good eating. Her mother, Betty Ann, was a homemaker and "traditional Canadian cook," who, Karen notes, "experimented along gourmet lines." There was a shared appreciation of food. "We'd sit around as a family," she continues, "and critique our mom's cooking. She would never be offended." Food has, Karen adds, "always been a passion." After seven years as a flight attendant, it also became her career.

After moving to Toronto in 1976, Karen began taking cooking classes. In 1983, she signed up for a three-month course at Le Cordon Bleu in London. "It was classic French cuisine," she recalls. "I learned all the basics: stocks, sauces, omelettes, puff pastry." Crucial, she adds, "was timing—how to make every part of a meal arrive at the same time, in the best possible condition."

Back in Toronto, Karen and I soon met. Naturally, it was because of food. In January, 1984, I had just begun my newspaper career as food editor for the *Toronto Sun*. Karen heard I was looking for someone to test recipes and style food for photos. "One of the first things I tested was Pimblett's bread pudding," she recalls, referring to the eccentric British restaurant still going strong in Cabbagetown. Soon, Karen had her own food column. For five years, "Open Kitchen" featured restaurant recipes requested by readers. "It was so exciting interviewing chefs and watching them make the dish," she says.

Karen then spent several years selling and demonstrating the high-end, cast-iron AGA oven and giving hands-on barbecue lessons at her home. During four years living in London, she taught cooking and took classes in England and Europe before returning to Toronto. For five years, Karen has been a real estate agent for Re/max Hallmark, working out of the company's Pape and Mt. Pleasant offices.

Re-enter that Incredible Carrot Cake.

Karen, who can cook almost anything with ease and has a magic touch when it comes to baking, has found a way of melding her two careers. She brings food to the open houses she hosts regularly for other agents. "I try to get the agents in the door to see my property," she explains. "That gives my clients as much exposure as possible." Her bait: mouthwatering food. It started with dishes like tandoori chicken and fudge brownies. When she first served the popular carrot cake, "it disappeared—and people always ask for the recipe." She now brings the cake to every open house. "If you want to make people happy, feed them," she claims with a grin, adding quickly, "especially dessert."

Incredible Carrot Cake

Use greased parchment paper to line cake pans if desired.

1 cup (250 mL) coarsely chopped
   walnuts or hazelnuts
4 eggs
1 cup (250 mL) granulated sugar
1 cup (250 mL) dark brown sugar
1½ cups (375 mL) vegetable oil
2 cups (500 mL) all-purpose flour
2 tsp (10 mL) baking powder
1½ tsp (7 mL) baking soda
2 tbsp (30 mL) ground cinnamon
1 tsp (5 mL) salt
2½ cups (625 mL) grated carrots,
   about 5 medium carrots

1 cup (250 mL) unsweetened crushed
   canned pineapple, undrained
1 tsp (5 mL) vanilla extract
1 cup (250 mL) dark raisins

CREAM CHEESE ICING
1 lb (500 g) cream cheese, at room
   temperature
½ cup (125 mL) unsalted butter, at
   room temperature
Grated rind of 1 lemon
2 tbsp (30 mL) fresh lemon juice
2 cups (500 mL) icing sugar, sifted

1. Preheat oven to 350°F (180°C).

2. For cake: Butter and lightly dust with flour three 9-inch (23 cm) round cake pans.

3. Add walnuts to dry skillet over low heat. Cook, shaking at intervals, about 5 minutes or until aromatic.

4. Using electric mixer, in large bowl, beat eggs until combined. Add sugars and oil. Beat until light and creamy.

5. Into separate bowl, sift flour, baking powder, baking soda, cinnamon and salt. Stir into egg mixture until blended. Stir in carrots, pineapple, toasted nuts, vanilla and raisins. Divide batter evenly among prepared pans. Bake 30 to 40 minutes or until toothpick inserted in centre comes out clean. Cool 5 minutes in pan. Invert onto wire racks. Cool completely.

6. For cream cheese icing: Using electric mixer, beat cream cheese in large bowl until light and fluffy. Add butter, lemon rind and juice; beat until blended. Add icing sugar; beat until smooth.

7. Spread thin layer of icing over two cake layers. Place on top of each other; place third layer on top. Spread remaining icing over top and sides of cake.

MAKES 12 TO 16 SERVINGS.

FASHION PLATE

✳ MONTREAL—I PLAN TO STAY IN TOUCH with Thierry Loriot—
and not just because he's easy on the eyes.

Loriot is a 27-year-old male model who is a mine of information when it
comes to my favourite topic: food. Joining him for a late-morning cappuccino here a few weeks ago at the pleasant Café Tramezzini on Rue de la
Montagne just below Sherbrooke, I'm rummaging for a pen in the depths of
my handbag when I mention needing some tips on where to eat that night.
My interviewee, dressed comfortably in jeans, pale blue shirt and running
shoes and speaking English with the charming accent of a true Francophone,
immediately rattles off about a dozen local places—complete with addresses—that he recommends for one culinary specialty or another.

Loriot travels for at least seven months of the year to places like Milan,
Paris, London and New York. And, although he's not a fan of flying, globe-
trotting to runway gigs and doing ads for the likes of Armani, Moschino, GAP
and Banana Republic offer this lanky young man with the glowing skin,
small features and spiky hair ample opportunity to sleuth out top-notch dining haunts around the world. In Montreal, he tells me confidently, the current hot spot is "Rosalie at 1232 Rue de la Montagne near Ste. Catherine. The
food is good and I know the chef, David McMillan. Along with Globe and
Buona Notte, which have the same owners, it's where I like to eat when I'm
home." He quickly adds a useful tidbit. "You'd better make a reservation if
you want to sit on the terrasse."

Admitting he has "a photographic memory," Loriot then mentions "Chez
L'Epicier, 311 Rue St. Paul in Old Montreal—very cool but too many tourists,"
and urges me to try a new vegetarian eatery in Outremont called Les Chevres
that's "pricey but really worth it."

For drinks, it's Bily Kun—"It means 'white horse' in Polish—on Mont
Royal East." He also insists I check out Le Petit Italien, located in Outremont,
where he's a regular. "While you're there," he continues, "you must have an ice
cream from Le Bilboquet which is beside it." All this talk about restaurants
has almost made me forget why I'm here: to quiz Loriot about the cupcakes
he bakes for this café and catered events like birthdays and weddings.

As I nibble on one garishly iced with bright blue icing and dotted with neon pink sprinkles, I note that it's properly moist, tasty and not too sweet. "It's my late grandmother's recipe," explains Loriot who concedes his cakes, which come only in vanilla flavour and two sizes, look homemade and a little kitsch. "It's a tacky dessert so you should make them tacky," he says with a smile. In New York, he found a shop on 25th St. at 8th Ave. "where they sell great decorations for my cupcakes—orchids, birds, flowers."

Born and raised in Quebec City, Loriot comes from what he calls "an intellectual family. My father is a diplomat at the U.N. and my mother is an international lawyer."

He had been studying architecture for a year when a woman friend suggested he try modelling. He likes the job for its "travel and meeting people," then adds, "It'll be fine for a few years." He's quick to note that he enjoys dining out with his peers while on assignment. "It's a myth about models not eating," he explains. "They eat and eat well."

London, where "there's really good food and a lot of great new chefs," is his favourite city. Here, along with the Madonnas of this world, he's a regular at The Ivy. Asked how he obtains a reservation, he replies: "My agency gets my table." He also likes the Japanese noodle house chain Wagamama in Covent Garden, especially menu item #72: Chicken with Curry and Rice. Also Shrimp with Creamy Spicy Sauce at Nobu in the Metropolitan Hotel.

In New York, Loriot enjoys the macaroni at Balthazar and lunch at Fred's in Barney's "where they have great French fries and the best Ricotta Spinach Ravioli." In Edinburgh, he recommends The Witchery: "Scottish food in a spooky atmosphere located near the castle." Casa Bini on Rue Gregoire in Paris is where "Catherine Deneuve or someone is there every time I go. It's good and very simple."

As our interview winds up, Loriot can't resist chiming in with one more Montreal dining tip. "Le Reservoir on Duluth at St. Laurent is great for brunch," he notes with a grin. By the way, when he's out of town, owner Vito Salvaggio and his crew at Café Tramezzini bake the cupcakes from Loriot's recipe. Here it is, from *The Magnolia Café Cookbook*.

Vanilla Cupcakes

Brodie's self-raising flour is sold at most supermarkets. Use a few drops of food colouring in the icing, if desired.

1 cup (250 mL) unsalted butter, at
    room temperature
2 cups (500 mL) granulated sugar
4 eggs
1½ cups (375 mL) self-raising cake
    and pastry flour
1¼ cups (300 mL) all-purpose flour
1 cup (250 mL) milk
1 tbsp (15 mL) vanilla extract

ICING
½ cup (125 mL) unsalted butter, at
    room temperature
1 lb (500 g) icing sugar
¼ cup (50 mL) milk
½ tsp (2 mL) vanilla extract

1. Preheat oven to 350°F (180°C).

2. Line two 12-cup muffin tins with large paper liners.

3. For the cupcakes: In bowl and using electric mixer, beat butter until creamy. Beat in sugar until fluffy. Add eggs one at a time, beating well after each addition.

4. Into another bowl, sift together flours.

5. In small bowl, combine milk and vanilla extract.

6. Using wooden spoon, stir flour mixture and milk mixture into butter mixture, making three additions of dry and two of wet. Fill paper liners about three-quarters full. Bake in centre of oven 20 to 22 minutes, or until tops are firm to touch. Turn out on to wire rack; cool.

7. For icing: In bowl and using electric mixer, beat together butter and half of icing sugar until smooth. Beat in milk and vanilla extract. Beat in remaining icing sugar until smooth. Spread about 1½ tbsp (22 mL) icing over top of each cupcake. Decorate as desired.

MAKES 24.

YOU SHOULD EAT

❋ LIKE MANY A JEWISH MOTHER, I cook largely according to the wishes—and occasionally the whims—of my children. When my older daughter Esther, now married and living in Vancouver, became a vegetarian in her early teens, I would rush home from work and attempt—mostly with questionable results—yet another way to incorporate soy into our evening meal. Happily for us all, she became an excellent cook as soon as she left home and has, over the years, taught me how to make a mean meatless pizza crowned with goat cheese, sun-dried tomatoes and fresh herbs, a delectable salad based on that mineral-packed, curly vegetable kale and yummy pasta tossed with black olives and a sauce of puréed, well-seasoned tofu.

Ruthie, my 15-year-old, has had an impeccable palate from an early age. While her "beige period" was no fun for me, she thrived for several years on a diet of pasta—it ran the gamut from bow-ties (farfalle) to "drill bits" (fusilli) to ears (orechiette)—garnished only with butter and a little grated parmesan. During this trying time, her other favoured foods were chicken, cheese, white bread ("No seeds, please, mum") and vanilla ice cream.

Eventually, my budding offspring began listening to her inner gourmet.

Her current penchants for cappuccino yogurt, barley risotto, fine dark chocolate desserts, croissants from French bakeries, local field tomatoes in season and chickpeas in any shape or form are proof. Which brings me to the subject of this column: chickpeas and other nifty items I keep on hand to make quick, easy meals that are popular with family and friends. All of these are non-perishable convenience foods that can be found at your local supermarket and are a boon when you want to put a tasty, nutritious meal together at short notice.

Canned chickpeas: Like Ruthie, I love this perfect pulse. Blend them up with a little olive oil, the optional tahini, lemon juice, salt and pepper to create that luscious dip: hummus. Drop them into soup, toss into salads and add them to vegetable curry for the perfect vegetarian protein hit. Other canned beans—in particular, romano, cannellini and black beans—are, along with lentils, indispensable standbys in my kitchen cupboard.

Dried mushrooms: Small packages of porcini, portobello, oyster and mixed mushrooms are widely available these days. Reconstituted, they can be tossed with pasta, used in soup or added to the liquid for braised meat, poultry or vegetables. To reconstitute, simply place in a bowl, add boiling water and soak for about 15 minutes. Strain the liquid (there may be grit) through a coffee filter. Do not discard; use in whatever sauce you're making as it adds flavour and deep colour.

• FROZEN PUFF PASTRY AND PHYLLO DOUGH: There are a few things I refuse to make with the view that others do it much better and for a reasonable price. Among them are wine, cappuccino, bread, yogurt, puff pastry and phyllo dough. Both of the latter are easy to find in the supermarket freezer section. Puff pastry makes a delicious, impressive-looking dessert when you top squares of it with ground almonds, thinly sliced fresh fruit and a little sugar, then bake about 20 minutes at 350°F (180°C). Phyllo is great for creating quick and easy hors d'oeuvres like mini-pizzas or spanakopita layered with feta and spinach. It can also be used, like the aforementioned puff, as a cheater's pie crust.

• IMAGINE ORGANIC BROTH AND SOUP: These top-quality Tetra-Pak products are now staples in my pantry. The soups, especially the Creamy Portobello Mushroom, are delicious as is. I also like to add the latter, along with some dry white wine, to roast chicken during the second half of roasting to make a wondrous sauce. The Vegetable and Chicken Broths are superb for all manner of soups, sauces and braised dishes. Bonus: no MSG.

• PRESIDENT'S CHOICE THINDIDO FLATBREAD: This is my favourite ready-made base for a quick pizza. I like to top it with grilled veggies, goat and mozzarella cheeses and lots of fresh herbs. A simple pizza of olive oil, snipped fresh rosemary, paper-thin prosciutto, shaved Asiago and a few optional, halved cherry tomatoes is also wonderful.

• RENEE'S CAESAR LIGHT AND NATURALLY LIGHT JAPANESE DRESSINGS: These two, sold in the produce section of most supermarkets, are rarities in the store-bought salad dressing department. They taste good and, in particular, are not too sweet. I add a little balsamic vinegar to the Caesar and sometimes combine it with the Japanese dressing for a creamy Asian rendition.

Pasta e Fagioli

This big-batch dish, a cross between a soup and a stew, is a cinch to make. The Imagine brand of Vegetable or Chicken Broth is a super shortcut. Use whatever canned beans you prefer or have on hand; I like the mixed beans by Unico in this. Puréeing some of the soup before adding the pasta is optional. A great lunch or supper served with salad and crusty bread, this is filling but not heavy. This recipe makes a lot; you can freeze some, if desired.

2 tbsp (30 mL) olive oil
1 small onion, finely chopped
1 small carrot, peeled, finely chopped
3 cloves garlic, chopped
1/4 tsp (1 mL) hot pepper flakes
4 cups (1 L) vegetable or chicken stock
28 oz (796 mL) can diced tomatoes or stewed tomatoes with Italian seasoning, undrained

19 oz (540 mL) can chickpeas, undrained
19 oz (540 mL) can romano beans, undrained
19 oz (540 mL) can cannellini or other white beans, undrained
2 cups (500 mL) short dried pasta
Salt and freshly ground pepper to taste
Chopped fresh parsley
Freshly grated parmesan cheese

1. Heat oil in very large saucepan, stockpot or dutch oven over medium-low heat. Add onion, carrot, garlic and hot pepper flakes. Cook about 5 minutes, or until soft and golden. Add stock and tomatoes. Bring to boil; reduce heat and simmer, partially covered, 20 minutes.

2. Stir in chickpeas and beans. Simmer about 10 minutes, stirring at intervals.

3. In food processor, purée about 2 cups (500 mL) of mixture. Return to saucepan. Bring to boil; stir in pasta. Simmer over low heat, stirring at intervals, until pasta is tender, about 8 minutes. Add salt and pepper. Garnish with parsley. Serve plenty of parmesan on the side.

MAKES 8 TO 10 SERVINGS.

LIVER COME BACK TO ME

❊ LIKE THEIR HUMAN COUNTERPARTS, the Rodney Dangerfields of the culinary world—foods that "don't get no respect'—are often undeserving of their bad rep.

Take liver, for example. ("No, you take it," I hear you say.) Few foods, except perhaps its 90s meatless equivalent, tofu, are forced to endure so many upturned noses, heartfelt "yucks" and other vehement terms of abuse.

Then there are close runners-up to this unpopular offal: high-profile veggies on the list of oft-hated fare, such as Brussels sprouts, lima beans, cabbage and okra. Of course, there's my personal unfavourite food—the avocado. (To me, it tastes like soap and is loaded with calories from fat.) Obviously, I'm out of sync with the times, since this vile veg seems to be on trendy menus all over town in everything from pork panini to California-style salads, to that tried-and-true dip which even I enjoy, guacamole. Which brings me to the point of this column: the most hated foods and whether they can be rescued from the gastronomic mire in which they wallow.

If I can savour the flavour of a ripe avocado once it's been gussied up with tangy chunks of tomato, onion, jalapeño pepper, fresh coriander and lashings of lemon juice, then surely other unpopular foods could be elevated to higher status with the right recipe for success.

Who in their right mind could refuse a dish of chicken livers seared, then lusciously simmered with onion, garlic, plum tomatoes, fresh sage and a splash of balsamic vinegar?

What could be better than Brussels sprouts perfectly steamed with some sprigs of fresh mint—bright green, gorgeous and the perfect sidekick to roast lamb? As for cabbage, it's my top-rated veg these days when stir-fried with ginger and garlic, then finished with chicken stock and soy sauce. This wonderfully healthful, low-cal dish is ideal to serve with stew, roast chicken or curried chickpeas on a chilly day.

And, in response to our recent survey, here are the foods you, my trusty readers, hate most. And the winner is: liver! Close on the heels of the unloved liver in our Top 5 most hated list were: parsnips, Brussels sprouts, turnips and eggplant, in that order.

Honourable mentions must be given here to other organ meats like tripe, tongue and lungs, along with reviled delicacies like jellied eels, blood pudding, tapioca, marmite (a British yeast extract), tofu and caviar. In the veggie department, okra, spinach, coriander, vegetable marrow, lima beans, zucchini and mushrooms took their share of abuse.

And those who called did not mince words. "Dry and tasteless," "Tastes like sawdust," "Hated it my whole life," and "Smells awful and is slimy" were just some of the epithets heaped on liver.

Childhood memories explain why many of you want no part of parsnips. "A yucky vegetable I was forced to eat because they grew in our garden," and "Had too many growing up," were reasons given.

Likewise for Brussels sprouts. "As a kid, I stuffed them under the chair," said one caller. Another deemed them "bitter, squishy and gaseous" and added "Nothing can be done to make them taste good."

As for turnips, their high score also has childhood roots for many. "The taste is disgusting. My mom would try to hide them in potatoes but I always caught her," was a typical comment.

Eggplant, said someone with undisguised disgust, "is tasteless with no texture—just watery and edible only if covered in sauce."

So you've had your say. Now, as promised, I happily rush to the defense of these much-maligned foods. Actually, I do this with genuine enthusiasm as all five most hated foods are big hits with me. Roast turnips, cooked on their own or alongside roast chicken, are simply divine. Come summer, I can't wait to brush eggplant slices with olive oil and grill them to crisp perfection on the barbie. As for liver, I'm a fan, especially when it's sprinkled with coarsely ground pepper, quickly seared in a pan and then smothered with my rendition of caramelized onions.

So here are some mouthwatering, winning ways to cook two of the most popular "winning" foods: chicken livers and Brussels sprouts. The Caramelized Onions are a nice sidekick for any liver dish. Try them, you might like them. *Bon appétit!*

Chicken Livers au Vinaigre

This dish was inspired by one I saw ace chef Jacques Pepin prepare at a demonstration some years ago. I like liver on the rare side; if you like it well-done, cook it a minute or two longer. A superb, nutritious, quick and inexpensive meal, it's great served with boiled potatoes, rice or pasta and a salad. I sometimes make this for myself as a weeknight meal and just eat it with salad and some crunchy French bread to sop up the delectable sauce. It would also be a fine dinner party dish. I use organic chicken livers whenever possible.

1¼ lb (625 g) chicken livers
2 tbsp (30 mL) olive oil
1 small onion, chopped
3 cloves garlic, minced
2 tbsp (30 mL) red wine vinegar
2 tbsp (30 mL) balsamic vinegar
½ cup (125 mL) chicken stock
1 large tomato, chopped

1 tbsp (15 mL) chopped, fresh sage
   or ½ tsp (2 mL) dried
Salt and freshly ground pepper to
   taste
Dash hot pepper sauce, optional
2 tbsp (30 mL) chopped, fresh parsley,
   chives or green onions

1. Trim fat and green bits from livers (they have a bitter taste). Snip each pair of lobes to separate.

2. Heat 2 tsp (10 mL) of oil in large, heavy skillet over high heat. Add half the livers, in a single layer and cook for about 4 minutes, or until browned and cooked through. Transfer to sieve placed over bowl to catch juices. Repeat with another 2 tsp (10 mL) oil and remaining livers. Set aside cooked livers in sieve.

3. Reduce heat to medium. Stir in remaining oil and onion; cook, stirring, 4 minutes or until soft and golden. Add garlic, cook about 1 minute, without browning. Add vinegars; cook about 2 minutes or until thickened. Add stock, tomato, sage and juices from livers. Bring to a boil, reduce heat and simmer about 3 minutes or until slightly thickened. Stir in salt, pepper, hot pepper sauce, if using, and livers; cook until heated through.

4. Sprinkle with parsley, chives or green onions.

MAKES ABOUT 3 SERVINGS.

Caramelized Onions

This terrific sidekick will make a liver lover out of anyone. Just season your choice of liver (calf's liver is my favourite) with salt and coarsely ground black pepper, then grill or pan-fry using high heat (treat it as you would a steak) to desired doneness and serve smothered with caramelized onions to make a wondrous '90s version of liver with onions.

2 tbsp (30 mL) olive oil	1 tbsp (15 mL) balsamic or red wine
1 tbsp (15 mL) unsalted butter	vinegar
4 medium onions, coarsely chopped	1 tbsp (15 mL) brown sugar
Pinch each salt and pepper	

1. Heat oil and butter in skillet over medium heat; add onions, salt and pepper. Cook, stirring occasionally, about 15 minutes, or until onions start to brown. Reduce heat to low; cook about 20 minutes more or until onions are golden and very tender. Stir in vinegar and brown sugar; cook 5 minutes more.

2. Taste and adjust seasoning.

MAKES ENOUGH FOR 4 TO 6 SERVINGS OF LIVER.

Hashed Brussels Sprouts

A superb recipe from The Union Square Cafe Cookbook *by Danny Meyer and Michael Romano guaranteed to make a convert of even the most die-hard opponent of Brussels sprouts. The original recipe used poppyseeds; we used toasted sesame seeds instead, since I find poppyseeds look unattractive and get stuck in your teeth. Use large Brussels sprouts; they're easier to "hash."*

1 tbsp (15 mL) sesame seeds
1 lb (500 g) large Brussels sprouts
Juice of ½ lemon
2 tbsp (30 mL) olive oil

2 cloves garlic, chopped
¼ cup (50 mL) dry white wine
Salt and freshly ground pepper
   to taste

1. Toast sesame seeds in small frying pan over medium-high heat until golden brown, 3 to 5 minutes; shaking pan often. Remove from pan.

2. Trim stems from Brussels sprouts; halve each sprout lengthwise. Slice each half in thin slices. Add to large bowl; toss with lemon juice.

3. Heat oil in large frying pan over high heat; stir in Brussels sprouts, garlic and sesame seeds. Add white wine; stir-fry 3 minutes or until sprouts are cooked but still a little crunchy. Reduce heat to low, season with salt and pepper and cook 1 minute. Transfer to warm serving bowl.

MAKES 4 TO 6 SERVINGS.

A PIEROGI PRIMER

❋ THE VOICE AT THE OTHER END OF THE PHONE was unmistakable. Those dramatically rolled r's, the sing-song Eastern European accent and that exuberant enthusiasm. All were clues it was Kazik Jedrzejczak (pronounced Ka-zheek Yen-jay-chuk) calling to tell me about his latest project. And when my cheerful friend recently explained that this year's imminent 9th Annual Polish Night would involve two of my favourite things—raising money to help underprivileged children and pierogies—how could I resist?

Jedrzejczak, who came here from Poland in 1979 and has a PhD in organic chemistry, works as a forensic technologist for the Centre of Forensic Sciences in Toronto. "Unexpected deaths, unknown deaths, suicide, criminal cases—that kind of thing," he answers matter-of-factly when I ask about his day job. But, in his spare time, this irrepressible man turns his considerable energy and talents to having fun—and doing good.

In past years, the Polish Gay and Lesbian Association of Toronto, of which he is president, has donated thousands of dollars from their annual January wing-ding to adults and children suffering from AIDS in Poland.

This year's event will raise money for To Save a Life—a new charity that Jedrzejczak can't wait to explain. To Save a Life is the brainchild of retired Polish physician Jadwiga Wojtczak, who is now based in Toronto. In 2001, she founded the organization after travelling to several former Soviet republics—in particular, Lithuania, Byelorussia, Georgia and the Ukraine. When she saw the poor quality of health in those countries and, most sadly, children in orphanages dying from lack of medical treatment, she swung into action. In her native Poland, she persuaded 11 hospitals to treat terminally ill children and many afflicted with TB, at cost. Here in Canada, her foundation raises money to pay for that treatment.

Enter those pierogies.

At the fundraiser, Bozena (pronounced Bo-zhe-na) Srubarek—Toronto's reigning pierogi queen—served up 1,200 of her delicious dumplings along with Polish staples like cabbage rolls and hunter's stew that are her specialties. You guessed it: This was the perfect excuse for me to go to the source and learn how to make the perfect pierogi.

When I arrived at Srubarek's suburban home, I followed her to her second kitchen in the basement: an immaculate room furnished with the bare essentials for pierogi production.

This includes a large gas stove, sink, a hand grinder, two commercial mixers, a couple of big stockpots and skillets and a well-stocked walk-in fridge. As I sipped a cup of rich coffee from a dainty Royal Dalton cup and nibbled on a yummy *rugelach* cookie filled with nuts, Srubarek calmly spooned flour onto the counter from a giant container.

She came here in 1987 from the small Polish village of Anielin near Lublin where her family had a large farm. Growing up, she learned to cook from her late grandmother Agnieszka Kopec. And Srubarek, whose company Business Class Catering specializes in Polish fare, still makes her pierogies the way her beloved granny did. "The dough is very important," she says, speaking softly and deftly moving the fingers of one hand in a circular motion to combine the egg yolks, oil and water she's placed in the middle of the flour. "It must be not too hard but not too sticky." Like any good cook, she uses her senses to check if the amounts are right. In this case, she adds a little hot water at a time until the dough, which she feels and squeezes, has just the right consistency before she begins to knead it. Once that's done, it's wrapped in plastic wrap to be chilled.

Next, it's over to the walk-in fridge to bring out bowls of fillings and a batch of dough made the day before. "You can make pierogies with almost anything," Srubarek notes. "The dough must be made a certain way. The filling is up to you." I don't know if I'll ever master her one-handed technique of stylishly crimping the edges of each filled pierogi but, then again, this is a woman who reckons she makes at least 2,000 of them a year. Many are for the Polish Consulate, which she has been supplying with catered food for the past eight years.

Now it's time to cook the perogies, which have been filled with a selection of fillings: potato and cheddar, ground chicken and sauerkraut with mushrooms. As the water comes to a boil, Srubarek chops and fries a batch of bacon that will be the pierogies' glorious garnish.

As I sit down to a plate of these divine dumplings crowned with a dollop of sour cream, I'm convinced life doesn't get much better than this.

Here is Srubarek's prescription for producing perfect pierogies every time.

I've designed the fillings to make about 2 cups (500 mL)—the right amount for the dough recipe given here. Feel free to design your own fillings. Srubarek makes one that combines sautéed onions, dry cottage cheese and potatoes and another that's a mixture of fresh cabbage and dried mushrooms. She says you can grind up any leftover meat or vegetables you have on hand to create a filling, adding that you can even make one using lentils.

Pierogi Dough

This makes a wonderfully pliable, sturdy dough that's a pleasure to work with. The amount of water—taken from the tap, it should be hot rather than warm—will vary depending on the type of flour (I used unbleached all-purpose) and size of eggs. I wound up using about two-thirds of a cup (150 mL).

2 cups (500 mL) all-purpose flour
1/2 tsp (2 mL) salt
2 large egg yolks
2 tbsp (30 mL) vegetable oil

1/2 to 3/4 cup (125 to 175 mL) very
    warm water
1 lb (500 g) bacon fried, chopped

1. Place flour on counter or wooden board; sprinkle on salt. Make well in centre. Place egg yolks and oil in well. Using tips of fingers, stir in circular motion, working from middle of flour mixture out and adding water with your other hand, a little at a time, as you go. You have added enough water when dough begins to hold together and is just slightly sticky. Form into ball, scraping up and adding any bits that stick to counter.

2. Knead dough (adding a little more water if necessary) 20 to 25 times or until soft and elastic. Wrap in plastic wrap; chill at least 1 hour or overnight.

3. To fill pierogies, divide dough into 3 or 4 pieces. Using hands, shape into logs about 1 inch (2.5 cm) in diameter. Slice each log into pieces about 1 inch (2.5 cm) wide. Dust each piece lightly in flour. Using hands, shape each piece into round disc, then pull gently as you would pizza dough. When dough is thin, place a rounded spoonful of filling in centre. Using fingers, gently pull dough over filling to form half-moon shape. Pinch edges together carefully but tightly, crimping as you go, to seal.

4. To cook pierogies, bring large saucepan of salted water to boil. Reduce heat so water simmers and does not boil rapidly. Add pierogies, one at a time, taking care not to crowd them. (Srubarek recommends a maximum of 15 in a large saucepan.) Cook, uncovered, 4 to 5 minutes stirring occasionally and gently with wooden spoon to loosen from sides of saucepan. Drain.

5. Place on unheated platter brushed lightly with oil. Garnish with chopped, fried bacon and serve with sour cream on the side.

MAKES 2 TO 3 DOZEN.

Potato Cheese Filling

Basically mashed potatoes with grated cheese. Feel free to add a little butter to the mashed potatoes.

2 medium potatoes, peeled, cut in
  chunks
2 tbsp (30 mL) sour cream, plain
  yogurt or milk

1 cup (250 mL) grated cheddar
  cheese
Salt and pepper to taste

Boil potatoes (in water to cover) until soft; drain water. Add sour cream; mash with potato masher or ricer. Stir in cheese. Add salt and pepper.

MAKES ABOUT 2 CUPS (500 mL).

Chicken Filling

This is one of Srubarek's favourites. You could use ground beef or other meat.

1 tsp (5 mL) vegetable oil
2 large skinless boneless chicken
    breasts, cut in chunks
½ medium onion, chopped

1 clove garlic, chopped
2 tbsp (30 mL) water or chicken stock
Salt and pepper to taste

In medium skillet, heat oil over medium heat. Add chicken, onion and garlic. Cook, stirring, until chicken is cooked through and onion browned, about 3 to 4 minutes. Reduce heat to low; add water. Cook about 1 minute stirring and scraping browned bits from bottom of skillet. Grind coarsely in meat grinder or food processor. (If using food processor, do not over-process or chicken will become mushy.) Add salt and pepper.

MAKES ABOUT 2 CUPS (500 ML).

Sauerkraut Filling

I used a tasty Polish sauerkraut sold in jars made by Krakus, with great results. You can rinse the sauerkraut and squeeze dry before using, if desired.

1 tsp (5 mL) vegetable oil
2 cups (500 mL) coarsely chopped
    mushrooms
1 tbsp (15 mL) water

1½ cups (375 mL) sauerkraut,
    chopped
Freshly ground black pepper to taste

1. In non-stick skillet, heat oil over medium-high heat. Add mushrooms; cook, stirring, until browned, 3 to 4 minutes. Add water, stirring to scrape up browned bits from bottom of skillet, and cook about 1 minute more.
2. Place sauerkraut in bowl. Add cooked mushrooms. Stir to combine. Add pepper.

MAKES ABOUT 2 CUPS (500 ML).

GET POTLUCK-Y

❋ My reputation as potluck host par excellence proves yet again: I'm not just a pretty face.

However, I will admit my penchant for dinner parties at which each guest brings a dish was borne of necessity rather than a brilliant brainwave. A single mother with a busy life, I realized some years ago that preparing and serving a multi-course meal is more frazzling than it is fun.

What's the point, I began to ask, in gathering an interesting group of compatible people chez moi if I spend much of the evening in the kitchen slaving over a hot stove and hovering nervously over assembled invitees as they chat, chow down and generally have a rip-roaring good time? Happily, serendipity and synergy come into play when I "organize" one of these soirees. Except for a last-minute phone call to potluck participants, I let the chips fall where they may when it comes to the food they bring. Somehow, the meal that results is always a stellar success.

Friends are now known for their trademark dish. There's the sublime squid ink risotto prepared on site by one pal as an appetizer. Puréed squash and tofu soup laced with scotch bonnet peppers is another's specialty. Lasagna layered with homemade pasta, a voluptuous salad inundated with chunks of cheese and toasted nuts, and luscious mushroom eggplant tart are popular offerings from assorted buddies.

If the meal has gaps, I fill them in with the likes of crostini topped with goat cheese, spicy stir-fried shrimp and apple crumble with ice cream. The food is laid out, buffet-style, on my kitchen table. With plates full, we all adjourn to the dining room where the communal meal, peppered with laughs, is usually a huge hit. This nifty dining paradigm is contagious. A group of us now host such dinners regularly at each other's homes.

Here are two of my favourite potluck recipes. Both are best made a day or two ahead. Prunes give the sauce in my unorthodox version of Beef Bourguignon a hint of sweetness; they also add rich texture and colour. This yummy dried fruit appears in the second recipe: a toothsome creation based on Chicken Marbella from *The Silver Palate Cookbook* by Julee Rosso and Sheila Lukins.

185

Beef Bourguignon

I like the beef in big, irregular pieces and sometimes cut up a chuck roast for this. I like Imagine chicken or beef stock sold in cartons at most health stores and supermarkets.

3 lb (1.5 kg) stewing beef, cut in big chunks

3 cups (750 mL) full-bodied dry red wine

About 6 tbsp (90 mL) olive oil

1 tsp (5 mL) salt

1/2 tsp (2 mL) freshly ground black pepper

1 medium onion, chopped

3 medium carrots, peeled, chopped

4 garlic cloves, chopped

1 cup (250 mL) pitted prunes

1 1/2 cups (375 mL) half a 28 oz (796 mL) can plum tomatoes

1/4 cup (50 mL) beef or chicken stock

2 tbsp (30 mL) fresh thyme leaves

Salt and freshly ground black pepper to taste

2 tbsp (30 mL) unsalted butter

1 lb (500 g) mushrooms, thickly sliced

10 oz (284 g) bag pearl onions

1/3 cup (75 mL) beef or chicken stock, water or white wine

Chopped fresh parsley

1. A day ahead, place beef and wine in large bowl; let marinate in fridge at least 12 hours. Drain marinade into saucepan. Bring to boil; cook, uncovered, over medium-high heat about 5 minutes or until slightly reduced. Reserve marinade.

2. Place beef on paper towel; pat dry. Sprinkle with salt and pepper.

3. Preheat oven to 325°F (160°C).

4. Add 1 tbsp (15 mL) of olive oil to large skillet over medium heat. Add onion and carrots; cook, stirring at intervals, about 10 minutes or until golden brown. Add garlic; cook about 3 minutes more. Add reduced marinade; cook, scraping up browned bits from skillet, about 1 minute.

5. Add 1 tbsp (15 mL) of oil to large dutch oven over high heat. Add about one-third of beef, making sure pieces are not crowded. Cook, turning once, until browned all over, about 5 minutes. Transfer to bowl. Repeat, using 1 tbsp (15 mL) of oil per batch, until all beef is browned. Return beef to dutch oven. Over high heat, add prunes, tomatoes, stock, thyme and carrot/onion mixture with its liquid. Bring to boil, scraping up browned bits from bottom.

6. Bake in oven, covered, about 2½ hours or until beef is tender but not falling apart. Using tongs, transfer beef to large bowl. Place large sieve over bowl. Pour in sauce, pressing it with spoon until no liquid remains; discard solids. Taste sauce; add salt and pepper if necessary.

7. Add 1 tbsp (15 mL) each of olive oil and butter to large skillet over high heat. Add mushrooms. Cook, shaking at intervals, until browned, about 10 minutes. Add to beef mixture.

8. Add pearl onions to saucepan of boiling water. Cook over high heat about 2 minutes. Drain under cold water; peel.

9. Add remaining 1 tbsp (15 mL) each of olive oil and butter to large skillet over medium-high heat. Add pearl onions. Cook, stirring, about 12 minutes or until browned. Reduce heat to low; add stock, water or wine and cook 5 minutes more or until tender. Add to beef mixture. Reheat before serving. Garnish with parsley.

MAKES 6 TO 8 SERVINGS.

Potluck Poulet

If using skinless chicken, add some oil to the skillet when browning.

Two 3-lb (1.5-kg) chickens, quartered
   or cut in pieces
1 cup (250 mL) pitted prunes,
   quartered
1 cup (250 mL) halved pitted green
   olives
1/2 cup (125 mL) sundried tomatoes,
   sliced
1/4 cup (50 mL) chopped fresh
   oregano or marjoram, or 4 tsp
   (20 mL) dried

2 tbsp (30 mL) capers
6 cloves garlic, finely chopped
1/4 cup (50 mL) olive oil
2 tbsp (30 mL) balsamic vinegar
2 tbsp (30 mL) red wine vinegar
1 tsp (5 mL) salt
1/2 tsp (2 mL) freshly ground black
   pepper
1/2 cup (125 mL) packed brown sugar
1 cup (250 mL) dry white wine
1/4 cup (50 mL) chopped fresh parsley

1. With poultry shears or sharp knife, halve chicken legs into drumstick and thigh. Halve chicken breasts crosswise. Place in single layer in one or two large baking dishes.

2. In bowl, combine prunes, olives, sundried tomatoes, oregano, capers, garlic, olive oil, vinegars, salt and pepper. Pour over chicken. Cover with plastic wrap. Refrigerate overnight. Remove chicken from marinade and pat dry; reserve marinade.

3. Preheat oven to 350°F (180°C).

4. In large non-stick skillet, cook chicken in batches over medium-high heat until browned on all sides, turning occasionally, about 5 minutes. Return to marinade, skin side up. Sprinkle with brown sugar. Pour wine around edges of dish.

5. Bake, uncovered, in centre of oven, basting occasionally, until chicken is cooked through, about 45 minutes. Transfer chicken to platter; sprinkle with parsley. Skim fat from sauce. Pour sauce around chicken.

MAKES 8 TO 10 SERVINGS.

MIAMI SPICE

❋ MIAMI—I CALL THIS WONDROUS PLACE, where I shared a March break of sun and fun with my daughter Ruthie—"New York on the beach." Although teenagers and their moms don't always see eye-to-eye, we agree on this.

A snapshot: The longest stretch of windswept, sandy beach I've ever seen. Lively crowds comprising folks of every age, shape and colour. Rundown neighbourhoods and shabby-chic hotels amid the high-end hype. Beautiful art deco buildings painted in soft pastels. Wall-to-wall shopping and hucksters peddling everything from lobster dinners to para-sailing. Bronzed, dolled-up babes swishing their hips in hot pink mini-skirts. The sun-hatted geriatric crowd who shuffle in couples along the boardwalk in their running shoes.

There are quiet side-streets off the beaten track where you can come upon a sandwich shop serving yummy baguettes stuffed to bursting. Meanwhile, restaurant rows Ocean Drive and Lincoln Rd.—South Beach's top spots to see, be seen and do the stroll—offer everything from sushi to stone crab to thin-crust pizza.

"Look, there's Armani's house," I hear a woman exclaim as we elbow our way along Ocean Drive at dusk, stopping outside the walled-in, mini-chateau that was Gianni Versace's home. We're en route to the nearby News Café where the late designer was wont to have his morning coffee. Ruthie grabs my arm as I make a move to edit the clueless tourist's remark with a succinct correction. Instead, we focus on more important things: our next meal. There's a vast, eclectic choice of food here and much of it is great.

Today, the News Café's luscious Chicken Fajita Salad—mixed greens crowned with grilled chicken, seared veggies, melted cheese and tortilla chips—beckons. We share it amid the happy hubbub at an outdoor table. In keeping with American's demand for giant portions, it's so big even I of the hearty appetite cannot finish this dish alone. Dinner the following evening is at glorious Haitian eatery, Tap Tap, on a slightly seedy street a few blocks away. Here, in a room splashed with vibrant murals, I savour another addictive food: chewy, roasted goat tidbits with spicy dipping sauce. Latino, especially

Cuban, culinary influences are everywhere. Some dishes, including the ubiquitous rice, beans and overcooked pork, I can live without. However, tres leches (three-milk) cake at South Beach's landmark David's Café is a sweet tooth's dream, especially washed down with a shot of sugary, smooth-as-silk café con leche.

Delicacies lurk in some unlikely spots. The food court at the sprawling Aventura Mall—about an hour's bus ride from South Beach—is where persistent vendors hawk heaping helpings of grilled beef, sauce-slathered ribs and chorizo sausage; honey mustard chicken with a side of couscous; Cuban roast pork avocado sandwiches, and mountains of salad.

The Fontainebleau Hilton is at the north end of South Beach. Famous playground of the Rat Pack (Marilyn Monroe and pals) in its '50s heyday, and location of movie *Goldfinger*'s brilliant opening scene, the hotel has lost some of its former glitz. However, the bountiful Sunday brunch buffet is worth a visit and the $45 (U.S.) price for its "wall of seafood," big bowls of caviar and superb roast beef. It's here, at a pool-side barbecue, that we first taste *yuca con mojo*. On a foray into Miami proper's Little Havana, we discover this taste sensation again amid the piled-high steam table at amazing little Nicaraguan eatery Yambo.

Yuca, also called cassava, is a starchy root veg with a buttery flavour and creamy texture that's Cuba's equivalent of boiled potatoes. Back in Toronto, we discover a fabulous rendition doused in the traditional oil, lemon and garlic sauce at west-end Julie's Cuban Restaurant, served with a moist-crisp, deep-fried whole snapper. The aromatic, mint-laced mojito I sip reminds me of the primo South Beach version at Lario on the Beach owned by Gloria Estefan.

Versions of fish soup or stew, sometimes called bouillabaisse, *zuppa di pesce* or *cioppino*, are on many Miami menus. Here's an easy recipe to try at home.

Seafood Stew

If using fish stock from a cube, you may not need salt. You can use fresh toma-toes in season. For a soupier version, add more fish stock and/or wine.

2 tbsp (30 mL) olive oil
1 medium onion, chopped
2 cloves garlic, finely chopped
19-oz (540 mL) can or 2 cups
    (500 mL) tomatoes with juice,
    chopped
2 cups (500 mL) fish stock
    (recipe below)
1½ cups (375 mL) dry white wine
1 tbsp (15 mL) each: chopped fresh
    basil, oregano and thyme OR
    ½ tsp (2 mL) each: dried
½ tsp (2 mL) hot pepper flakes
Pinch saffron (optional)
Salt and freshly ground black pepper
    to taste
6 cups (1.5 L) bread cubes

¼ cup (50 mL) olive oil
4 cloves garlic, finely chopped
8 oz (250 g) cod, haddock, bluefish
    or grouper, skinned, boned, cut in
    chunks
8 oz (250 g) salmon, skinned,
    boned, cut in chunks
8 oz (250 g) monkfish, skinned,
    boned, cut in chunks
8 oz (250 g) scallops
8 oz (250 g) large shrimp, peeled,
    deveined
Salt and freshly ground black pepper
    to taste
Sour cream for garnish
Chopped fresh parsley or coriander

1. In large saucepan, heat oil over medium heat; cook onion and 2 cloves garlic 5 minutes, stirring occasionally, until soft. Stir in tomatoes, fish stock, wine, basil, oregano, thyme, pepper flakes and saffron. Bring to boil. Reduce heat to low; simmer, uncovered, 20 minutes or until thickened slightly. Add salt and pepper. (May be made ahead to this point.)

2. Preheat oven to 350°F (180°C).

3. In large bowl, toss bread cubes with olive oil and 4 cloves garlic. Spread on baking sheet. Bake in oven 15 to 18 minutes or until golden. Set aside.

4. Stir cod, salmon and monkfish into simmering stock mixture; cook, uncovered, 3 minutes. Stir in scallops and shrimp; cook, uncovered, 2 to 4 minutes or until seafood is opaque. Taste; add salt and pepper if necessary.

5. Ladle into large bowls. Top with croutons, a dollop of sour cream and parsley.

FISH STOCK

1½ lb (750 g) fish bones and heads
½ cup (125 mL) dry white wine
1 small onion, unpeeled

1 stalk celery
1 clove garlic, unpeeled
Pinch of dried thyme

In large saucepan, cover fish bones and heads with cold water. Bring to boil over high heat. Reduce heat to low. Add remaining ingredients; leave onion and garlic unpeeled. Simmer, partially covered, about 1 hour. Strain, discarding bones and vegetables.

MAKES ABOUT 6 SERVINGS.

Key Lime Pie

While in Miami, I conducted a serious survey of a regional specialty: Key Lime Pie. The clear winner is Joe's Stone Crab Restaurant, 11 Washington Ave. Opened in 1913, this dining landmark is famous for its prized, pricey stone crabs. Avoid huge line-ups and try their unequalled, creamy, crunchy-crusted pie at the adjacent take-out/café. At Joe's, they half-freeze their pie wedges and let them sit at room temp a few minutes before serving. This makes a large pie, so invite a crowd to share it.

CRUST
16 graham crackers
3/4 cup (175 mL) graham cracker
   crumbs
1/2 cup (125 mL) unsalted butter,
   melted

FILLING
Two 1 1/4 cup (300 mL) cans condensed
   milk
5 large egg yolks

3/4 cup + 2 tbsp (205 mL) key lime
   juice, or half fresh lime and half
   fresh lemon juice
1 tbsp (15 mL) lemon rind

WHIPPED CREAM TOPPING
1 cup (250 mL) whipping cream
1 tbsp (15 mL) icing sugar
1/2 tsp (2 mL) vanilla extract
Thinly sliced halved limes (optional)

1. Preheat oven to 350°F (180°C).
2. For crust: Wrap graham crackers in clean tea towel or place in seal-able freezer bag. Pound with mallet until they are coarse crumbs. (Or pulse a few times in food processor.) Add to bowl with ready-made graham cracker crumbs and butter. Stir to combine. Pat mixture in even layer over bottom and up sides of 9-inch (23 cm) pie plate. Bake for 8 minutes. Cool.
3. For filling: In large bowl using electric mixer, beat condensed milk and egg yolks until well combined. Beat in lime juice and lemon rind. Pour into pie shell. Return to middle rack of oven; bake about 20 minutes, or until filling is still jiggly but begins to set. Cool. Refrigerate until ready to serve.
4. For topping: Whip cream with sugar and vanilla in bowl using whisk or electric hand mixer, until firm. Spread over pie just before serving or serve on side. Garnish with lime slices, if using.

MAKES 8 TO 10 SERVINGS.

PUDDIN' N' SOUSE

"Gimme Saturdays seven days of the week! Saturday, when I was grow-ing up, was the day for making black pudding and souse, the best food in the world." – Pig Tails 'n Breadfruit by Austin Clarke.

✳ IF YOU WANT TO IMPRESS OR, BETTER STILL, bond with a person from Barbados, drop this key phrase: pudding and souse.

I first encountered that unique culinary creation—a Barbadian national dish—thanks to award-winning Toronto writer Austin Clarke. The occasion was New Year's Eve and Clarke, who hails from that Caribbean island, had brought a large pot of souse to a party hosted by mutual friends in a down-town restaurant. I, ever the intrepid food sleuth, was intrigued by the con-coction that half-filled a big pot Clarke had placed beside the dips and cru-dités: an unusual salad comprising unidentifiable, bite-sized chunks of meat tossed in a wonderfully aromatic dressing. It was delicious—in a chewy, tangy, tantalizing sort of way—and I chowed down on several helpings.

Unlike others at that soiree, I was not put off by the news Clarke cheerfully imparted when I quizzed him about the dish. This was that souse's main ingredients are weird and wonderful cuts of pork: ears, trotters and snout. Also that it's traditionally served with a sweet potato pudding.

A couple of weeks later, I happened to be staying at a popular resort on the northwest coast of Barbados for some much-needed R&R. On my second day, I mentioned pudding and souse to Heather Hinds, the resort's stat-uesque grill chef who makes a mean barbecued kingfish and killer omelettes. Her eyes literally lit up as she flashed me a big grin. "You know about pud-din' n' souse?" she said, noticeably surprised a Canadian tourist had such insider info about her country's food.

In minutes, a plan was hatched. She would take me to "Neville's place" on the east coast the following morning—a Saturday and the mandatory day for souse consumption.

We arrived by car in St. John's parish on the other, more rugged side of this wondrously warm, lush island that's gorgeously studded with the fiery orange, fuchsia and crimson blooms of bougainvillea trees. It was lunchtime and "Neville's place," it turns out, is "pudding and souse central." In an average rural, pastel-painted bungalow in the middle of nowhere, people come from all over to eat, take out and stock up on this Saturday mainstay.

Out back, an assortment of full-grown and baby pigs slept or casually cruised their spotless enclave. In the house's large kitchen, a crew of cooks prepared the dish of which they're the key component.

Hinds, her friend Tyrone and I slowly and quietly ate our large servings of pork and pudding from Styrofoam containers seated on a small deck at the rear of the building. Between delectable bites, we sipped the local beverage: a Banks beer.

Back in Toronto, I call Clarke to ask if I can come over to cook souse. He is about to leave for Barbados to talk up his new book *The Polished Hoe* and suggests I call his cousin Rose Paradis. When I arrive at her Willowdale home, Paradis is cooking up a storm. As her 98-year-old mother Menina Cozier—a major pudding and souse fan—gets into the joyful mood, I thank my lucky stars I'm a food writer. In no time, we're chatting, tasting and, best of all, having lots of laughs.

Paradis, who has six grown-up sons and works as a freelance event planner, was born and raised in Barbados and loves to cook. "It's a great dish," she says, chopping a cumber. Souse's origins, she adds, go back a long way. "On plantations, when pigs were slaughtered, the master got the good meat. The workers and slaves got what was left over: the head, the feet, snout and ears. They ate it at the end of the week. They learned to make do." The pudding, she reckons, is "a version of haggis since most Bajan early settlers were Scottish."

Here are Paradis's recipes. The sweetish pudding and tangy, salty souse are perfect together.

Pudding

I baked this in a baking dish instead of making a sausage, as Paradis usually does, by using the traditional "hog's casings," i.e., pork intestines. Use the red-skinned, white-fleshed, sweet potatoes sold in Caribbean stores.

2 medium sweet potatoes, peeled, cubed

1 small onion, cubed

3 green onions, trimmed, cut in pieces

1 tsp (5 mL) fresh thyme leaves, chopped

2 tbsp (30 mL) brown sugar

2 tbsp (30 mL) unsalted butter, melted

Salt to taste

1. Preheat oven to 375°F (190°C).
2. In food processor, process sweet potato until finely chopped. Add onion and green onions; process until puréed and smooth. Transfer to bowl; stir in thyme, brown sugar and butter. Add salt. Spoon mixture into buttered 9-inch (23 cm) square or round baking dish. Bake about 30 minutes or until tester comes out clean.

MAKES ABOUT 6 SERVINGS.

Souse

Caribbean stores sell pig parts; large supermarkets sell trotters. Vary pig parts as desired; a pork hock can be used, for example.

1½ lb (750 g) boneless pork roast
2 pig's trotters
1 pig's ear
1 pig's snout

DRESSING
1 large or 2 small cucumbers,
  peeled, chopped

1 medium sweet vidalia onion,
  chopped
Juice of 2 or 3 large limes
½ fresh scotch bonnet pepper,
  seeded, chopped
¾ cup (175 mL) fresh parsley,
  chopped
Salt to taste

1. In saucepan, cook pork roast by simmering, partially covered, in salted water to cover, until tender, about 1 hour. Transfer to bowl of cold water; cut in bite-sized pieces.

2. In another saucepan, cook trotters, ear and snout by simmering, partially covered in salted water, until tender, about 1½ hours. Transfer to bowl of cold water. Cut in bite-sized pieces, removing bones from trotters, if desired.

3. In large bowl, combine dressing ingredients. Add pork. Toss to coat. Let marinate at least a few hours. Serve at room temperature with warm pudding and crusty bread.

MAKES ABOUT 6 SERVINGS.

WOMEN WHO RULE THE ROAST

✳ THANKFULLY, MY LATE MOTHER-IN-LAW IDA KANE—a feisty Cockney Jew who proudly and accurately described herself as "a good, plain cook"—initiated me into the "pinch of this," "handful of that" style of cooking prevalent among grandmothers. When asked how much sugar went into her tasty Walnut Slice—an old-fashioned British bar cookie baked for large gatherings of extended family—Ida's reply was terse, tight-lipped and to the point: "Enough." When grilled about how long to cook her famous roast potatoes (the secret, I eventually found out, is to parboil the spuds, then roast them to crisp perfection in a very hot oven), her response was equally enigmatic: "'Til they're done."

However, even this didn't prepare me for the hot water I recently got into when tackling recipes from Canadian TV cooking show, "Loving Spoonfuls." After sharing a particularly sad story of botched baking with the show's charming, witty host, David Gale, in which a large batch of would-be cookie dough wound up in my garbage can—the result of following an otherwise lovable granny's recipe to a T—he offered a couple of theories.

An actor with a background in theatre, musicals and comedy, Gale could not resist a sympathetic chuckle at my plight and reckons that, in many cases, grandmothers have no written recipes. "Then, when they go to give a recipe to someone," he explains, "they genuinely forget the exact amounts." But, he's quick to note, some cases are not so innocent. "Often, they're very protective," he continues, adding darkly, "and there can be sabotage." The latter tends to occur, he says, "when a woman who is famous in the family for her coffee cake wonders: 'What if someone else makes it?'"

Gale has become increasingly comfortable with his role on the show as the always affable chatterbox, occasionally inept co-cook and frequently funny kibitzer-in-chief. He has won a Gemini for his efforts, with the weighty title Best Host in a Lifestyle or Performing Arts Program or Series.

"I don't have a generation problem," he explains. "I grew up with three grandmothers in my life—one was my great-grandmother—and I was particularly close to my mother's mother, Bobi Clara, who died last year. She gave me the training for this. She was a homemaker and a great cook of knishes, blintzes—simple food that tasted good."

Gale's affection for the women (there is an occasional grandfather) with whom he shares a kitchen is clear as he waltzes around the room with a giggling granny and flirtatiously accepts an affectionate but firm rebuke about his sifting or whisking.

"It can be very taxing work," he says. "When we shoot, I'm spending the day with people I've just met—but it's hugely rewarding. I usually come away from their homes with people wanting me in their life. I get a new grandmother each time." And that powerful emotion—the magical bonding that happens when people share a love of food and cooking—is what hooked me on "Loving Spoonfuls."

Allan Novak is the show's clever creator and executive producer. He calls himself "a TV comedy person" who writes, edits and directs and has worked with the likes of CODCO, Mike Myers and Ken Finkleman. He and Gale have been friends since they met teaching drama at summer camp near Winnipeg in 1974. "The idea for the show came to me in one of those moments of inspiration," says the soft-spoken Novak. "I saw it as a sort of post-*Two Fat Ladies* cooking show that doesn't have to be just straight cooking."

The twin themes of ethnically diverse grandmothers and cooking have proven to be a winning combination. "They're the heart and soul of food," says Novak, "of character and life. Both are pure and met in this idea."

But what about those recipes?

After hearing my plea for a seasonal recipe from the show that would actually work, Novak put me in touch with Hilda Kuhteubl whose Austrian holiday cookies, Vanilla Kipferl, were sent out with kits promoting the "Loving Spoonfuls" Holiday Special and were a huge hit. Kuhteubl and I talked by phone, I baked, the cookies were delicious, I danced around the kitchen singing her praises and we talked some more. You guessed it: this one's a winner. Novak assures me that, in future, recipes will be tested for the show's terrific website.

Hilda's Vanilla Kipferl

Kuhteubl, who came to Canada in 1954, used to make these festive crescents (kipferl) with her mother when she was growing up in a small town near Vienna. They're easy to make, taste divine and stay wonderfully crisp stored in the fridge or a cool cupboard in an airtight tin. Vanilla sugar by Oetker, sold in most supermarkets, comes in packages of 9-gram envelopes. I was skeptical about mixing the dough using my hands. It's messy but works well; take off your rings and don't answer the phone as I foolishly did. Let the butter soften for a few hours; Kuhteubl leaves it out overnight. She uses an old-fashioned hand grinder for the walnuts (don't substitute other nuts); the food processor does a fine job.

1 cup (250 mL) ground walnuts
3/4 cup (175 mL) granulated sugar
2 1/2 cups (625 mL) all-purpose flour
1 1/2 tsp (7 mL) vanilla extract

1 cup (250 mL) unsalted butter, softened, cut in pieces
1/2 cup (125 mL) icing sugar
9 g envelope vanilla sugar

1. Preheat oven to 350°F (180°C).

2. In large bowl, stir together walnuts, granulated sugar, flour and vanilla extract. Add butter. With fingers (you can start with a wire pastry blender), blend in butter until mixture resembles coarse crumbs and forms a dough. Pinch off pieces of dough; shape into crescents about 1 1/2 inches (4 cm) long. Place on ungreased cookie sheet(s) or Silpat liner placed on cookie sheet; bake until light (not dark) brown on bottom, about 15 minutes. Cool on wire rack(s).

3. On plate or in large, shallow bowl, combine icing and vanilla sugars. Dredge cooled cookies in mixture until lightly coated.

MAKES ABOUT 5 DOZEN.

CREATING A STIR-FRY

✳ Luckily, i arrive late—an atypical event caused by bad weather and, I'm convinced, a full moon—to interview Shirley Lum at her house one recent afternoon. I am thus saved the Type A conniption that would likely have ensued had I been there to witness the struggle she and the *Star* photographer have gone through in an effort to coax flames from her small, vintage gas stove. The pair, taking it all cheerfully in stride, are laughing and chatting in the tiny kitchen as Lum tosses chunks of chicken breast she has marinated briefly in Chinese cooking wine into her well-used wok. It is sitting precariously atop a ring of flames that threaten to disappear at any time.

The diminutive, energetic Lum grew up in downtown Toronto not far from where she now lives. When asked about her heritage, she grins: "I'm a true cbc—Canadian-born Chinese." This background—along with a prodigious gift of the gab and adventurous spirit—are excellent qualifications for her current job as owner/operator of A Taste of the World, the nifty business she founded in 1993. As the company's tour-guide-in-chief, Lum regularly leads groups—a mixture of tourists and curious Torontonians—on an assortment of walking and biking tours of our city's downtown core with the emphasis heavily on two areas: food and Chinatown.

Of course, as any well-travelled resident of our city knows, there are currently several sizable Chinatowns in the gta. Lum breathlessly rhymes off six: "The original two downtown Chinatowns—near Old City Hall and Dundas/Spadina; Broadview/Gerrard; Scarborough/Agincourt/Markham; Richmond Hill/Downsview, and Mississauga."

She conducts tours of the three downtown ones, concentrating on their culinary attributes, and recommends these choice spots amid the bustling hub at Dundas/Spadina:

- woks, cleavers and other cookware: Tap Phong Trading Co., 360 Spadina Ave.
- groceries: Tai Kong Supermarket, 310 Spadina Ave.
- tea, herbs and dried ingredients: Po Chi Tong Natural Herbs & Dry Seafood, 460 Dundas St. W.

When it comes to cooking at home, Lum, who is the eldest of four children, has been helping her mother—"an excellent cook"—since childhood. She loves stir-frying. "It's all about movement and rhythm," she tells me as she stands over her stove, wielding a metal spatula and tossing a handful of slender baby corn cobs into the wok. "With one hand, you stir the sliced and chopped food with a spatula while, with the other, you rock and tip the wok back and forth," she says, doing just that.

The object of a stir-fry, she explains, is "to cook foods only to the point at which they still retain flavour, colour, texture and nutritional value." She then offers these tips:

- Although Lum often stir-fries for her family of six, she recommends thinking small. "Ideally, stir-fry for one or two," she says. "It's easier to keep the food at a high heat if there is not too much in the wok."
- "Be prepared. Have all your ingredients ready—sliced, diced and chopped—and your sauce mixture ready to go, before heating up the wok."
- "A gas stove is best for stir-fries and can accommodate a wok with a rounded bottom. An electric stove is fine but you'll need a flat-bottomed wok. In both cases, turn your burners up as high as they will go."
- "It's a good idea to heat the empty wok over high heat until it's barely smoking. Then add the oil and wait until it's barely smoking before adding your other ingredients."
- "Vegetables should be dry, not wet, when added to the wok. Firmer vegetables like carrots, cabbage and broccoli should be cooked slightly longer than softer ones like bok choy or red and green peppers."
- "Stir-fry meat until almost cooked through—70 to 80 percent. The final cooking will happen when it's added back to the stir-fry with the sauce."

Lum, who claims Chinese cooking is "intuitive and doesn't usually involve recipes" devised this chicken stir-fry. The colours of the veggies are auspicious for Chinese New Year. "The green of the bok choy symbolizes long life," she explains. "The yellow corn means prosperity and the red pepper is for good luck." On New Year's Eve, Lum's family typically enjoy a multi-course feast prepared by her mother. "There will be a fish dish," she begins, "one chicken, one pork and always a platter of long, un-cut noodles which symbolize long life."

Chicken Stir-Fry

Use as a guideline, with ingredients you have on hand.

MARINADE
1 egg white, lightly beaten
1 tsp (5 mL) Chinese cooking wine
1 tsp (5 mL) cornstarch
¼ tsp (1 mL) each salt and granulated
   sugar
1 skinless, boneless chicken breast,
   cut in strips

SAUCE
1 tsp (5 mL) oyster sauce
1 tsp (5 mL) soy sauce
1 tsp (5 mL) hoisin sauce
1 tbsp (15 mL) Chinese cooking wine
½ tsp (2 mL) granulated sugar
¼ tsp (1 mL) ground pepper
1 tsp (5 mL) cornstarch

3 tbsp (45 mL) chicken or vegetable
   stock or water
1 tsp (5 mL) sesame oil

STIR-FRY
About 3 tbsp (45 mL) vegetable oil
1 cup (250 mL) canned baby corn
2 cups (500 mL) baby bok choy,
   stem ends removed
1½ tsp (7 mL) grated fresh ginger
   root
1 clove garlic, grated or chopped
1 red pepper, sliced
1 tsp (5 mL) Chinese cooking wine
Fresh coriander, parsley or green
   onion, chopped
2 tbsp (30 mL) toasted sesame seeds

1. In medium bowl, combine marinade ingredients. Add chicken. Let marinate at least 30 minutes in fridge.

2. In small bowl, combine sauce ingredients.

3. Heat wok over high heat until barely smoking. Add about 1 tbsp (15 mL) of oil. Add corn; cook, stirring, about 1 minute. Add bok choy, ginger root and garlic; cook, stirring, about 1 minute. Add red pepper; cook, stirring, about 30 seconds. Transfer mixture to plate. Wipe wok with paper towel.

4. Heat wok over high heat until barely smoking. Add remaining oil, tilting wok to coat. Add chicken with marinade, spreading in single layer; cook about 45 seconds. Turn; cook about 1 minute or until browned and almost cooked through. Add cooking wine, stirring.

5. Return vegetable mixture to wok; cook, stirring, 1 to 2 minutes. Make well in centre; stir in sauce mixture; cook, stirring, until food is coated and sauce thickened, about 1 minute. Garnish with chopped coriander and toasted sesame seeds. Serve over noodles or steamed rice.

MAKES 2 GENEROUS SERVINGS.

VEG HAS THE EDGE

❋ You know a woman is serious about things culinary when she arrives at your door clutching a small package, raving about the Japanese food shop down the street and uttering these words: "I'm so glad I found that place—I'm right out of burdock."

Lisa Voutt, the foodie in question, uses this unusual herb in a Japanese carrot dish called *kinpira gobo*. It's a recent Saturday and she's driven to my home, pumped and perky, to take me on a mission: food sleuthing in our city's northern 'burbs. Usually, I loll about on weekend mornings nursing a cup of coffee and reading the paper. However, I've ditched this cherished ritual after hearing about Voutt's culinary credentials from an impeccable source: my daughter Ruthie.

Ruthie is a friend of Voutt's daughter Justine and regularly regales me with raves like these: "Justine's mom made an incredible dessert with plums," "I had this delicious squash soup at Justine's house," or "Mom, you should get together with Lisa—she's a fantastic cook."

When I accepted an invitation for a weeknight dinner at the Voutts' downtown loft, I found that, as usual, Ruthie is right. After a busy day at the software company she co-owns and operates with her husband Rob, Voutt effortlessly prepared a wondrous meal. The family, which includes younger teenage daughter Serena, is vegetarian. Voutt's reasons are down-to-earth. "I don't think I need to eat meat or fish to live in this part of the world," she says. "If I lived in Iceland or Canada's far north, I would definitely eat them for survival." She cannot condone mass production of meat and fish for human consumption. Likewise for fruit and vegetables, so she opts for organic produce whenever possible. "My reasons are purely environmental," she explains, asking, "What is the state of the earth going to be like for future generations?"

Dinner proved how delectable a meatless meal can be: a luscious soup of kale, spinach and lentils; yummy pasta tossed with broccoli; a vibrant cherry tomato and bocconcini salad, followed by two British cheeses—robust Lincolnshire Poacher and pungent Stilton—with wholegrain organic bread from St. John's Bakery. Afterwards, Voutt brought out two jars of *mostarda*

—a spicy fruit chutney—she brought back from a recent trip to Italy along with 15 bottles of sea salt, four bags of dried porcini and several jars of truffles.

Voutt (née Colucci) grew up in Mississauga, the eldest of three children of a working single mother. As we drive north, heading for Bologna Pastificio on Dufferin south of Lawrence, she tells me her passion for food and cooking began early. "My mother gave me free rein in the kitchen," she recalls. "I scored highest in my grade 10 family studies class for making the most nutritious, tasty meal." But she credits both sets of grandparents, who came from different regions of Italy, with "handing her the torch" when it came to food.

Voutt has shopped at Bologna Pastificio, a spotless little shop specializing in fresh pasta and sauces, for 15 years. We stock up on three excellent renditions of agnolotti stuffed with butternut squash, sweet potato, and porcini respectively. She likes to have their veggie lasagna on hand to serve with salad and dips. The gnocchi are amazing. So are several pestos and a nifty tofu sundried tomato spread.

Soon we're on the road again en route to Sababa, located in Thornhill, a super Middle Eastern food emporium with adjacent restaurant where Voutt is a regular. We pick up ground sumach seeds (a wonderfully aromatic seasoning), Moroccan veggie phyllo "cigars" similar to spring rolls, and glazed chestnuts which she serves over caramelized pineapple and Gelato Fresco crème caramel ice cream.

It's lunchtime, so we settle in next door to savour sublime, lemon-laced fried eggplant, crisp falafels and the deservedly famous, spicy lentil soup. Back in the car, we return downtown via Bayview Ave., where Voutt wants to stop at Alex Farm's North Toronto location to check out their excellent array of cheese. On the way, she cites dishes from her repertoire: corn chowder, oyster mushroom cutlets, pasta with rapini and raisins, fusilli with tomato carrot sauce, lentil loaf and pecan pie. She usually improvises with local ingredients in season but often uses recipes for dessert, in particular from *In the Sweet Kitchen* by Regan Daley. She would love to be a chef and dreams of opening her own restaurant.

Here's her recipe for a vegetarian salad that's packed with flavour.

Mid-East Chickpea Potato Salad

Voutt often uses store bought Delouis Fils aioli for the dressing. I used baby organic Yukon Gold potatoes, brushed, then cooked with the skin on. Serve warm or at room temperature.

3 medium potatoes, peeled, cut in
  1/2-inch (1 cm) cubes
3 tbsp (45 mL) olive oil
1 tsp (5 mL) mustard seeds
1/2 tsp (2 mL) each salt and freshly
  ground black pepper
1 tsp (5 mL) cumin seeds
1 onion, coarsely chopped
1/4 tsp (1 mL) ground turmeric
19 oz (540 mL) can chickpeas,
  rinsed, drained

1/2 cup (125 mL) raisins, coarsely
  chopped (optional)
1/2 cup (125 mL) chopped fresh
  coriander leaves

DRESSING
1 clove garlic, minced
2 tbsp (30 mL) mayonnaise
1 tbsp (15 mL) extra virgin olive oil
1 tbsp (15 mL) fresh lemon juice
1/4 tsp (1 mL) salt

1. Bring potatoes to boil in saucepan with water to cover; simmer over low heat until cooked but still firm, 8 to 10 minutes. Drain.

2. In large skillet, heat 2 tbsp (30 mL) of olive oil over medium-high heat. Add mustard seeds; when they pop, add potatoes, salt and pepper. Cook, shaking skillet at intervals, until browned all over, about 8 minutes.

3. Add cumin seeds to small skillet. Cook over medium-low heat until browned, 3 to 4 minutes. Grind in mortar and pestle or small grinder.

4. Add remaining olive oil to skillet over medium heat. Add ground cumin, onion, and turmeric. Cook, stirring at intervals, until caramelized, about 15 minutes. (Lower heat slightly if onions begin to burn.)

5. For dressing: Whisk together all ingredients until combined.

6. In large bowl, combine cooked potatoes, caramelized onions, chickpeas, raisins (if using) and coriander. Stir in dressing. Taste; add salt and pepper, if desired.

MAKES 4 TO 6 APPETIZER SERVINGS.

ঞ৩

Chapter Six

HAIL TO THE CHEF

❋ Call it synergy, co-operation without words or synchronized cooking.

There's a special magic about the way chefs work together in a professional kitchen that never ceases to amaze me. Whatever the explanation—and I'm not sure there is one for this almost mystical phenomenon—being in a room with a group of men and women, all dressed in whites, working as a team to prepare food for others is a wonderful feeling.

It has something to do with being nurtured. After all, that's what feeding people is, in essence, all about. But the beauty of a busy restaurant kitchen is in the preparation.

It's the getting ready for the madness that is mealtime when, make no bones about it, things are far from peaceful. It's the soothing, quiet way things somehow come together during that calm before the storm and how each chef knows what to do without being told.

It may be Jewish guilt but, after more than 30 years of standing on the sidelines, pen and notebook at the ready, as those around me chop, slice, stir, peel and baste, I still feel like a bit of an intruder who watches and listens while others do the real work. However, that guilt is usually fleeting. Eventually, I find myself both energized and uplifted by the communal spirit, not to mention the lessons and tips I learn from studying chefs in action. Then, of course, there are those wonderful aromas and, if I get a chance, straight-from-the-pan flavours that emanate from that steamy, bustling room.

In addition, I've become pals with many of our city's chefs over the years. It is a privilege for me and often a boon to them when I write about who they are and what they do. Sometimes, they're well-known, even celebrity chefs, who've made a name for themselves through rave restaurant reviews or other media attention. On occasion, I discover, usually by word of mouth, a young or simply unknown chef with outstanding talent.

Mostly, they're flattered and occasionally overwhelmed at this attention. Used to working quietly behind the scenes, many of them are shy and unassuming. However, when it comes to talking about their passion, I've found chefs to be amazingly articulate, incredibly well informed and, almost without fail, eager to share their expertise.

Take Tony Barone, for example. I had eaten his magnificent potato gnocchi—one of my favourite dishes of all time—at a downtown restaurant I used to frequent once a week on the way to pick up my daughter Ruthie from her dad's. Seated at the bar, I would savour these toothsome little dumplings, either bathed in a fresh tomato sauce topped with grated parmesan or tossed in a much richer, equally luscious gorgonzola cream. One night, this affable chef with the handsome, cherubic face came out to meet me after hearing from the waiter how I felt about his gnocchi. I vowed then and there to get his recipe. He agreed.

It was at least two years later, by which time Barone had opened his own restaurant, that I took him up on that offer. During a lull between lunch and dinner—the best time to commune with any chef—I watched, using my own measuring cup and spoons to check amounts, as he prepared his delectable little potato dumplings amid the bustle of his restaurant's kitchen. The next day, I made them myself at home and wrote the recipe, which subsequently appeared, in my column.

A few weeks later, I was on the streetcar when I met a fellow chef and friend of Barone's who had cooked with him in a couple of restaurants. She grabbed my hand, thanking me profusely for documenting that gnocchi prescription. Apparently, she had seen him make them many times but had never been able to reproduce the yummy morsels until she tried the recipe I'd learned at the chef's apron strings.

Some stories about chefs are laced with laughs.

Such was the case when, on one of my regular trips to New York, I dropped by the gorgeous, historic Waldorf-Astoria with my brother Eric to try their famous Waldorf Salad.

Perched on bar-stools in the hotel's recently renovated—and far too modern for my taste—Oscar's restaurant (named after maitre d' Oscar Tschirky who invented the Waldorf Salad at the turn of the century), we savoured our salad lunch washed down with a little too much white wine. Back in Toronto, while researching this originally four-ingredient dish, I phoned the executive chef of the hotel to ask for his recipe and to discuss his delicious but noticeably updated version. His response was a hoot. After many years at the hotel, he heartily dislikes the Waldorf Salad and only has it on the Oscar's and room service menus because there was a public outcry when he tried to have it removed.

The tale told by chef Pascal Ribreau isn't in this jolly vein. However, it turned out to be an uplifting one. I met Ribreau by chance at a lunch for food writers and chefs to chat about an annual food festival held in Montreal where he had owned and operated a successful restaurant for several years after coming to Canada from France. I noticed this sweet-faced, pale young man for two reasons. First, he was in a wheelchair and had to be lifted up some stairs by two men to reach the barely accessible, second-floor room. But, more important, it was the mixture of gentleness and steely determination that emanated from him. As coffee and dessert were being served, I approached him and asked about his story. He readily and calmly described the serious car accident a year earlier that had cost him the use of his legs.

Then he shared some amazing news. He told me he was planning to open his own restaurant in Toronto and that some experts in the field were designing him a first-of-its-kind, hi-tech wheelchair that would enable him to stand upright while cooking. A year later, again by chance, I heard Ribreau's restaurant Celestin was about to open. I called; he agreed to an interview and photo session. After that poignant but positive column appeared, several other media outlets picked up the story. As I write, three years later, Ribreau, his upright wheelchair and busy restaurant are all going strong.

⟨⁂⟩

KNOCKOUT GNOCCHI

✻ MY PRIMARY WORK STATIONS ARE AS FOLLOWS: the computer (my least favourite, especially since it irretrievably ate a recent column), supermarket aisles (usually enjoyable and crucial for culinary sleuthing); the grocery store counter (a great spot for ingredient info and recipe exchange with other customers), and—my preferred perch for culinary research—the restaurant bar stool. The latter is where I discovered wonderful chef Tony Barone and, more to the point, his amazing gnocchi.

It was about three years ago and Barone was cooking at Cantine—one of inimitable Toronto restaurateur Joey Bersani's excellent eateries—on the lively downtown strip of flower shops and dining haunts known as Ave. & Dav. That evening, seated at Cantine's comfortable bar, I ordered gnocchi— they were in a simple tomato sauce, as I recall—to accompany a deliciously quaffable glass of Italian Merlot. As I popped those light-as-air, melt-in-the mouth little potato pillows into my mouth, savouring each one as I went, I resolved to find out the source and secret of these divine dumplings.

Fast forward to a chilly mid-afternoon when Barone and I finally fulfilled a pact made that night: that he would show me how to make gnocchi.

And what a great way this turned out to be to beat the blahs.

Barone opened his own restaurant called Toba (the combined first syllables of his names) at 243 King St. E. When I arrive there at the appointed time between busy lunch and dinner the kitchen is hot and hopping. "We love coming to work," says sous-chef Ling Zheng who is wearing a red bandana on her head and a big grin on her face. "Every day is like a party in here," she adds, placing two long sides of fresh salmon on a cutting board in the smaller front kitchen. Chatting with me in the adjoining prep kitchen, pastry chef Michelle Massey, who is scooping a batch of crème fraîche ice cream she's just whipped up into a large bowl, agrees and has the wide smile to prove it.

As my gnocchi mentor places four baked potatoes, still piping hot, on the wooden chopping block in front of us, my three-day headache wanes and my spirits lift. Soon we're cookin'.

Barone, who has attracted a loyal, talented kitchen crew, has the key ingredients for his career of choice: equal amounts of skill and passion. He recalls helping his mother Angelina—who has cooked at the family business, Stooges Sports Bar in Scarborough, for more than 20 years—prepare pasta when he was five years old. He has worked in restaurants since age 14. His parents are from the small village of Anzano at the heel of Italy; he was born and raised in our city's east end.

It was while working in Italy for a year in the mid-'90s that Barone learned to make gnocchi. "They don't make them in Puglia where my family is from," he explains, "but we made them in Tuscany, Umbria and Lombardia." Gnocchi styles vary. "Sometimes, we just cut the gnocchi and cooked them," Barone adds. "In other places, we made ridges by rolling them on the back of a fork. But the farther north I went, the heavier the sauce."

Roughly translated, the word gnocchi (plural of gnoccho) means "knot of wood, or lump." They can be made with just flour and water, with ricotta instead of potatoes or with semolina. They can be boiled, boiled then fried or baked in the oven with sauce and cheese.

As he cooked and I watched, Barone made gnocchi production look easy as pie, from baked potato to lusciously sauced dish.

When I tried them at home the next day, I had one disaster (see potato notes below), then gnocchi nirvana with a different batch of spuds for that night's dinner. The potatoes you use are crucial. Your basic baking potato—it could be Idaho or russet—is your best bet as it yields dry, fluffy flesh when baked. Yukon Golds, which Barone likes to use for their good flavour and pale yellow colour, are excellent as long as they aren't young ones with a thin skin. Baking the spuds is key to ensure a light dough. It can be flavoured with chopped fresh basil, pesto, grated cheese or blanched, drained, chopped or puréed spinach.

Potato Gnocchi

Add the last half-cup or so of flour gradually when making the dough; how much you need depends on the amount of moisture in the potatoes. The dough can be made ahead and kept in the fridge; let it sit at room temperature about 30 minutes before using. The gnocchi can be frozen and cooked from that state. Add your favourite pasta sauce or pesto to the cooked gnocchi or use the simple recipe below. Barone melts a slice of taleggio cheese on top of his sauced gnocchi, then sprinkles them with shredded fresh basil. He also makes a sauce by cooking a mixture of half whipping cream, half gorgonzola cheese, covered, in a 350°F (180°C) oven for about 30 minutes.

4 to 5 medium potatoes, about
   2 to 3 lb (1 to 1.5 kg)
2 large eggs
½ tsp (2 mL) salt

½ tsp (2 mL) ground nutmeg,
   optional
About 2 cups (500 mL) all-purpose
   flour
Freshly grated parmesan

1. Preheat oven to 400°F (200°C).

2. Prick skin of potatoes with fork in several places. Bake about 1 hour or until soft. Let sit until cool enough to handle. Halve; scoop flesh into large bowl with spoon. You should have about 4 cups (1 L). Discard skins. Add eggs, salt and nutmeg. Mash with potato masher. (Do not use mixer or food processor.) Add flour, stirring with fork; shape into dough using hands, adding a little more flour if mixture is sticky. Turn dough onto counter. Knead gently a few times; shape into ball that springs back when pressed with finger. Let rest about 15 minutes.

3. On counter or wooden board lightly dusted with flour, slice off about one-sixth of dough. Using palms of hands, roll into long, thin sausage about ½ inch (1 cm) in diameter. Using sharp knife, slice into ½-inch (1 cm) pieces. Roll each piece along tines on back of fork to create ribbed effect. You can make rounded gnocchi with an indentation to hold sauce by pressing one finger into middle of each to create a hollow. Toss gnocchi in just enough flour to dust.

4. Bring large saucepan of salted water to boil. Add gnocchi. Do not stir. Cook over medium-high heat until they rise to top, 2 to 3 minutes. Drain. Add to heated sauce in skillet or saucepan. Toss. Serve with freshly grated parmesan.

MAKES 4 TO 6 SERVINGS.

Easy Tomato Sauce

I learned this from American cookbook author Biba Caggiano. It's ideal for the time of year when tomatoes are out of season. I like Pastene or Strianese canned tomatoes, imported from Italy. In summer, make a sauce of chopped raw tomatoes, salt, pepper, basil and a little olive oil, mashed with a fork.

28 oz (796 mL) can plum tomatoes,
   drained
1 tbsp (15 mL) unsalted butter
Salt and pepper to taste

Purée tomatoes in food processor. Add to saucepan; bring to boil. Reduce heat; simmer until thickened, about 10 minutes. Add butter, salt and pepper.

MAKES 4 TO 6 SERVINGS.

TWO HOT TAMALES

❋ LAS VAGAS—IT WAS MID-MEAL, at some point between the third and fourth courses, that I found myself fondling the exquisitely soft, crushed silk burgundy tablecloth and realizing that Las Vegas is easily the best proof I've seen that nothing succeeds like excess.

I was attending a food writers' convention here and the sumptuous dinner we were savouring, by special invitation, was at The Mansion, in the heart of The Strip. This over-the-top, rococo, swathed and draped, gilded and glittery reproduction of an 18th century Italian villa was built in 1999 by MGM Grand as a private residence in which to entertain high rollers, in particular those happy to drop a million—or two, or three—during what is often a mere weekend of serious gambling.

And where there are big bucks, there are likely to be fancy restaurants. Hence the presence of many of America's top chefs and restaurateurs who have flocked here in the past few years to relish the boom generated by visiting big spenders.

It also explains why well-known names like Wolfgang Puck, Joachim Splichal and Todd English, all of whom have recently opened Las Vegas dining spots, were manning The Mansion's stoves that splendid evening and turning out dainty delicacies like these: Mandarin Quail with Fire Roasted Eggplant, Venison Medallions with Celery Root Foie Gras Remoulade and Napoleon of Yellowtail Ahi with Osetra Caviar.

After that surreal meal, our group's lunch the following day—at Border Grill, located at the hub of the huge new Mandalay Resort & Casino—came as a relief. Heaping platters of homey, flavourful Mexican food, served family-style, arrived at a leisurely pace as we basked in the sun on the airy eatery's palm-treed patio.

Here's a taste. Tender-crisp *empanadas* (half-moon-shaped pies) stuffed with chile-spiked beans and plantains. Ceviche of raw sea bass delicately laced with lime juice and serrano chiles. A yummy salad of grilled cactus paddles doused in a spicy dressing. Green corn tamales crowned with salsa and sour cream. Grilled turkey breast bathed in a silky, dark mole (chocolate-based) sauce. And an array of small desserts that included the lusciously sweet and creamy Three-Milk Cake made with evaporated, condensed and regular milk.

Afterwards, I had a chance to talk with the restaurant's chatty owners: Mary Sue Milliken and Susan Feniger. Feniger noted that business has been down in this tourist town since September 11. "Sales have dropped dramatically," she says. "It's 25 to 30 percent, though things are picking up now on weekends." But she and Milliken have the experience and savvy to roll with the punches.

Both are classically trained chefs who met in the 1970s while working in Chicago at a restaurant called Le Perroquet. "As women working in a French kitchen in those days," recalls Milliken with a grin, "we were often relegated to the shallot- and garlic-peeling station." But what seemed like a disadvantage had a bright side. "We became friends with the prep cooks who were from Latin countries like Mexico, El Salvador and Guatemala," she continues. "They taught us how make their food, which we immediately liked—for example, salsa made with dried chiles which we put on the boiled meat we often had at staff meals because it was cheap."

In 1981, the pair opened City Café on Melrose Ave., in Los Angeles, the town in which they both still live. Here, the menu was an eclectic ethnic mix gleaned from their travels—mostly Thai and Indian dishes along with the Mexican fare that would soon become the duo's trademark.

Research trips followed. "We often stayed in Mexico City with the family of one of our employees," Milliken explains. "We would go the local market, choose ingredients we'd never tried before and an aunt or uncle would show us how to cook it." Adds Feniger, "I fell in love with Mexico's intricate, hand-held street food like *panuchos*: handmade flour tortillas that puff up when they're cooked and are stuffed with black beans topped with spicy tomato sauce."

Gradually, the pair's passion for what Milliken calls Mexican cuisine's "bold, big flavours and the wonderful contrasts of taste and texture" grew and evolved. "The cooking we've come up with over the years is not Tex-Mex," she explains. "It's not always strictly authentic. I'd call it modern Mexican food."

Today, City Café is no more, but the pair own and operate three Mexican-themed Border Grills: one in Las Vegas, another in Santa Monica and a third in Pasadena. A fourth opens next month near Las Vegas in the small town of Henderson. They also have a restaurant in downtown L.A. called Ciudad that features Latin food, in particular, dishes from Spain, Cuba, Brazil and Mexico.

Talk about having plenty on one's plate—and this for two women who are avidly hands-on, working in the kitchens of their eateries, developing new dishes and perfecting existing ones, all the while working on other projects.

Like me, you may remember these cheerful chefs as the Too Hot Tamales from their terrific tv cooking show by that name. It, along with "Tamales World Tour," aired from 1995 to 1999 on Food Network and proved their natural gift as teachers. Happily, a new series called "Border Girls" featuring their dynamic dicing, slicing and spicing is in the works to be aired soon on PBS.

Earlier this year, Milliken and Feniger worked as consultants on the movie *Tortilla Soup*. The film had mixed reviews but, with these two in creative control and doing all the cooking for the many elaborate food scenes, Mexico's cuisine stole the show.

They have also written five cookbooks. The only one I could find locally is the excellent *Mexican Cooking for Dummies*. In it, you'll find a version of this delicious salad that's typical of Milliken and Feniger's tasty take on Mexican food.

Mexican Chopped Salad

I knew this was a winner when Ruthie requested I make it for dinner every night. I serve it with homemade chili and warmed flour tortillas. Omit the red onion—as I do because of Ruthie's delicate palate—if you don't like the heat. Pumpkin seeds are sold in major supermarkets and most health food and bulk food stores. I like to use a mixture of romaine and iceberg lettuce. The pumpkin seed dressing can be made ahead; store any left over in the fridge. Use more crushed tortilla chips, as I usually do, if desired.

⅓ cup (75 mL) pumpkin seeds (*pepitas*)
1 tsp (5 mL) ground cumin
¼ cup (50 mL) red or white wine vinegar
½ cup (125 mL) extra virgin olive oil
Salt and pepper to taste
1 medium head romaine or iceberg lettuce, sliced or diced
2 plum tomatoes, diced

1 small red onion, coarsely chopped
1 medium apple, peeled, cored, diced
¾ cup (175 mL) corn kernels
1½ cups (375 mL) crushed tortilla chips
1 avocado, peeled, pitted, thinly sliced (optional)
Chopped fresh coriander or parsley (optional)

1. Toast pumpkin seeds in small heavy skillet over low heat, stirring until lightly browned and beginning to pop, about 4 minutes. Add cumin; cook, stirring, about 1 minute. Remove from heat. Add vinegar, oil, salt and pepper. Stir until combined. Cool.

2. In large salad bowl, mix together lettuce, tomatoes, onion, apple and corn. Just before serving, toss with pumpkin seed dressing, using just enough to coat salad. Top with crushed tortilla chips. Sprinkle with avocado and chopped coriander, if using.

MAKES 4 TO 6 SERVINGS.

Mango Black Bean Salsa

In the spirit of Mexican cuisine, here's a fantastic appetizer that would be great served with tortilla chips as a snack with drinks or served on a bed of lettuce as a dinner party starter. It comes from the "Friends" cookbook Cooking with Friends *by Amy Lyles. For more heat, use two serrano or jalapeño peppers.*

3 medium ripe mangos, peeled, pitted, cut into ¼-inch (5 mm) cubes

19 oz (540 mL) can black beans, drained, rinsed

1 small red onion, diced

¼ cup (50 mL) fresh coriander, chopped

¼ cup (50 mL) fresh lime or lemon juice

1 medium fresh serrano or jalapeno pepper, seeded, minced

1 tsp (5 mL) ground cumin

In medium bowl, combine mangos, beans, onion, coriander, juice, pepper and cumin. Mix gently.

MAKES 4 TO 6 APPETIZER SERVINGS.

❧

EAT, DRINK AND BE MARRIED

❋ It's a clear case of the way to a man's heart—but, in this instance, we're not talking your average stomach. The object of Karin Desveaux-Potters' affection is her husband of three years and one of Toronto's top chefs: Michael Potters. Seated in the cozy living room of their west-end house while the couple's 11-month-old daughter Mia takes her afternoon nap, I chat with them over coffee about their food/love connection.

"My favourite cuisine is Karin's food," says Potters, 41, glancing affectionately over at his wife and looking uncharacteristically relaxed in jeans and a sweater. That's high praise coming from a man whose credentials include stints heading up kitchen crews at Winston's, The Left Bank and The Rosewater Supper Club. "There was always a plate of food waiting for me when I came home at night," he continues, referring to his former job of three years as executive chef at Accolade, the high-end dining room in the Crowne Plaza, which he recently left to take a well-earned hiatus. "I can't eat my food after cooking all day long," he adds. "Karin's roast chicken, a little pasta or a plate of pierogies was the warmest greeting I could have."

It's no surprise that Desveaux-Potters, whose cooking repertoire includes Polish fare from her mother's family and Quebecois staples on her father's side, makes a mean meal.

She's a chef of some standing herself—who met her husband-to-be in the kitchen of the short-lived Yorkville nightclub, Ivory, in 1995—and currently works as personal chef for a family in Rosedale and at restaurant/caterers To Go. "I've mostly been a pastry chef," she explains, adding, "I'm very detail-oriented." Her spouse and biggest fan chimes in, "She has great hands when it comes to pastry," he says softly. "She makes the best puff pastry I've ever seen."

The two then worked together at the Rosewater where she trained under pastry pro Dean Cole who has since returned home to Britain. After a year-and-a-half, she "wanted to move on and decided to quit." Potters took her out for dinner and persuaded her to stay. "I also came on to her," he says with a grin. "That was the beginning of our relationship."

But working together had its ups and downs. "I was the butcher under Michael at Winston's," she recalls. "It was disastrous." He reckons, "The chemistry was wrong—something about being a couple."

Things really blew up when they teamed up, once married, to do a catering job. "There was an ego problem," quips Potters, adding provocatively, "She was such a control freak." His wife, who had hired her hubby for that gig, was not amused. "He left before the dessert buffet," she claims with mock anger. "I was left with one cook to put out dessert for 300."

Potters admits the ego problem in question belonged to him. "There's the 'Yes, chef' mentality in a restaurant kitchen," he explains. "I was her boss for so long. It was hard to adjust to a new power structure."

Both feel that living with another chef has pluses and minuses. "You understand each other's job and its demands," he notes, adding with a smile: "And both of you can cook so you're never hard up for a good meal." On the downside, she notes: "For most chefs, there's no Valentine's, no New Year's Eve. You're lucky if you get a birthday off." Talking of birthdays, her 30th last December was one occasion when Desveaux-Potters truly appreciated her talented partner. To celebrate, Potters prepared a sumptuous, eight-course dinner for six served in fine style with the help of a sous-chef and a waiter. The soiree kicked off at 10 P.M. as the birthday girl had a catering job for 40 to do that day.

It began with osetra caviar and buckwheat blini served with 1985 and 1989 vintages of Salon champagne and wound up at 4 A.M. after a finale of chocolate cake with raspberries followed by four kinds of French cheese. In between, there was foie gras terrine; oysters two ways—raw with fresh salsa and cooked with sabayon; fresh dover sole in lemon sauce and a roasted lobster tail with sliced truffles; yogurt Gewurztraminer sorbet; and beef tenderloin Chateaubriand carved at the table. Two wines accompanied each course. Between each, the linen was changed. "It was the best meal Michael's ever cooked," claims his beaming wife, recalling that she nursed little Mia through most of that memorable feast.

Perhaps that's why their young offspring already shows signs of an impeccable palate. "I think she's going to be a good cook," says Potters proudly. "She loves playing with pots and pans and is a good eater. She loves dim sum, especially congee." Apparently, the budding chef is also a fan of the pasta with Bolognese sauce her dad learned to make from his ex-wife's Italian mother Grace Schiavone. Naturally, dear readers, I got you the recipe.

For four main course or six smaller servings, toss 1 lb (500 g) of cooked pasta with about 2 tbsp (30 mL) of its cooking water and 1½ to 2 cups (375 to 500 mL) of this wondrous sauce. You can do as Potter recommends and toss the pasta with about three-quarters of the sauce and pour the rest on top.

Big Batch Bolognese

Mashing the ground meat, then the tomatoes, gives fine texture. Purée the tomatoes in a food processor before adding to the sauce and substitute more ground beef for pork, if desired. This freezes well.

4 tbsp (60 mL) olive oil
1 lb (500 g) lean ground beef
1/4 lb (50 g) ground pork, optional
1 tsp (5 mL) salt, or to taste
1/2 tsp (2 mL) freshly ground black pepper
4 large cloves garlic, thinly sliced
1 medium onion, finely chopped
1 tbsp (15 mL) dried oregano
1/4 tsp (1 mL) crushed red pepper flakes

1/4 cup (50 mL) whisky (scotch, bourbon or rye)
Three 28 oz (796 mL) cans whole or diced plum tomatoes, undrained
5 1/2 oz (156 mL) can tomato paste
1 bunch fresh basil leaves, chopped or 1 tbsp (15 mL) dried
2 large bay leaves
Salt and freshly ground black pepper to taste
Freshly grated parmesan

1. In large, heavy saucepan with lid or dutch oven, heat 2 tbsp (30 mL) of olive oil over medium-high heat. Add ground beef, pork (if using), salt and pepper. Mash with potato masher to break up lumps until mixture browns and becomes granular, stirring with wooden spoon at intervals, about 5 minutes. With slotted spoon, transfer mixture to bowl.

2. Reduce heat to medium-low; add remaining olive oil to saucepan. Add garlic; cook, stirring, until golden brown, about 3 minutes. Add onion, oregano and pepper flakes; cook, stirring, until onion is soft, about 4 minutes. Return beef mixture to saucepan; add whisky. Cook, covered, until whisky is absorbed, about 5 minutes. Add tomatoes; mash with potato masher until broken up. Stir in tomato paste, basil and bay leaves. Bring mixture to boil; reduce heat to very low and simmer, partially covered and stirring at intervals, about 5 hours or until thick and rich in flavour. (Add a little water on occasion if sauce becomes too thick.)

3. Remove bay leaves. Add salt and pepper, if necessary.

4. Serve with cooked pasta as described above and plenty of freshly grated parmesan cheese on the side.

MAKES ABOUT 8 CUPS (2 L).

THE ART BEHIND OPRAH

❋ OPRAH WINFREY IS A LUCKY DUCK.

Or more likely, hiring Art Smith to be her personal chef is just another sign that the woman is one smart cookie. I know this because I had the good fortune of having this charming, gentle bear of a man cook for me in my own kitchen.

It all came about when the Toronto publicist for Smith's book *Back to the Table* called to ask if I would like Oprah's chef to come to my house the following Monday to cook me lunch. Stunned by this unprecedented offer—one I obviously couldn't refuse—I muttered something about the Pope being Polish. Sure enough, at the appointed time, the 6 foot 3, burly, smiling chef was on my doorstep, publicist in tow.

A brief chat about recipes ensued—we opted for Green Pea Soup and Classic Southern Cornbread, both from his book—followed by a whirlwind tour of Kensington Market to buy ingredients, during which the gregarious Smith made friends with several merchants. Soon, Smith's size 12 shiny loafers were neatly positioned near my front door and he was in my kitchen. By now, realizing there was a serious case of foodie bonding at work, the publicist has gone.

The loquacious Smith, chatting away in his soft, sing-song Southern drawl, is standing by my stove arranging pots and pans, readying his ingredients on the counter and acting very much like a man who knows what he's doing. His luggage, which included his chef's whites, had been lost two days before on a flight here from Moncton, N.B., Smith tells me cheerfully while chopping an onion. At the *Star* photographer's request, Smith solves that. One of his new Kensington friends hops on a bike to pick up an extra-large chef's jacket from a nearby restaurant. "That's an act of kindness," Smith pronounces, turning to me and pausing for emphasis. "It's like last week, when I was making breads for *Canada AM*, the assistant manager of the local Dominion helped me take two full grocery carts several blocks to the B&B where I was staying. Pausing again, then looking me in the eye, he adds: "It's the power of food. Good food always attracts great people."

As he meticulously but effortlessly cuts a carrot into tiny dice, Smith, as happens often throughout his visit, returns to a previous train of thought.

Moncton was one stop on the informal tour to Canada he instigated to promote his book and visit friends during this one-month vacation from work
at Winfrey's. "Moncton's a wonderful place," Smith gushes, creating a small,
tidy mound of finely chopped garlic on the chopping board. "The mayor
invited me to a lovely potluck dinner. The most amazing lobster and crab—
and they've got a fabulous market. I always go to markets when I travel." By
now, Smith and I are having fun.

While he chops, slices, stirs and whisks, I occasionally leave my perch at the
counter where I'm taking notes to find a measuring cup, to rummage through
cupboards in search of a hand blender and to make a quick foray to buy baking soda. Smith, who addresses me as "honey" between the initially unsettling
but by now endearing "Yes, Ma'am's," is sifting flour into a bowl for the cornbread. As he grates the crumbly raw milk, four-year-old cheddar we bought
on the advice of the young man at Cheese Magic, he pops a piece into his
mouth. "Honey, this is a real find. You could never find this in the U.S."

Smith grew up on his family's farm near Jasper in north Florida. His
grandmother owned and operated a boarding house where his mother
worked and cooked for many years.

"I was raised with a lot of love," he says, measuring milk and sour cream
together as a substitute for buttermilk. "There were very strong women in my
life who were all great cooks: two grandmothers, my mother Addie Mae, who
I speak to almost every day, and the African American woman Leila who
raised me while my mother was at work."

And, of course, now there's Oprah. Unfortunately, this is the only topic on
which Smith is a man of few words. "I'm sorry, honey, I can't talk about those
things," he says looking genuinely stricken but moving right along. "It's a
matter of privacy, a code of honour. I'm happy to say that all the families I've
worked for are still friends." And that's no mean feat since Smith has worked
as a personal chef, often for celebrities, for more than 20 years. He will say
that he got the gig cooking three meals a day for Winfrey and her partner
Stedman Graham five years ago after meeting her at a Washington party
given by his former boss Senator Robert Graham.

When asked about Rosie Daley, Winfrey's previous chef whose low-fat
cookbook *In the Kitchen with Rosie* was a huge bestseller in the mid-'90s,

Smith is mum. "I feel you should cook what you know," he says, an allusion to Southern food, most of which is not low-fat. "Choice in food is a personal matter," he adds elusively. "People should eat what they want and decide how much."

Smith, who lives in Chicago but frequently commutes to New York, worked as a teacher for several years for Williams-Sonoma and regularly caters special events for Martha Stewart on a freelance basis.

But being a personal chef is his vocation. "I like working for families who have a dog, children, music in their lives," he says, adding: "That's what life's about." The job requires a nurturing nature, which he obviously has in spades, and, in his case, is reinforced by spiritual beliefs. These pepper his book in chapters with headings like "Bless the Table", "Food as Love" and "Friends as Family".

Smith recently practiced what he preaches when he cooked for a family in which the father was killed on September 11. "They're African Americans who live in Brooklyn," he explains. "He was a delivery man who was on the loading dock at one of the towers when the planes hit—the wrong place at the wrong time." At the family's request, his dinner comprised the pot roast, Scalloped Potatoes with Tomato Pesto and Salad with Pecans, Blue Cheese and Pears (recipe below) from his book. Two young daughters, aged four and 10, helped him bake his grandmother's 12-Layer Cake.

That night, at a friend's house, Smith baked 500 cookies and the following day took them to the church at Ground Zero where food is distributed to rescue workers. "They said, 'Thank you for the homemade food,' which I thought was wonderful," he says.

By now, our soup is ready ("I'm having a Martha moment," quips Smith as he adjusts its mint garnish) and the aroma of freshly baked cornbread fills the room. Smith has washed the bowls, utensils and pots he's used. All are stacked on a tea towel spread carefully on the counter beside the sink.

I pour us each a glass of Pinot Noir then put on my new CD of the wondrous Cesaria Evora singing soothingly and seductively in Portuguese. She has barely uttered two bars when Smith chimes in. "I love her," he proclaims, launching into a story about drinking a cold Heineken some years ago on the Cape Verde island off the coast of Africa that is Evora's home. How did he wind up there? No prize for guessing: He was personal chef to a family who were travelling the world in a private yacht.

Here are three recipes from *Back to the Table* to help you enjoy the spirit of communing at the table with family and friends.

Green Pea Soup

It's important to use tender, young frozen peas such as Green Giant's Sweetlets or fresh peas in season. You could swirl buttermilk or plain yogurt thinned with milk over each bowl of soup with a plastic squeeze bottle.

2 tbsp (30 mL) olive oil
1 medium onion, chopped
2 celery stalks, chopped
2 cloves garlic, finely chopped
1 medium potato, peeled, chopped
About 6 cups (1.5 L) vegetable or
 chicken stock, homemade, from
 cubes or canned

2.2-lb (1 kg) package frozen green peas
 or 6 to 7 cups (1.5 to 1.75 mL)
1 large or 2 medium carrots, peeled,
 finely diced
2 tbsp (30 mL) fresh lemon juice
Salt and freshly ground pepper to
 taste
Fresh mint leaves (optional)

1. In large heavy saucepan, heat oil over medium heat. Add onion and celery; cook, stirring, until soft, about 8 minutes. Add garlic; cook 1 minute more. Stir in potato, then stock. Bring to boil over high heat, reduce to low and simmer, partially covered, until potatoes are very tender, about 15 minutes.

2. Add all but 1 cup (250 mL) of peas; return to boil over high heat. Reduce heat to low and simmer, partially covered, until peas are tender, about 5 minutes. Meanwhile, to make garnish, bring medium saucepan of salted water to boil. Add reserved 1 cup (250 mL) peas; cook until tender/crisp, about 2 minutes. Drain; rinse under cold water. Repeat with carrots, cooking about 3 minutes.

3. Purée soup to desired consistency with electric hand blender or in blender. Add lemon juice, salt and pepper. Return to heat; cook until piping hot. Serve sprinkled with blanched peas and carrots and mint, if using.

MAKES 6 TO 8 SERVINGS.

Classic Southern Cornbread

A shallow, crisp skillet cornbread that's great with soup or stew. You can substitute 1½ cups (375 mL) milk mixed with ½ cup (125 mL) plain yogurt or sour cream for buttermilk.

2 tbsp (30 mL) vegetable oil
2 cups (500 mL) cornmeal,
   preferably stoneground
¾ cup (175 mL) all-purpose flour
2 tbsp (30 mL) granulated sugar
2½ tsp (12 mL) baking powder
½ tsp (2 mL) baking soda
1 tsp (5 mL) salt
½ tsp (2 mL) freshly ground black
   pepper

2 cups (500 mL) buttermilk
2 large eggs, beaten
¼ cup (50 mL) vegetable oil
½ tsp (2 mL) dried thyme
½ tsp (2 mL) dried oregano
½ cup (125 mL) old white cheddar,
   grated
8 sundried tomatoes, soaked
   20 minutes in hot water, sliced

1. Preheat oven to 450°F (230°C).

2. Coat 9 to 10-inch (23 to 25 cm) heavy ovenproof skillet with 2 tbsp (30 mL) vegetable oil. Place in oven 5 minutes.

3. Meanwhile, in large bowl, combine cornmeal, flour, sugar, baking powder, baking soda, salt and pepper. Make well in centre.

4. In separate bowl, whisk together buttermilk, eggs, ¼ cup (50 mL) vegetable oil, thyme and oregano until combined. Pour into well in flour mixture along with cheddar and tomatoes; stir just until mixed. (Don't over-mix). Pour mixture into hot skillet. Bake until tester comes out clean, about 15 to 20 minutes. Cool about 5 minutes. Invert on to plate.

MAKES ABOUT 8 SERVINGS.

Salad with Pecans, Blue Cheese and Pears

A flavour-packed salad that looks as good as it tastes. Smith uses Late Harvest Riesling vinegar for the dressing but raspberry, sherry or the yummy fig with lemon version I found at Loblaws will do. This makes extra dressing; store in the fridge in an airtight container. You can substitute a crisp, tart apple for the pear.

½ cup (125 mL) pecan halves
1 tbsp (15 mL) maple or corn syrup
1 tbsp (15 mL) mayonnaise
2 tbsp (30 mL) Dijon mustard
1 clove garlic, minced
¼ cup (50 mL) fruit vinegar

1 cup (250 mL) extra virgin olive oil
Salt and pepper to taste
2 heads Boston lettuce
2 oz (50 g) blue cheese, crumbled
1 ripe Anjou pear, peeled, cored, cut
   in matchsticks

1. Preheat oven to 350°F (180°C).

2. Spread pecans on baking sheet. Bake about 5 minutes. Transfer to bowl. Add syrup. Stir to coat. Return to oven for 5 minutes. Cool.

3. In bowl, whisk together mayonnaise, mustard, garlic, vinegar and olive oil until well blended. Add salt and pepper.

4. Remove tough outer leaves of lettuce; discard. Wash and dry inner leaves; tear into bite-sized pieces. Place in large salad bowl. Just before serving, add only enough dressing to coat lettuce, and toss salad. Sprinkle pecans, cheese and pears on top.

MAKES 4 TO 6 SERVINGS.

PASCAL'S SPIRIT FEEDS CELESTIN

✳ THIS IS AN UPLIFTING STORY—IN MORE WAYS THAN ONE.

It's about a French chef, his state-of-the-art, upright wheelchair and a brand new restaurant he named after the grandfather who inspired his dream. And as he sits beside me at Celestin, in the hi-tech, everyday wheelchair Pascal Ribreau calls his "Ferrari," this impressive young man with the pale skin and dark brown eyes tells a tale of fate, fortitude and a formidable passion for his chosen métier.

Ribreau came here in the late 1980s after meeting his Canadian wife Laurie Anderson in Paris where he was born, raised and trained as a chef. "I like to say I'm from the mountains in Auvergne," he's quick to note. "That's where my grandfather lived and where I stayed for several months every summer when I was growing up." A farmer with nine children, his beloved grandfather taught Ribreau "respect and dignity. He loved the woods and the mountains. He was very bright and open-minded."

Ribreau honed his skills in classical French cuisine while attending culinary school by apprenticing at Paris landmarks like the Palais de Luxembourg and the Chamber of Commerce.

After arriving in Toronto in 1988, Ribreau took two full-time jobs: as pastry chef at the Royal York Hotel and chef de partie at Sutton Place.

In 1993, Ribreau and Anderson moved to Montreal. Two years later, he opened his own restaurant called Allumette in the heart of restaurant row on downtown Rue St. Denis.

For two years, business boomed. Then fear of Quebec's separation led to an exodus and a dip in the local economy. "I came to Montreal for the people and left for the people," Ribreau says. "I'll always be grateful to the city because they adopted me as a chef."

He sold Allumette and moved to Toronto. Here, he worked as executive chef at Provence, the Cabbagetown dining spot he calls "my favourite and the most beautiful restaurant in the city."

Then came the fateful day: October 11, 1999. Ribreau and his wife had travelled to Montreal for the weekend to celebrate the purchase of their

Toronto home with friends. On Thanksgiving Day, en route to Dorval airport after a picnic in the countryside, their car swerved to avoid an oncoming vehicle. Ribreau, who was in the back seat, was ejected in the crash. "Flying was fine," he comments quietly with a half-smile. "Landing was not that great." He has been paralyzed from the waist down ever since.

For the first month, he recalls "pain, pain, pain." But soon, Ribreau's steely determination and positive approach to life kicked in. Many months of gruelling rehab, much of it instigated by Ribreau, mean he can now walk using leg braces and exercise on the treadmill, both with the help of a physiotherapist. "I can't walk naturally," he notes, "but I can walk. I'm stubborn." He moves around in a high-performance wheelchair that he gets in and out of 20 to 30 times a day and in his Dodge Caravan specially fitted with a swivel driver's seat, hand controls and ramp.

But how, I hear you ask, has he managed to open his own restaurant? How, in particular, can he cook in its kitchen for several hours at a time? First, there's that fierce drive inspired by the grandfather who died eight months after his accident. "Two years ago, I did the Golden Horseshoe Marathon from Fort Erie to Toronto," Ribreau explains. "I was on the road in my wheelchair for five days. I felt my grandfather's presence—pulling me like he used to pull trees with a chain after he'd chopped them down—for those last 5 kilometres. This restaurant is a tribute to him."

As for his ability to cook, this is thanks to an amazing upright wheelchair—a prototype designed and built by engineers at Motion Specialty according to his specifications. "I'm basically standing on my legs," says the six-foot Ribreau proudly as he sails into the dining room of Celestin from the kitchen, looking comfortable in his clever contraption with straps just below the knees and a harness around his chest. He insists he isn't "a dreamer" but that "by the time I'm 40, I hope to be walking again. I also hope the next generation won't suffer paralysis. It's a matter of commitment, research, money."

Celestin's kitchen has been adapted to accommodate his unusual stance. The fridge slides open, shelves and counters are higher than usual and the gas stove is flat on one side to avoid an open flame. "There are no frites in my place," he says of the menu featuring his trademark Rabbit Ravioli and Crab Soup that he calls "French with my twist."

Lemon Tart

PASTRY
1 cup (250 mL) all-purpose flour
2½ tbsp (37 mL) granulated sugar
½ tsp (2 mL) salt
½ cup (125 mL) cold unsalted butter, cubed
2 large egg yolks

LEMON CURD FILLING
¾ cup (175 mL) granulated sugar
3 large eggs
1 large egg yolk
¾ cup (175 mL) fresh lemon juice
6 tbsp (90 mL) unsalted butter, cubed
4 tsp (20 mL) finely grated lemon rind

1. For pastry: In bowl of food processor, combine flour, sugar, salt and butter. Process until mixture resembles fine crumbs. Add egg yolks; process until dough comes together. Shape into a disc. Wrap disc in plastic. Chill for about 1 hour.

2. Between two sheets of lightly floured waxed paper, roll dough into circle ¼-inch (5 mm) thick. Fit into 10-inch (25 cm) round tart pan with removable bottom, folding over to create double thickness up sides. With fork tines, prick dough shell on bottom and sides. Cover with plastic wrap. Chill for about 30 minutes.

3. Preheat oven to 375°F (190°C).

4. Remove plastic wrap from dough. Place sheet of foil in dough shell. Fill with ceramic pie weights or dry beans. Bake in centre of oven for 15 minutes. Remove foil and weights. Bake another 10 minutes or until golden. Cool on wire rack.

5. For filling: In heatproof bowl set over, not in, simmering water, whisk together sugar, eggs, egg yolk and lemon juice until mixed. Whisk in butter. Cook, whisking, for 12 to 14 minutes or until mixture thickens. Strain curd into a clean bowl. Stir in lemon rind. Place sheet of plastic wrap directly on surface of curd. Chill for at least 1 hour.

6. For assembly: Fill pastry shell with lemon curd, smoothing top. Chill before serving.

MAKES 10 TO 12 SERVINGS.

❧❦❧

THE MAN WHO COOKED FOR KINGS

✳ JOHN HIGGINS IS CERTAINLY USED TO HAVING plenty on his plate. As executive chef of the King Edward Hotel for almost 14 years—a job he reckons took up 12 hours a day six days a week—he became well acquainted with hard work. As we chat over lunch at one of his favourite restaurants—a terrific little family-run eatery called Mammina's on Wellesley St. just east of Yonge—Higgins explains why he recently resigned from that position and how come he's just as busy at his new job. "At the hotel, it was tough," he admits, adding quickly, "There was lots of responsibility but lots of fun. What kept me going was the creativity of doing something different every day and of working with a team."

He pulls a business card from his current place of employment, The City College George Brown, and points to his mouthful of a title: Coordinator, New Initiatives—Culinary Programs, Faculty of Hospitality and Tourism. "I have a lot of knowledge to pass on," he says, the rolled 'r's and sing-song tone of his native Glasgow barely muted after 20 years in Canada. "I like working with students," he continues, "and George Brown is looking to move forward. I think I can help." Higgins, who will stay connected with the King Eddy as a consultant, admits he's on a learning curve and that he's been extremely busy readying himself for the work ahead, an explanation I happily accept for the seemingly endless telephone tag I endured to finally arrange this interview. His duties include teaching various levels of budding chefs and instructing kitchen crews at Siegfried's—the college's cheap and cheerful restaurant that's open to the public—a couple of days a week.

"I've wanted to be a chef since I was 10," he recalls. "My grandmother was a great cook of stews and Scottish dishes like Mince and Tatties. She baked wonderful scones, soda bread and fruitcake. Even her boiled eggs tasted good." But it was while caddying for his uncle who played golf at the spectacular Gleneagles Hotel near the Higgins home that a specific ambition was born. "I decided that was where I wanted to work." That dream came true when he spent two years as chef de partie at Gleneagles soon after graduating as a chef from Motherwell College in his hometown.

Already, Higgins, who believes in setting goals—and, it turns out, methodically achieves them—had found his niche. There were several stints working in large hotels in Scotland. Then, in 1980, he successfully applied for a job as Junior Royal Cook at Buckingham Palace. "I had to sign the Official Secrets Act before starting work," he says. Then with a chuckle: "It was the best address I ever had."

As part of a team who prepared the Royal Family's breakfast, lunch and dinner, he lived in the servants' quarters, which weren't too shabby. "My room was like a plain hotel room. It was cleaned every day." There was a staff kitchen and a bar inside the palace. The Royal menu, he continues, consisted of "simple English food cooked well: Poached Leg of Lamb with Caper Sauce for Sunday dinner and lots of cakes and breads made in the Palace's pastry shop."

He decided to emigrate after his mother received a postcard from a friend in Canada showing "beautiful red maple trees and gorgeous blue sky." Here, he quickly attained another goal. "I'd decided to be an executive chef of a major hotel by age 30," says he. "I achieved it at the King Eddy when I was 29."

It's no secret Higgins has had problems with his weight which, five years ago, peaked at 300 pounds. Not long after, I wrote a column about one of his temporarily successful attempts at dieting. It bore the headline: "Chef reduces hefty portions—of himself." "It's a hazard of the job," he concedes cheerfully, pointing out what I'd already noticed—that he's currently in excellent shape and a burly, healthy size. The reasons: ongoing help from a nutritionist and regular work-outs at the gym. "I cook because I love food," he adds. "Being a chef, it's difficult. You have to taste things and try new ideas."

And chef Higgins does it well. One of his specialties—Scottish Salmon Smoked over English Breakfast Tea—is among my favourite dishes.

At home, he shares cooking duties with his wife Arlene. "She makes terrific chili," he enthuses. "And her meatloaf is so good—she uses a mixture of beef, pork and veal—we once had her come into the kitchen at the King Eddy and help make it for 200 managers from the hotel chain who were having dinner." "I don't care if it's truffles and foie gras or bacon and eggs," says this down-to-earth chef, "as long as it's done as well as possible."

Here's a sweet, simple recipe for scones like those Higgins ate growing up.

Old-Fashioned Scones

Serve with whipped cream, crème fraîche or Yogurt Cream (see page 119), made by letting the yogurt sit in a coffee filter set over a cup about 30 minutes, then sweetened with a little maple syrup. Fruit compote or good quality jam are also good accompaniments—and, of course, a nice cup of tea. You can use the food processor to cut the butter into the flour mixture.

2 cups (500 mL) all-purpose flour
1 tbsp (15 mL) baking powder
1/2 tsp (2 mL) baking soda
Pinch of salt
1/2 cup (125 mL) cold unsalted butter,
 cut in pieces

1 cup (250 mL) raisins
2 tbsp (30 mL) granulated sugar
1 egg, separated
3/4 cup (175 mL) buttermilk or plain
 yogurt
Granulated sugar for dusting

1. Preheat oven to 375°F (190°C).

2. In large bowl, combine flour, baking powder, baking soda and salt. Using wire pastry blender or two knives, cut in butter until mixture resembles coarse crumbs. Stir in raisins and sugar.

3. In small bowl, whisk together egg yolk and buttermilk. Stir into flour mixture with fork until soft dough forms. Gather into ball; turn on to floured surface and knead a few times. Roll out to about 3/4 inch (4 cm) thickness. Using a glass or cookie cutter, cut into 2 1/2-inch (6.5 cm) rounds. Brush with egg white; dust with sugar.

4. Baked on greased cookie sheet or on Silpat plastic liner 18 to 20 minutes or until golden brown.

MAKES ABOUT 16.

TARTE TATIN: APPLE OF MY EYE

❋ I BAKED MY FIRST TARTE TATIN LATE LAST FALL. I had come across the recipe in *Kitchen Wisdom*, Julia Child's cookbook, a nifty, compact collection of her favourite recipes. Little did I know at the time that this famous French dessert—a luscious caramelized, upside-down apple pie created more than 100 years ago by the Tatin sisters at their hotel in Lamotte Beuvron in the Loire Valley—was about to become a sweet obsession that would consume many weeks of my life.

My first stab at the wondrous Ms. Child's recipe was as easy as pie. The result: an attractive, tasty tart that was a hit when I served glossy wedges of it crowned with crème fraîche to friends that night at dinner. But my second attempt—using the same recipe, the same ingredients and the same utensils—was a complete bust.

On this occasion, I failed to make it past the initial stage prescribed in Child's recipe: melting the butter and sugar in a skillet to produce Tarte Tatin's most crucial element—caramelization. And things did not improve. Three batches of butter and sugar later, I had experienced these three culinary disasters: crystallization, separation and, finally, incineration. The last—and definitely worst—of these had me wondering whether to laugh or cry as I abandoned the kitchen and stood on my back deck holding in my oven-mitted, outstretched hand a charred skillet from which was emanating pitch-black smoke.

I was a damsel in distress, a victim of botched baking, a cook with a conundrum—but help was imminent. The next day, I bumped into Joanne Yolles at the downtown Y. Well known locally for her excellent work as a pastry chef of long-standing at Scaramouche and now at Pangaea, Yolles has taken time out for the past few years to raise her two young children. When I mentioned Tarte Tatin, her eyes lit up.

In no time, the two of us were eagerly making plans to share recipes, pool pie info and meet for a joint Tarte Tatin baking session. Yolles has fond memories of her first encounter with the dessert she first saw demonstrated at Tante Marie's Cooking School in San Francisco about 20 years ago. "I had no idea what Tarte Tatin was until then," Yolles confessed a few days later as we peeled apples in her bright, airy kitchen. "The person making it—her name was Jean Brady—was using an incredible amount of apples that were cut in halves and a huge amount of butter and sugar." The result, she recalled, was "outstanding. The tart turned out looking like a golden crown and tasted delicious."

The tart Yolles and I made that day was good—but good is not enough for two cooks on a quest for the best. In the following weeks, we baked a plethora of pies, alone and together, at her house and mine. We experimented with apples: Red Delicious, Mutsu, Golden Delicious, Courtland and, finally, the winner—Royal Gala, a fruit with full-bodied flavour and ideal texture that remains firm but not hard after lengthy cooking. Instead of halves, we found the apples cooked best when quartered.

We tried different skillets: cast-iron, stainless steel and then, on the emailed advice of Julia Child, a 10-inch (25-cm) non-stick skillet. I discovered the Martha Stewart version sold at Zeller's and simply wrapped the handle in foil before placing it in the oven. Yolles splurged and purchased a stainless steel-lined copper Tarte Tatin pan and loves the results.

We played around with pastry. Our final version is a buttery dough that's just the right amount for one crust. Using the food processor makes it foolproof. Rolling the dough out and chilling it before baking makes the tricky step of placing it on the hot apples much easier.

Then there was the pesky caramel. After many tries, we wound up rating the Tante Marie stovetop method in which the apples are slowly caramelized in a skillet on top of the butter and sugar before baking—a method not used in most recipes—easily tops.

So here's the fruit of our labour: Yolles' and my recipe for Tarte Tatin.

The Ultimate Tarte Tatin

Serve tart warm with crème fraîche, vanilla ice cream or sweetened plain yogurt.

PASTRY
1 cup (250 mL) all-purpose flour
½ tsp (2 mL) salt
1 tsp (5 mL) granulated sugar
½ cup (125 mL) cold unsalted butter,
   cut in pieces
¼ cup (50 mL) ice-cold water

APPLE LAYER
3 lb (1.5 kg) about 7 medium Royal
   Gala tart, firm apples, peeled, cored,
   quartered
Juice of half a lemon
½ cup (125 mL) unsalted butter,
   softened
1 cup (250 mL) granulated sugar

1. For pastry: Add flour, salt, sugar and butter to food processor. Process, pulsing about 6 times, until mixture resembles coarse crumbs. Transfer to bowl; add water and stir with fork until combined. Shape dough into ball with hands. Cover in plastic wrap; chill 1 hour or until needed.

2. About 1 hour before baking, roll dough into circle about 11 inches (28 cm) in diameter; transfer to round baking pan or flat metal disc (the bottom of a quiche pan works well), crimp edges and pierce all over with fork. Chill.

3. Meanwhile, for apple layer: In large bowl, toss apples with lemon juice.

4. Preheat oven to 400°F (200°C).

5. Smear butter evenly in heavy-bottomed, 10-inch (25 cm) non-stick skillet that's at least 2 inches (5 cm) deep. Sprinkle evenly with sugar. Arrange apple quarters on their sides on sugar in concentric circles, wedging together tightly. You will have a few quarters left; place on top of first layer. Cook, uncovered, over medium-low heat about 45 minutes or until syrup thickens and turns a rich, toffee brown. (Mixture should bubble steadily but not vigorously during caramelization. If syrup threatens to bubble over, remove some with bulb turkey baster. Be careful not to burn caramel by cooking too long or over too high a heat.) Remove skillet from heat; let stand about 10 minutes.

6. Carefully slide chilled dough on top of apples in skillet. Place skillet on cookie sheet to catch drips. Bake in oven about 30 minutes or until pastry is golden brown. Remove from oven; let stand 10 minutes. Place large plate (preferably with lip around edge) over skillet; invert.

MAKES 8 TO 10 SERVINGS.

THE WALDORF'S SALAD DAYS

"Peel two raw apples and cut them into small pieces, say about an inch square, also cut some celery the same way, and mix it with the apple. Be careful and don't let any seeds from the apple be mixed with it. The salad must be dressed with a good mayonnaise."

– Waldorf Salad recipe from
The Cook Book by "Oscar" of the Waldorf
(circa 1896) by Oscar Tschirky

❈ JOHN DOHERTY, WHO'S BEEN EXECUTIVE CHEF at The Waldorf-Astoria for almost 20 years, has never seen the hilarious episode of the British TV series *Fawlty Towers* bearing the sweet and simple title: "Waldorf Salad." For this reason, I spare him my Basil Fawlty (a.k.a John Cleese) imitation. But I do explain why this side-splitting show, featuring an irate American who demands that easy-to-make salad for a late night snack, never fails to cheer me up, no matter how bad my day.

I'm even more surprised when this agreeable chef, speaking with a distinct New York twang, follows his admission with a brutally frank assessment of the famous dish that originated more than 100 years ago at his renowned 1,400-room, midtown Manhattan hotel and is still served there. "I've never liked it," Doherty says succinctly. "It's apples, celery, mayo, walnuts. I think that's rather unappealing. It's not for me." If he had his way, the salad would not appear on any of the hotel menus. But some beg to differ. "I have to have it," he continues, with just a trace of weary resignation. "People ask for it. It's a big seller."

So he uses innovation to make this all-American classic his own. "I've always played with it, changed it," he explains. "I often use it as a seasonal garnish for entrées like smoked duck or smoked trout rather than serve it by itself as an appetizer or main course."

His often updated, constantly evolving rendition of Waldorf Salad appears regularly on buffet tables and is a staple on the room service menu. On occasion, it meets with mixed reviews. "Somebody called to complain last week," Doherty tells me with a smile. "The guy was beside himself. He was appalled that we'd used Granny Smith, not Red Delicious, apples and that there was no mayonnaise or celery in it."

Over the years, the hotel has offered a Waldorf Salad made with smoked chicken and currants, one that came accompanied by Maine crab and another that incorporated crispy calamari, winter greens and a lime walnut vinaigrette. But I have no gripes about the upscale concoction placed in front of me when I recently visit Oscar's—the renovated American brasserie on the Waldorf-Astoria's main floor—where an appetizer of Waldorf Salad, at $8 (u.s.) a pop, is served. It is a wondrously elegant sight to behold.

Thin shards of unpeeled apple coated in a glistening dressing are mounded in the centre of the plate. Around it are amorphous chunks of toasted walnuts. On top are dainty dots of something black. These turn out to be the high-end, crowning touch: fine shavings of black truffle. In between sips of a fruity white wine, I savour each bite. The delicate contrasts of soft and crunchy, sweet and sour, crisp and smooth are a taste sensation. I have no doubt, wiping the last trace of creamy, lemon-laced dressing from my plate, that Doherty has improved on the original, three-ingredient Waldorf Salad.

That was the dish invented, so the story goes, by the Waldorf-Astoria's original maitre d' Oscar Tschirky: a man with several culinary claims to fame. In 1893, Tschirky, an ambitious Swiss immigrant to the Big Apple, left his job at the city's fashionable Delmonico's restaurant, to join the staff of a new hotel opened by William Waldorf Astor. Here, he dreamed up the idea of a sweet, savoury, simple salad comprising cubed apple and chopped celery tossed with mayonnaise. It was an instant hit. The addition of walnuts came some time later—an innovation of which Tschirky did not approve. In fact, word has it, if he saw a walnut-garnished Waldorf Salad leave the kitchen, he would send it back.

Two barely recognizable versions of his salad are currently available at The Waldorf-Astoria. One is on the room service menu; the other is served at Oscar's, the brasserie named after Tschirky. Chef Doherty describes its fare as "American by means of local ingredients prepared with classical French technique." Most recently, he has come up with the luscious rendition I enjoyed in that lively dining room. In it, he uses equal amounts of Granny Smith and Red Delicious apples bathed in his own mayonnaise made with egg yolks and walnut oil. He uses celery root instead of celery. The shaved truffle garnish is a spectacular addition but beyond the reach of most home cooks.

When in the Big Apple, stop by Oscar's for that amazing salad. Meanwhile, this one, which was being served at Oscar's a couple of years ago, is easier to make—and just as delicious.

By the way, should you want to duplicate Tschirky's original salad and the one featured on "Fawlty Towers," simply mix equal amounts of unpeeled diced apple with chopped celery and toss with enough mayonnaise to coat. Walnut chunks and green grapes are two traditional options.

Waldorf Salad

Substitute sour cream for crème fraîche, if desired. To toast walnuts, cook over low heat in a dry skillet 2 to 3 minutes or until aromatic and crisp.

2 unpeeled Royal Gala apples, cored, cut in julienne strips
2 unpeeled Granny Smith apples, cored, cut in julienne strips
2 stalks celery, diced
1/3 cup (75 mL) mayonnaise
1/3 cup (75 mL) crème fraîche (next page)

1/4 cup (50 mL) plain yogurt
2 tbsp (30 mL) fresh lemon juice
Salt and white pepper to taste
8 radicchio or lettuce cups
3/4 cup (175 mL) coarsely chopped walnuts, toasted
Sliced strawberries

1. In large bowl, stir together apples and celery.

2. In small bowl, whisk together mayonnaise, crème fraîche, yogurt and lemon juice. Pour over salad; toss to coat. Add salt and pepper.

3. Place radicchio or lettuce cups on salad plates. Fill with salad. Sprinkle walnuts on top. Garnish with sliced strawberries.

MAKES 8 APPETIZER SERVINGS.

Crème Fraîche

This makes the small amount needed for the salad; it can easily be doubled or tripled. For a low-fat version, substitute low-fat sour cream for the whipping cream.

3 tbsp (45 mL) whipping cream
3 tbsp (45 mL) plain yogurt or
    buttermilk

In small bowl, combine whipping cream and yogurt. Cover; let sit 24 hours at room temperature or until thickened.

MAKES ⅓ CUP (75 mL).

WHEAT-BERRIED TREASURE

❋ HEALTHFUL EATING, ALONG WITH A LOVE of good food, runs in my family.

"My mother was ahead of her time in being very diet-conscious," says my mum chatting by phone from her home in London, England, about my pediatrician grandmother Agnes Nisse. "We always ate lots of fruit and vegetables," she continues, a reference to her childhood in Riga, Latvia. "In winter, there were no greens for salad. That was when we had root vegetables and lots of apples." The latter inspired a clever concoction devised by my granny to make fruit consumption more palatable for unsuspecting children: homemade applesauce inundated with dark chocolate chunks. This dish delectably combines sweet, bitter, soft and crunchy with a healthy dose of nutrients and was a popular dessert at home when I was growing up.

Like her mother before her, my biologist mum insisted on dishing out spoonfuls of cod liver oil—a noxious-tasting liquid offered free by the socially conscious government in England during post-war years—nightly before bed. On a happier note, my brothers and I had rye or wholewheat toast with cheese or eggs for breakfast, milk at every meal and always a mixed salad bathed in lemony vinaigrette with dinner.

My pleas for cream buns or steamed pudding with custard—sweets that rounded off the early evening meal called "tea" at friends' homes where English cooking was the norm—fell on deaf ears. Instead, we had fresh fruit salad, baked apples made with windfall Cox's from our North London garden or the aforementioned chocolate-laced applesauce.

At this time of year, I often make it by baking sliced, unpeeled apples that are past their prime with a little sugar and lemon juice, then gently mashing them so toothsome lumps remain. A bar of bittersweet chocolate smashed with a meat hammer yields those chocolate chunks.

Since my daughter Ruthie is not a milk fan, I find ways to slip calcium into her food. A dollop of yogurt or vanilla ice cream is delicious with that applesauce au chocolat. Tropicana's nifty orange juice spiked with this important mineral is our breakfast mainstay. I've also discovered a medium white cheddar of which my offspring approves to accompany her current favourite bread: a delicious wholegrain, high-fibre muesli baguette.

Which brings me to our dish du jour: Wheat Berry Salad. I was only a little surprised when, at dinner about 10 years ago, she enthusiastically chowed down on two helpings of the Wheat Berry Barley Risotto I was testing: a recipe from stellar chef Mark McEwan of North 44 and Bymark fame.

It was McEwan who first introduced me to the wheat berry: a grain that is fast becoming fashionable for its taste, texture and nutrient value. Simply hulled kernels of wheat, these berries are high in fibre, vitamins and minerals. What's more, the nutty-tasting, slightly chewy grains are easy to prepare and incredibly versatile. One of my favourite ways to use them is in salad, various versions of which I've been making since coming across the idea in u.s. cookbook author Steven Raichlen's *High-Flavor Low-Fat Vegetarian Cooking*, now sadly out of print.

In fact, this salad is one of Ruthie's favourite foods. "It's fresh and light," my daughter explains. "You just feel healthy eating it. It's not like you're eating something bulky but you're still full afterwards." It's quickly become a school lunch staple she can make herself. "You don't have to warm it up," says Ruthie, "and it makes a nice change from things I sometimes buy like pizza, falafels or chicken wraps."

So here it is: a great meatless lunch, light supper, potluck or buffet dish that can be made ahead and is always a hit because of its fresh taste and yummy combination of textures.

I often make double this amount. Ruthie tosses hers—a balanced meal that contains the protein hit of beans—with dressing before taking it to school.

Wheat Berry Salad

I buy soft Ontario wheat berries sold in most health and bulk food stores. They take a little more than 1 hour to cook. I like canned President's Choice Organics Bean Medley. Grape tomatoes, corn kernels, dried cherries, lightly steamed chopped green beans or tiny broccoli florets and toasted sunflower or pumpkin seeds are nice additions. Use your favourite non-creamy dressing, homemade or bottled, if desired.

1 cup (250 mL) wheat berries
19 oz (540 mL) can red kidney,
    pinto, soy or mixed beans,
    drained, rinsed
Half an unpeeled English cucumber,
    diced
1 large red bell pepper, seeded, diced
3 green onions, chopped
Seeds of 1 pomegranate (optional)

Salt and freshly ground black pepper
    to taste
1/4 cup (50 mL) extra virgin olive oil
2 tbsp (30 mL) balsamic vinegar
2 tbsp (30 mL) freshly squeezed
    lemon juice
1 tsp (5 mL) Dijon mustard
Few drops of Tabasco sauce
1 cup (250 mL) fresh herb leaves
    (mint, coriander, parsley)

1. In bowl, soak wheat berries at least 4 hours or overnight in enough cold water to cover by about 1 inch (2.5 cm). Drain. Place in saucepan with cold water to cover by about 2 inches (5 cm). Bring to boil; reduce heat to low and simmer, partially covered, about 1 hour or until al dente. Drain; cool.

2. In large bowl, combine cooked wheat berries, cucumber, red bell pepper, green onions and pomegranate seeds. Add salt and pepper.

3. In small bowl, whisk together olive oil, balsamic vinegar, lemon juice, mustard, and Tabasco until combined.

4. Store salad and dressing separately in fridge. Before serving, stir dressing and fresh herbs into salad.

MAKES 4 TO 6 SERVINGS.

❀

—⁓ *Chapter Seven* ⁓—

TABLE TALK

❊ THE BEAUTY OF BEING A FOOD WRITER is you never know when or where you're going to come upon a story. As I often say, occasionally to the dismay but often to the joy of family and friends who wind up in them, "Everything and everyone's a column."

One of my favourite examples is the tale of how I discovered, by sweet happenstance, the original home of Canada's most famous fruit: the McIntosh apple. It was the summer of 1998 and I had travelled to Brinston, a tiny St. Lawrence Valley village in the heart of lush, quiet farming country about an hour's drive south of Ottawa. The mission: to visit my erstwhile nanny Evelyn Smail. A popular member of this tight rural community, she has lived in this area for more than 70 years and knows everyone and everything.

She wants to show me the local sights. Like me, she has a nose for news. So one morning, we drive to the small town of Dundela not far from her home. There, we stop outside a tumble-down, old wooden house which was uninhabited and suffering from years of neglect. Standing in front of it near the small dirt road was a large sign that read: John McIntosh, 1777–1846. This, Evelyn tells me proudly, was the home of the Mr. McIntosh who, almost two centuries ago, found some seedlings in the nearby forest, transplanted them into his garden and the rest is Canadian apple history. But Evelyn's not finished. She tells me that, somewhere behind the house, near a rickety greenhouse and overgrown with weeds, is another plaque marking the spot of that first McIntosh tree.

Ever the intrepid sleuth when it comes to food, I venture back. Sure enough, almost completely obscured among thick foliage, is a rectangular stone with this inscription, all in capital letters: THE SITE OF THE ORIGINAL MCINTOSH APPLE TREE. There are also two dates: 1811 and 1900, during which years, I assume, the tree lived before being burned down in a fire.

Soon, clever Evelyn has put me in touch with Nancy McIntosh, John's great-great granddaughter, a schoolteacher who has been trying to save the family's historic house and garden in Dundela. The discovery of the Mac apple has been declared an event of historical significance. However, even after my feature article about this appeared in the *Star* in the fall of 2002, there has been no move to repair, restore or preserve this important heritage sight although a couple of lively murals featuring the McIntosh apple have appeared on outdoor walls in Dundela.

Edna Staebler, almost 100 and still kicking at time of writing, is another key figure in Ontario's culinary history. A feisty woman who was born and raised in Kitchener, she spent many years living with Mennonites, writing about them and documenting their food—a cuisine big on pies, simple roast meat and yummy potato dishes—in a series of hugely popular cookbooks. I visited her one sunny spring day at the lovely, homespun cottage on a lake where she's lived happily with several cats for many years. Smart as a whip and a lively woman who loves to joke and gossip, Staebler is one of our country's most important food writers, but has no time for pretension of any kind. For lunch, we all munched on pizza I and a friend brought with us. Then there was tea and Staebler's sweet, simple crumble made from home-grown rhubarb she'd frozen the year before.

Dropping by people's homes for food and interesting chats is one of my job's best perks. So is dropping by to watch them cook. That's what I did after hearing that cookbook author and ace Jewish cook Norene Gilletz is a pro at making latkes: those yummy potato pancakes that are de rigueur at Hanukkah. In the tiny kitchen of her suburban condo, I hurriedly took notes as she casually peeled potatoes, then shredded them in the food processor along with onions and a couple of other ingredients. A few cored, unpeeled apples were nuked in the microwave for applesauce and "presto" the best latkes I've ever eaten.

After watching a pro prepare something firsthand, then testing it at home myself, I can, with a clear conscience, offer my readers a foolproof method.

Talking of first-hand, I know who to consult about one of the key tools of my trade: cookbooks. Alison Fryer and Jennifer Grange have both worked at The Cookbook Store in downtown Toronto since it opened in 1983. So they know of what they speak—and cook.

Over lunch at a favourite restaurant, they spilled the beans about which cookbook authors have the best recipes, which tomes are riddled with recipes that don't work—and everything in between. Naturally, I picked their brains and shared this invaluable info with my readers.

Like I said, everyone and everything's a column!

THE REAL BIG MAC

❋ DUNDELA, ONT.—THE TOPIC IS APPLES and we've just reached the core of the matter. "I like my apples to cook up in a pie," announces Nancy McIntosh firmly, adding, "I don't want any chunks in it at all. The filling should be almost like applesauce." This is best achieved, she continues, by using McIntosh or Wealthy apples.

Sensing a culinary controversy, I turn to Barb Smail and ask for her opinion on this crucial question. Her reply is quick and unequivocal: "Oh yes, they should definitely be cooked up. I don't like apple pieces in my pie."

As a lone city slicker visiting apple-growing country in the St. Lawrence Valley about an hour's drive south-east of Ottawa, I'm nervous about weighing in on the "cooked up" or not issue. However, I note that the two women are both looking at me—so I do. "Actually, my favourite apples for pie are Spys," I offer tentatively. "They have really great flavour—nice and tart—though it's true, they don't tend to dissolve when cooked." Receiving no response, I add swiftly, "But, of course, it's all a matter of taste." Happily for all concerned, that, at least for now, is that on the apple debate and we proceed with our leisurely lunch.

It's a sunny fall day and we're seated around the table in Barb and Ron Smail's big, bright kitchen. They raise dairy cattle on a more than 250-hectare farm that's been in the family for several generations. The sweet and simple meal we're enjoying is an assortment of sandwich fixings spread out before us: tuna salad, wholewheat bread, mayonnaise, sliced cucumber and dainty cherry tomatoes from the garden and a dish of Barb's yummy apple salad made with just-picked Macs from Smyth's, a nearby orchard. Dessert is angel food cake with shiny white frosting. The beverage is tea accompanied by sugar and milk. The latter comes crowned with a layer of cream and is, says Barb, "straight from the cow."

Both McIntosh and I are enjoying the food and conversation. We've spent the morning in Dundela—a nearby village in Matilda Township. The place isn't notable for much except its unfair share of rural poverty and a historic landmark: her family's former home and the site of the original McIntosh apple tree.

Nancy McIntosh is the great-great granddaughter of John McIntosh who was a young farmer when he came to Canada from the United States in 1796. After settling in the small town of Iroquois and a failed marriage, he moved to Dundela with his new wife and began clearing the land he'd traded with her brother. In 1811, so the story goes, he came upon some feisty little seedlings growing like weeds amid the forest. For some reason, he spared what turned out to be tiny apple trees and transplanted about a dozen of them to his garden.

Only one survived. It grew and eventually bore fruit: the round, tasty, red-and-green apple we know as McIntosh.

After lunch, Nancy, a retired high school science teacher, picks up her family's story as she takes sepia photos, vintage newspaper clippings and the odd fascinating artifact out of an old wooden grafting box. "In about 1835, a hired hand came along and showed John and his son Allan how to graft," she says, showing me some of the latter's handwritten order sheets from the nursery he ran with his brother Sandy. She pulls out a withered, gnarled piece of wood that is, she explains, "supposed to be part of the original McIntosh tree."

Allan became skilled at grafting and produced several orchards of what were then called "Granny" apples after his mother Hannah, the apple expert of her generation. They soon became known as McIntosh Reds.

It took many years for the McIntosh apple to become established. Although it had several things going for it—hardiness, attractive colour, crunchy texture and tangy taste—the trees were susceptible to "scabs" and had to be carefully nurtured. The apple finally became famous in the mid-19th century while Allan's son Harvey was in charge of the family's flourishing farm. Today, the Mac, as it's affectionately known, is produced in greater quantities than any other Canadian apple and is popular around the world. It ranks second behind only Red and Golden Delicious in the United States.

Theories about its heritage abound but it's generally agreed that one of its parents is the Fameuse, known in English Canada as the Snow apple. Its other ancestor is thought to be the Detroit Red. Traipsing through long grass behind the dilapidated house in Dundela where Nancy grew up, she shows me a gray stone monument buried beneath weeds. It says succinctly: "THE

SITE OF THE ORIGINAL McINTOSH APPLE TREE. 1811–1906. The original family home burned down in the late 1800s," she explains. "The fires also damaged the original tree. It died some years later."

Returning to the front of the house, now privately owned and in a sad state of disrepair, I check out a plaque and monument identifying this as a historical site. Nancy also points out a colourful mural recently painted on the wall of Dundela's community centre nearby. It shows John McIntosh, Bible in hand, and a plethora of apples. But that's it. These are the only efforts to preserve the legacy of a place and people that gave our country its foremost fruit. Nancy, who worked in the family orchards until her parents sold them along with the house in 1974, is trying to change all that.

Together with her cohorts in a small but stalwart group called the McIntosh Heritage Committee, she hopes the house, its grounds and monuments can be saved "either by a charitable group like us or a private owner who respects and honours the history." Her fear is that the quickly deteriorating home will be condemned and then torn down. "The discovery of the Mac apple in Dundela has officially been declared an event of historical significance," she adds, and there have been recent celebrations of it there attended by the likes of Sheila Copps. Now she'd like to see that heritage preserved.

"The house could be restored and become a museum with, perhaps, a shop on the grounds," she suggests. "There could also be a heritage orchard planted, using DNA, with heirloom apples that are no longer commercially viable." Sounds like a top-notch plan. I, for one, can't think of a better way to bring jobs and energy to an underprivileged part of the province and save our heritage at the same time.

Apple Crumble

This is my favourite apple dessert. I insist on using Northern Spys, available in late fall, but the addition of lemon juice and/or cranberries to Cortland, Mutsu or Royal Gala apples can almost achieve the tartness crucial to contrast with the sweet topping from Regan Daley's In the Sweet Kitchen.

³/₄ cup (175 mL) all-purpose flour

³/₄ cup (175 mL) old-fashioned or quick-cooking (not instant) rolled oats

³/₄ cup (175 mL) packed brown sugar

³/₄ cup (175 mL) cold unsalted butter, cut in pieces

2 tbsp (30 mL) granulated sugar

¹/₂ tsp (2 mL) ground cinnamon

6 or 7 large Spy apples, cored, peeled, sliced

1 to 2 (15 to 30 mL) tbsp fresh lemon juice

1. Preheat oven to 375°F (190°C).

2. In large bowl, combine flour, rolled oats and brown sugar. Add butter. Using wire hand pastry blender or two knives, cut it in until mixture resembles coarse crumbs.

3. In small bowl, combine granulated sugar and cinnamon.

4. Lightly butter a 12-cup (3 L) shallow ceramic, earthenware or glass baking dish. Arrange apple slices in dish. Sprinkle with lemon juice and sugar/cinnamon mixture. Spread evenly with topping mixture. Bake for about 50 minutes, or until browned on top and apples are soft.

MAKES ABOUT 6 SERVINGS.

Barb's Apple Salad

Barb Smail uses whatever eating apples are in season. At Christmas, she likes unpeeled Red Delicious and Granny Smith for a festive touch. She insists on homemade or Hellmann's mayo. Great with pork, turkey and as an accompaniment to or in sandwiches. Sprinkle a little lemon juice on apples before adding other ingredients to prevent browning if making ahead.

3 to 4 apples, cored, peeled, finely diced

1 celery stalk, finely chopped

2 tbsp (30 mL) chopped vidalia or other sweet onion

2 tbsp (30 mL) mayonnaise

In bowl, combine all ingredients.

MAKES ABOUT 6 SIDE-DISH SERVINGS.

BAMBOOZLED

The now-defunct BamBoo restaurant was a landmark in Toronto's hip Queen Street West scene. I wrote this before the BamBoo closed in 2002.

❋ My brother Eric Schachter, who lived here briefly in the 1980s before returning to reside happily in Montreal, isn't a fan of our city. However, there are two things he loves about Toronto: downtown's irrepressible Kensington Market and that Queen West landmark, the BamBoo. "It's delightful," he says fondly of the latter. "It's the food, the company, the whole ambience." When pressed, my teacher-turned-filmmaker sibling elaborates. "The BamBoo is bohemian in the very best sense," he continues. "Not hip bohemian—free, fun and expressive. And it's maintained that. I would go back and find it the same time after time." As is often the case, my bro' and I agree.

After all, that establishment festooned its dining room with hot pink streamers when my daughter Esther chose it for her Sweet Sixteen party many moons ago. My teenage offspring Ruthie's affinity for the spacious, child-friendly spot dates back to infancy when my afternoon ritual during maternity leave was to tuck her baby seat into a chair beside me while I slowly sipped a glass of wine.

But sadly, our favourite haunt has only a few weeks to live. At the end of this month—on Hallowe'en—the BamBoo winds up 20 years as Toronto's most eclectic, eccentric, incredible nightclub-cum-restaurant when it closes its doors for good.

Patti Habib has owned and operated it with friend and business partner Richard O'Brien since they leased the former Wicker World location at 312 Queen St. W., in July of 1982.

When it officially opened a year later, complete with funky Caribbean-inspired décor and a menu that ran the lively gamut from *callaloo* to *pad thai* (thai noodles), it was an instant hit.

"At that time, there was only the Peter Pan and Le Select," Habib notes when I ask about the Queen West dining scene in those days. Seated on the BamBoo's sun-drenched, leafy patio as she sips black coffee and I put the chopsticks to a heaping plate of chile-zapped, citrus-spiked pad thai, she explains how the tropical-themed, totally original dining/music venue she and O'Brien dreamed up came to be. "Richard and I used to walk along Queen Street past this place," she begins. "With the alley leading to a court-yard just off the street, it reminded us of Jamaica where we'd both lived and which we loved." O'Brien, who had operated a local after-hours booze can, suggested joining forces to open a reggae club in the location.

"We wanted it to be a nightclub with a Caribbean theme and live music," Habib says. Chuckling, she recalls, "We thought of calling it Liquor World but we knew the LCBO would nix that one." Then the pair came up with a name that stuck. It harked back to the building's former wares: bamboo. "In those days, the only way you could get a liquor license was to serve 60 percent food," she recalls. "That's how we ended up with a dining room." And so the happy marriage of live music—reggae, soca, jazz, funk and R & B—and exotic food began. Which brings us to the BamBoo's luscious *pad thai*, which I have, by now, polished off.

"We were the first place in Toronto to put Thai noodles on our menu," states Habib adamantly, taking another swig of coffee: "It was the dish that made us famous and has been a mainstay of our menu for 20 years." But she has a beef. "Certain young food writers in this city," she attests with a slight-ly menacing look, "aren't aware that the BamBoo was the only place in town to get a *pad thai* fix in 1983."

How that came about is part of Toronto's culinary history. In the early '80s, Habib met Wandee Young: a young woman who had recently arrived from Thailand and was cooking at her hole-in-the-wall Thai eatery on Eglinton Ave. W. "The place had no liquor license and special guests were served scotch in teapots," she says. "When it went out of business, Wandee's husband at the time asked if she could work here. We made her co-chef with Vera Khan who now owns one of the best restaurants in Costa Rica and whose specialties were dishes like curried chicken and *callaloo*." The menu the two created was a delicious melting pot of Asian and Caribbean fare that's stayed almost the same for 20 years.

Young moved on after eight years and now owns and operates several Young Thailand eateries in town. In her wake, she has left a legion of protégés who learned how to make *pad thai* from her and each other in the BamBoo's busy kitchen. Most of the restaurant's current kitchen crew hope to follow Habib and O'Brien to the north end of Pier 4 on our lakeshore where the pair plan to open Bambu by the Lake. The circumstances under which the BamBoo's lease was transferred to local entrepreneur and sometime restaurant owner Charles Khabouth, who will soon open a nightclub there under a new name, are grim.

Habib, who had a deal to sell the business some months ago, isn't happy about how the deed was done. "It's unfortunate the BamBoo has to close under such awful circumstances," she says diplomatically. But she has options. "I could always return to CBC where I worked as a story producer for 10 years, and be a restaurant critic," she says with a wicked grin.

Try this recipe and raise a glass of bubbly to the BamBoo: the magnificent place that put *pad thai* on T.O.'s culinary map.

Pad Thai (Thai Noodles)

I've substituted tamarind paste for some of the ketchup in the BamBoo recipe. Preserved tamarind comes in small rectangular blocks in Chinatowns and some supermarkets' ethnic sections. Use more or less chile paste (sometimes called chile sauce) depending on how spicy you like food. It, along with rice sticks, fish sauce and fried tofu are sold in any of our Chinatowns.

8 oz (250 g) rice sticks (noodles)
1 tbsp (15 mL) preserved tamarind
2 tbsp (30 mL) boiling water
1/4 cup (50 mL) ketchup
1/4 cup (50 mL) fish sauce
2 tbsp (30 mL) fresh lime or lemon juice
1 tbsp (15 mL) soy sauce
1 tbsp (15 mL) granulated sugar
2 tsp (10 mL) Asian chile paste
2 tbsp (30 mL) vegetable oil

8 oz (250 g) boneless, skinless chicken breast, cut in bite-sized pieces
8 oz (250 g) shrimp, peeled, deveined
4 oz (125 g) fried tofu, cut in bite-sized pieces
3 cloves garlic, chopped
2 eggs, beaten
3 cups (750 mL) bean sprouts
1/4 cup (50 mL) unsalted peanuts, coarsely chopped
3 green onions, coarsely chopped
1/2 cup (125 mL) fresh coriander, coarsely chopped

1. In large bowl, cover rice sticks with warm water; let sit about 20 minutes. Drain.

2. In small bowl, stir together tamarind and boiling water until dissolved. Press through sieve. Discard pulp; reserve purée.

3. In another bowl, make sauce by whisking together tamarind purée, ketchup, fish sauce, lime juice, soy sauce, sugar and chile paste.

4. Heat oil in wok over high heat until very hot. Add chicken, tofu and garlic. Cook, stirring, 1 to 2 minutes, or until chicken is no longer pink inside. Make a well in centre. Add eggs; let set for a moment, then stir. Add drained noodles, bean sprouts and sauce. Stir-fry, using tongs, 4 to 5 minutes, or until noodles are tender and all ingredients well coated.

5. Garnish with peanuts, green onions and coriander.

MAKES ABOUT 4 SERVINGS.

SCHMECKS OBJECT

❋ Edna Staebler sits regally in a rocking chair and flashes me one of her girlish, buck-toothed smiles. At her feet sit a couple of pastel-coloured, handmade catnip mice. They belong to her cat Mally, named thus because Staebler bought her at the local mall. The toy rodents match the homespun, Mennonite Country-meets-Beatrix Potter ambience of her cozy, cluttered living room that's a rag-tag mélange of colourful quilts, petit point wall hangings and braided rugs. Behind her, there's a gorgeous view of the lake, a small dock and giant cedar, spruce and tamarack trees. The only distraction is a lively, non-stop performance by assorted birds and squirrels who have devised an unorthodox, mostly harmonious arrangement for sharing two oversized, well-stocked bird feeders.

Staebler, who was born and raised in Kitchener, looks and acts about 20 years younger than her 96 years. She is obviously relishing the visit by me and a fellow food writer (who lives nearby and knows this neck of the woods) at the secluded, winterized cottage that has been her home for 45 years. Nestled in the woods overlooking Sunfish Lake just northwest of Waterloo, it's close to the Mennonite farmlands of Woolwich Township where her great-great-grandfather was the first permanent settler.

"My late husband Keith and I built this place in 1957 as a summer cottage," she explains. "I got unmarried to him a few years later and just stayed." As my friend prepares pizza we brought for lunch in the adjoining kitchen, Staebler announces that we might find her "a little vague." Not only did she get up early to make her famous Rhubarb Crunch as dessert, she expended a lot of energy the day before attending one of the many engagements that pepper the well-filled Milk Calendar hanging on her wall.

"Those blank spaces in March were really bad weather," she's quick to explain. "I'm nearly always busy—with visitors, neighbours, my cleaning lady, things in town. And every week, my biographer Veronica Ross comes out for half a day. That won't be finished until I'm long gone." It's fast becoming clear that Staebler is far from vague. She is as sharp as your proverbial tack.

Yesterday's event, she goes on to explain, was a reception for the new writer-in-residence at the Kitchener Public Library, a program now in its seventh year and one of several causes that she funds. "I should have given away more money when Nortel was high," she notes with a mischievous grin. "I'll be long dead before it comes up." But the plummet in high-tech stocks appears to be one small glitch in an otherwise wonderful life. After all, except for hearing aids in both ears, a partial denture and a recent diabetes scare, Staebler has her health.

She also has plenty of friends who regularly visit, food in hand. "People call and bring me dinner," she tells us with childlike glee as a piping hot pizza slice is placed before her. "I'm so spoiled. I'm a guest in my own home. I call it 'meals on wheels.'" She also has an impressive body of work that's earned her an array of honours. Many of those awards, certificates and honorary degrees line her narrow hallway in assorted frames, including the Order of Canada, which she received in 1996.

Staebler began her prolific writing career in 1948 when Scott Young, singer Neil Young's father, bought her first article—a first-person story about sword fishing in Cape Breton—for Maclean's. It was the first of many well-written articles, mostly for that magazine, about her intrepid adventures in communities across the country, a style of journalism she calls "creative non-fiction."

In the name of research, she lived with a fisherman's family in Neil's Harbour, in a miner's home in Wawa and on the French-owned islands of St-Pierre-Miquelon off the coast of Newfoundland. In 1949, the story of her experiences living with an old order Mennonite family on a farm near St. Jacobs won a Canadian Women's Press Club Award. According to Staebler, "I talked so much about the food, Maclean's assigned a story to me about Mennonite cooking."

Eventually, with the encouragement of her friends Pierre and Janet Berton and "an incredible amount of help from my Mennonite friends," she found herself writing a cookbook on that theme. In 1968, McClelland & Stewart published *Food that Really Schmecks*. It quickly became a runaway hit and is still available in paperback.

Less than a decade later came *More Food that Really Schmecks* followed, another decade later, by *Schmecks Appeal*, a compilation of recipes that didn't make it into the other two books and the most popular recipes that did. It has just been re-issued as a paperback. All three books are Canadian classics.

"Mennonite food is country comfort food," Staebler explains. "People like my recipes because they can go into the kitchen and make them. It's mostly stuff you have on hand. And they always turn out." Having tried several recipes from *Schmecks Appeal* with great success, I agree. Easy and delicious are her famous Schnippled Bean Salad—"frenched" green beans tossed with a traditional Mennonite dressing of sour cream, vinegar and sugar—and her award-winning Sour Cream Raisin Pie for which I use the book's foolproof Speedy Pat-In Pastry.

Staebler, who has also written several small, single-theme cookbooks, makes no bones about her culinary expertise. "I got into food-writing by accident," she says. "I'm not like the real foodies who spend their lives with food. I ask questions when I need to know." Over the years, she's received many letters from her cookbooks' fans. "Some people call them their bible," she says with a smile. "They say, 'Dear Edna, I have your book and I feel you are my friend.'"

As we get ready to leave, Staebler disappears into her bedroom. She returns with a pink and baby blue catnip mouse—one of the more than 30,000 she reckons she's knitted over the years. "My sister Ruby, who's 91, has pretty well denuded the Peterborough area getting me catnip for these," she notes with a chuckle. When I tell her I don't have a cat, she presses it into my hand. "Give it to a friend," she says sweetly. As we walk away, Staebler waves, smiling broadly, and urges us to come back soon for a swim in the lake. That's certainly in my plans.

Here's the recipe for the yummy rhubarb dessert she served us made from homegrown rhubarb she'd frozen. It's from an entire chapter on rhubarb, in her wonderful book *Schmecks Appeal*.

Rhubarb Crunch

This should be served warm or hot as the bottom layer becomes quite hard if served straight from the fridge.

1 cup (250 mL) all-purpose flour
3/4 cup (175 mL) quick-cooking
   (not instant) rolled oats
1 cup (250 mL) packed brown sugar
1/2 tsp (2 mL) salt
1 tsp (5 mL) ground cinnamon
1/2 cup (125 mL) unsalted butter,
   melted

4 cups (1 L) diced rhubarb, about
   5 stalks
1 cup (250 mL) granulated sugar
1 tbsp (15 mL) cornstarch
1 cup (250 mL) water
1 tsp (5 mL) vanilla extract

1. Preheat oven to 350°F (180°C).

2. Grease 9-inch (23 cm) square baking dish.

3. In bowl, combine flour, rolled oats, brown sugar, salt and cinnamon. With fork, stir in melted butter until mixture resembles coarse crumbs. Spread half of mixture in prepared baking dish. Layer rhubarb evenly on top.

4. In saucepan, whisk together granulated sugar, cornstarch, water and vanilla. Cook, whisking, over medium heat, 1 to 2 minutes, or until slightly thickened. Pour over rhubarb. Top with remaining crumb mixture.

5. Bake about 50 minutes, or until golden brown. Serve warm with vanilla ice cream, whipped cream, crème fraîche or plain yogurt.

MAKES ABOUT 6 SERVINGS.

LOTSA LATKES

✳ IT TAKES CHUTZPAH. BUT IT'S ALSO A PERK of my wonderful job that I can phone a professional cook like Norene Gilletz and say, "Hi, it's Marion Kane. Can I come and make latkes with you tomorrow?" Not surprisingly, even the good-natured, easy-going Gilletz was a tad taken aback by this sudden request but soon rallied when she realized a doctor's appointment had been cancelled for that day. "It must be beshert," she replied sweetly using the Yiddish word that roughly translates as "meant to be."

And so I found myself driving to the woolly wilds of North York one recent afternoon to learn the fine art of latke preparation: a culinary ritual that was sadly missing from the secular Jewish home in which I was raised. I was doing this partly for myself as, the older I get, the more I prefer Hanukkah as a winter celebration to the frantically over-hyped, commercialized alternative: Christmas. But as usual, dear readers, I was on this mission with you in mind. My goal: to share the joy of making—as well as eating—this wondrous holiday rendition of the potato pancake, a dish found in many of the world's cuisines and one beloved by my people.

I finally arrive at Gilletz's home where she and her two little Lhasa apso dogs greet me warmly. In her small but well equipped kitchen, the latke ingredients and our main tool—the food processor—are on the counter, at the ready. Moving slowly and calmly, my seasoned mentor begins peeling potatoes while I take notes. "Of course, I love latkes," answers Gilletz when I ask about our dish du jour. Then she momentarily stops peeling a potato, looks my way and adds with a smile, "Read my hips."

Gilletz (née Rykiss) was born and raised in Winnipeg. In 1960, she moved to Montreal. "Winnipeg is flat," she says by way of explanation. "I wanted some ups and downs in my life." Evidently, there were mostly ups. She "became enchanted" with her new home and stayed 37 years.

Gilletz has no formal training but is, she notes, "trained in eating" and has taken cooking classes with well known pros like Jacques Pepin and Anne Willan. She calls her style "Jewish fusion. I take food from other cultures and incorporate it to follow Jewish dietary guidelines and a taste that I like."

In Montreal, she catered, operated her own cooking school and began writing cookbooks. Two are still in print. The quirkily titled, self-published *MealLeaniYumm!* is a super collection of low-fat recipes and *The Food Processor Bible* is a compendium of recipes using that all-purpose kitchen tool.

The whir of the food processor reminds me of my mission. Gilletz pushes potato chunks and onion halves alternately through its feeder tube—"It helps stop the potatoes from oxidizing and turning brown"—then adds the eggs, flour and baking powder, pulsing, chatting and checking the mixture as she goes. "You can test baking powder to see if it's fresh," she notes, sharing the first of several nifty tips. "Just add half a teaspoon to half a cup of hot water. If it fizzes, it's fine." She adds salt and pepper, then stirs what is now a thick batter. "I always stop and take a peek," she explains, "just so the food knows I care about it."

When I ask about squeezing out the liquid collecting at the bottom of the work bowl, Gilletz is adamant in her response leaving no doubt where she stands on this controversial topic. "In the old days, grandmothers used to squeeze out the water," she concedes, "and save the potato starch they got for Passover." But she doesn't see the need. "I'm a quick cook. I don't have time for squeezing food," she adds with a smile. "I'd rather squeeze a person."

Gilletz, who's been making latkes for 40 years, is now heating her large, heavy non-stick skillet on the stove. "I start it on high," she says, "then turn the heat down to medium-high." Her frying medium of choice is olive oil. "It's the closest thing to schmaltz (chicken fat) I can find."

She has put down her well-loved metal "latke spoon" which holds about two tablespoons of batter and is wielding her favourite non-stick spatula to make sure the latkes don't touch each other as they cook. "I always fry small batches," she explains, trying to prise off one stubborn pancake that's threatening to stick. "My husband has a habit of doing things to my pans," she says affectionately of Soly Zamir, the former Israeli she married "because he brought me the most wonderful lemons and he makes a fabulous chopped salad."

As she cooks each batch, Gilletz adds a little more oil to the pan. When I notice liquid left at the bottom of her work bowl and wonder aloud about that "squeezing" debate, she smiles. "If you worry, food doesn't turn out well," she says softly. "You must be master of your food. Always show it you're in control." Those wise words and these recipes will ensure latke success.

Easy Potato Latkes

From Gilletz's The Food Processor Bible, *this produces a traditional latke that's part batter, part potato. She uses Idaho, sometimes called Russet, potatoes which are starchy and not too watery. I found Ontario-grown Yukon Gold worked even better. Use the shredder on your food processor instead of the steel blade or grate vegetables by hand for a lacier latke. Use the baking method for less fat but be sure to use a good quality, well-greased baking sheet so they don't stick. Traditional accompaniments are sour cream and applesauce.*

3 large or 4 medium baking potatoes, peeled, cut in chunks
1 medium onion, halved
2 large eggs
1/3 cup (75 mL) all-purpose flour or matzo meal

1 tsp (5 mL) baking powder
3/4 tsp (4 mL) salt
Freshly ground black pepper to taste
About 2 tbsp (30 mL) vegetable oil

1. Add potatoes, onion and eggs to food processor fitted with steel blade. Process, pulsing, until shredded, 20 to 30 seconds. Add remaining ingredients except oil. Process a few seconds more until combined.

2. Heat a teaspoon or two of oil in large, heavy non-stick skillet. Add potato mixture in large spoonfuls to form pancakes about 2 inches (5 cm) in diameter. Cook until golden brown on both sides, about 3 to 4 minutes per side. Add more oil to skillet as you cook and stir potato mixture before cooking each batch.

3. (To bake latkes, preheat oven to 450°F (230°C). Place racks in lower and middle positions. Drop potato mixture by large spoonfuls on to well-greased baking sheet; flatten slightly. Bake 10 minutes, or until edges are browned. Turn latkes over. Switch baking pans from middle to lower rack. Bake 8 to 10 minutes more.)

4. Drain cooked latkes on paper towels.

MAKES ABOUT 24.

Rosti

Gilletz calls this Swiss dish from The Food Processor Bible *"a giant latke."*

3 large or 4 medium potatoes,
  peeled
1 medium onion, halved

1 tbsp (15 mL) olive oil
Salt and freshly ground black pepper
  to taste

1. Using shredder attachment on food processor or by hand, coarsely grate potatoes and onion.

2. Spray or brush 10-inch (25 cm) non-stick skillet with oil. Add potato mixture in even layer. Press down with spatula; sprinkle with salt and pepper. Cook over medium heat 8 to 10 minutes, or until bottom is browned and crisp. Turn; cook until bottom is browned and crisp, 6 to 8 minutes more.

MAKES ABOUT 4 SERVINGS.

COTTAGE INDUSTRY

✳ SOMETHING'S COOKING IN COTTAGE COUNTRY and it's not your rubbery barbecued burger on a white-bread bun.

Finally, the well-heeled folks who flee our city each summer for some rural R & R are demanding the same high-end foods up north that have been de rigueur in neighbourhoods like Rosedale, Forest Hill and North Toronto for at least a decade. How else to explain the noticeable proliferation of gourmet food shops in Port Carling—a busy hub at the heart of magnificent Muskoka's cottage enclave—that have recently popped up to serve this need?

Take the chi-chi little store next to and operated by The Compleat Angler restaurant perched on a hill in that small town. Open just one month, this pristine, minimally stocked room resembles a mini-Pusateri's. Jumbo-sized live lobsters that filled a large tank to the rim were selling well on the recent Saturday I was there. Fresh foie gras, Arctic char and Angus beef lined the meat counter while small packages of the prized French salt fleur de sel, Le Puy lentils and sushi nori decked the shelves.

Nearby, on a leafy side street, there was a noisy line-up the same day at Stephen's Butcher Shop, a family-run store that has long been a magnet for cottagers and where rack of lamb, filet mignon and stuffed pork tenderloin are currently hot items.

Likewise for small containers of frozen hors d'oeuvres produced by Meagan and Charmaine Broughton whose fledgling catering company Gourmet on the Lake is the latest addition to the region's increasingly upscale food scene. The two sisters, who grew up in Markham, have spent every summer at the cottage built 20 years ago by their father Ray. It was here—overlooking the North Muskoka River at the end of a winding, one-lane road just north of Bracebridge—that I recently spent a couple of hours chatting with them at their picnic table.

Giant cedars, white pine, maple and birch trees surround the small, rustic, cedar home. Its lush garden has a carefully tended vegetable plot and is ablaze with bright orange day lilies, pink roses, peonies and daisies. The scenery is gorgeous. The mood is peaceful bliss. Until Meagan, 21, starts describing her average day. She begins by relating how she got up at midnight the night before to gather a bouquet for our table setting. "I read in a magazine that's the best time to pick flowers," she says sweetly.

Then this athletic young woman who loves to travel and spends her winters as a snowboard instructor on Grouse Mountain in B.C., explains how she fits her new culinary career into an already busy life. "I usually get up at 5 A.M," she begins. "Then I type up recipes, package up hors d'oeuvres to deliver to stores in Port Carling and go to my other job: managing the grounds on a 33-acre island on Lake Joseph." Just listening to this is making me a tad jittery but Meagan hasn't finished. "I then drive the small motor boat back across choppy Lake Joe and come home, making stops at our mailboxes, to pick up labels for our chutney and cookies and at Morley Stephen's store to buy ingredients." Back on home turf, Meagan adds with a grin, "I check out what Charmaine's doing and wait to be put to work by her."

It turns out Charmaine, a trained chef with a husband, a one-year-old son and another baby on the way, has an equally hectic schedule. Hers involves spending part of the week at her home in Keswick working part-time for Loblaws teaching cooking classes and developing products in their Test Kitchen. The rest of the time, she's up at the cottage where she and Meagan kicked off their business by selling her reheatable hors d'oeuvres to local shops. Her husband and family members help by looking after her young son Tyler.

The catering end of things began in late May. "We both enjoy working," Meagan says, something I had already deduced. And being sisters turns out to be a plus. "We're both determined to make this work and there's a trust thing," Charmaine explains. "We've never let each other down and we stay off each other's toes," chimes in Meagan. "I would never tell her how to cook and she knows I can take care of the packaging, promotion and designing logos like the ones on our shirts and the car."

And it looks like things are already happening for the dynamic duo. As I write, they're preparing dinner for six to celebrate a client's 50th birthday. On the menu are some of the pair's trademark appetizers like Brie and Leek Tarts, Curried Chicken Spring Rolls and Spinach Ricotta-Filled Phyllo. An antipasto platter includes fresh figs stuffed with blue cheese and caprese salad of tomatoes, bocconcini and fresh basil. The main dish is individual beef wellingtons with roast baby potatoes and grilled seasonal veggies. Charmaine is proud of all her food, which, she says, features "bold, strong flavours and simple ingredients" but she positively boasts about the meal's dessert: her rendition of little dark chocolate soufflés.

Here's a delicious dish from their repertoire:

Grilled Mushroom Salad

Grill the mushrooms in the oven under broiler, if desired. Use mostly portobellos for great texture. Button and brown mushrooms should be medium to large for easy grilling.

DRESSING
2 cloves garlic, minced
1 tbsp (15 mL) Dijon mustard
¼ cup (50 mL) balsamic vinegar
⅓ cup (75 mL) extra virgin olive oil

SALAD
1½ lb (750 g) mushrooms (a combo of portobello, button and brown)

1½ cups (375 mL) marinated artichoke hearts, drained, quartered
¼ cup (50 mL) chopped fresh parsley
1 tbsp (15 mL) chopped fresh thyme
Salt and freshly ground black pepper to taste
⅓ cup (75 mL) crumbled goat cheese

1. Preheat barbecue to medium.
2. In small bowl, whisk together dressing ingredients until combined.
3. Clean mushrooms thoroughly with damp cloth or mushroom brush. Remove and discard all but 1 inch (2.5 cm) of portobello stems. Place mushrooms in large bowl. Add half of dressing. Toss to coat well. Grill on barbecue, turning once or twice, until crisp and tender, about 15 minutes.
4. With tongs, transfer to cutting board. Cut in 1-inch (2.5 cm) cubes. Transfer to large bowl. While still warm, add artichoke hearts, parsley, thyme and remaining dressing; toss. Add salt and pepper. Transfer to serving platter. Top with goat cheese.

MAKES ABOUT 6 SIDE-DISH SERVINGS.

THE MOTHER OF QUEEN STREET

❋ "WE'RE THE JEWISH MOTHER'S TRAGEDY," quips Andre Rosenbaum with a grin. "Lawyers who gave up law to open a hole-in-the-wall café!" We're chatting at a corner table amid the usual lunchtime bustle at the Queen Mother Café, 208 Queen St. W., the former "hole in the wall" of which he speaks. Seated opposite me is Rosenbaum's longtime friend, business partner and fellow lawyer David Stearn with whom he has owned and operated this cozy, unpretentious Queen West landmark since the fall of 1978.

And with recent closures of the nearby BamBoo and Beverley Tavern—both much-loved, longtime neighbourhood haunts that will be missed be many—I find it heartwarming to see that, 25 years later, this place is definitely alive and cooking. Nor does it hurt that, as I chat with Rosenbaum and Stearn, who also own the Rivoli—an equally popular eatery, entertainment venue and pool hall a few blocks west—I get to eat. Dipping warm wedges of soft, chewy homemade pita bread into silky Artichoke Heart and Goat Cheese Dip in between bites of the café's famous Thai-inspired Ping Gai Chicken, I'm not surprised theirs is a success story.

Rosenbaum is the more talkative of the two and leaves much of the behind-the-scenes work to Stearn but both have been hands-on partners since day one. "We lived in this neighbourhood at the time," Rosenbaum begins, "and used to eat at Le Select a lot." The latter, along with the Peter Pan and the Beggar's Banquet, were already popular innovators on the soon-to-burgeon Queen West restaurant scene. He became friends with Le Select Bistro's owner Frederic Geisweiller. When Rosenbaum, a law grad already tired of his career, saw a "For Rent" sign on a tiny store called Tom's Submarines and discovered it was a mere $350 a month, he asked Geisweiller to be a silent partner in a café he had in mind. That didn't pan out.

However, Rosenbaum's sister, Anique, and Stearn did get into the act. Anique was in the biz until 1997 when, as her brother jokes, "She decided to be a psychotherapist and do professionally what she did here in an amateur way." At that point, his brother-in-law Jeff Strasburg stepped in to take her place. With no experience and little knowledge of the difficult biz they were about to enter, the enthusiastic young trio opened the Queen Mother Café at 11:30 A.M. in late October, 1978. The place was a third of its current size, had 18 seats, was furnished whimsically with thrift store bargains and had a minimal menu.

"On our second day, we had to close by 12:30 P.M.," Rosenbaum recalls, smiling. "We'd sold our six bagels and had to run to Lottman's Bakery in Kensington Market to get more." Their kitchen facilities were basic, to put it mildly. "Our style of cooking was two burners for soup, a domestic toaster for sandwiches and a sink," he explains. Why the royal moniker? "The night before we opened, we still didn't have a name," he continues. "We'd found three pictures of the Queen Mum in the garbage when we were cleaning up. They were war photos: two with George VI and one of her when she was young."

Decorating the walls of their tiny room with these and a few shabby chic items like a vintage wedding dress seemed like a good idea. "It was a bit tongue-in-cheek," Rosenbaum explains. "Then it clicked. We're trying to attract friends in the neighbourhood, we thought. This will be the 'mother of Queen Street.'" The Queen Mother Café quickly became a hit. Stearn admits they had "really opened the place as a lark," but it wasn't long before that notion was dispelled.

"In the first year, we realized we had to get serious," he continues, adding, "We expanded because we needed a stove." Rosenbaum chimes in, "We were tired of returning those toaster ovens to Eaton's." The place was rapidly becoming what he calls "an artsy, bohemian hang-out" frequented by artists, actors, musicians and students from the Ontario College of Art. They hired a proper chef, then another along with more servers and kitchen staff. Soon, the restaurant took over the adjacent store. In 1984, an outdoor patio was added.

Today, the Queen Mother Café has a total of 110 seats, employs about 40 people and is open seven days a week for lunch and dinner. The menu is an eclectic mix that's big on Asian and vegetarian dishes. The former date back to early years when the owners hired several Southeast Asian refugees, in particular Vanipha Sout. "There was very little Thai or Laotian food here at that time," says Rosenbaum, adding that their kitchen introduced Torontonians to dishes like *Pad Thai*, sticky rice and spring rolls. The still popular meatless Cosmic Burger made of grains, nuts herbs and vegetables, was also an early staple. Desserts came from Dufflet Rosenberg who, back then, was baking in her mother's basement. "We were her third and are now her longest continuous customer," notes Rosenbaum.

He's proud to say that many of their kitchen and dining room staff have worked at the café for many years. "We have mutual respect," he notes. "We let them do their job," adds Stearn. "We've never regretted opening this place," he says cheerfully. "It's like a child," adds Stearn. "Once it's there, it's always there. It becomes a part of you." That can be stressful. "Yesterday, a delivery truck hit our patio fence," Rosenbaum says. "It's always something." His partner agrees. "It's a details business: the physical plant, décor, staff, menu."

The pair acknowledge that Queen West has become gentrified in recent years but note that, so far, the restaurants and bars haven't "gone corporate." They cite the Peter Pan, the Stem, Le Select Bistro, the Rex Hotel and the Cameron House as institutions that, like them, are still going strong. These days, Rosenbaum's wife Kelly St. John helps with the "front of house" while, says Stearn, "I supervise accounting, building maintenance, office stuff and jump in and help if it's busy." Judging by today's lunch, busy is the operative word. The café is hopping with a group celebrating that day's wedding at nearby City Hall.

It was at one such event that a new bride recently explained why she chose to celebrate at the Queen Mother Café. "She said it was because of the longevity of the restaurant and its namesake," Rosenbaum tells me. "She thought coming here might be a good omen."

Here are two good recipes to give you a taste of what's kept diners happy at this excellent eatery for a quarter of a century.

Artichoke Heart and Goat Cheese Dip

The restaurant uses artichoke hearts packed in water. A tube of Woolwich Dairy goat cheese, sold in most supermarkets, is ideal. The amount of lemon juice will depend on the acidity of the canned artichokes.

2 tbsp (30 mL) olive oil
14 oz (398 mL) can artichoke hearts,
    drained
4 cloves garlic, finely chopped
1/4 tsp (1 mL) salt

4.5 oz (130 g) package soft goat
    cheese
1/4 to 1/2 tsp (1 to 2 mL) fresh
    lemon juice
Freshly ground pepper to taste

1. In saucepan, heat olive oil over low heat. Add artichoke hearts, garlic and salt; cook about 15 minutes. stirring occasionally, or until very soft. Cool slightly.

2. Add mixture to bowl of food processor with goat cheese and lemon juice; purée until smooth. Add pepper. Serve with wedges of warm pita bread, crackers or raw vegetable sticks.

MAKES ABOUT 1 1/3 CUPS (325 mL).

Ping Gai Chicken

This is usually served with steamed rice but is also delicious laid on top of a large salad.

4 lb (2 kg) chicken thighs

MARINADE
1 medium bunch fresh coriander, roots attached, washed
6 cloves garlic
1 tbsp (15 mL) whole black pepper corns
3 tbsp (45 mL) oyster sauce
2 tbsp (30 mL) soy sauce
2 tbsp (30 mL) vegetable oil

DIPPING SAUCE
1 cup (250 mL) water
½ cup (125 mL) granulated sugar
3 sprigs fresh coriander, roots removed, washed, chopped
2 cloves garlic, chopped
2 tbsp (30 mL) white vinegar
1 tbsp (15 mL) fresh lime or lemon juice
1 tbsp (15 mL) Asian chile garlic sauce
1 tbsp (15 mL) Asian fish sauce

1. Remove bones from chicken thighs using a sharp knife, leaving skin on.

2. For marinade: Reserve 3 sprigs of coriander for dipping sauce. Add remaining coriander, stems, roots and all, to food processor with garlic and peppercorns. Process until finely chopped. Add oyster sauce, soy sauce and oil; process until combined.

3. Place chicken in shallow glass baking dish; brush with marinade. Cover with plastic wrap. Marinate in fridge at least 1 hour or overnight.

4. For dipping sauce: In saucepan, combine water and sugar. Bring to boil over medium-high heat, stirring, until dissolved. Continue cooking 10 minutes, or until reduced and syrupy. Cool completely. Add to food processor with reserved 3 sprigs coriander, garlic, vinegar, lime juice, chile garlic sauce and fish sauce; process until smooth.

5. Preheat barbecue to medium-high.

6. Place chicken pieces, skin side down, on greased grill. Close barbecue lid. Cook about 8 minutes, or until skin is crispy and chicken is almost cooked through. Turn chicken. Close lid; cook chicken 6 minutes more or until cooked through. Chop into 1-inch (2.5 cm) pieces. Serve with steamed rice and dipping sauce.

MAKES 6 TO 8 SERVINGS.

READ 'EM AND EAT

❋ ALISON FRYER KNOWS A RECIPE FOR SUCCESS—and failure—
when she sees one.

As manager of The Cookbook Store, 850 Yonge St., since it opened in 1983,
she's seen her fair share of books devoted to food and cooking. More important, Fryer, who calls herself "a good at-home, self-trained cook," regularly
samples recipes from the 9,000-plus titles stocked in the compact store and
serves the results to resident tasters, her husband and two teenage daughters.
"Usually, I only need to read a couple of recipes to get an overall view of a
book," claims Fryer, who admits she still gets a thrill when opening a box of
new cookbooks. "I usually check out one baking recipe and one other."

As usual, the devil's in the details. "I make sure there are verbs in the directions," she continues with a smile, "and that the recipe reads well. Another
clue is the ingredient list. Are ingredients listed in the order used? If the list
is long, are they interesting herbs and spices or things you can't easily find?"

She reckons "there's no cookbook in which all the recipes are accurate—
although Julia Child comes close," and that "about 10 to 15 percent of recipes
in any book need tweaking." When a recipe doesn't work, she notes, "Most
people blame themselves, not the book."

Jennifer Grange has no formal chef's training but cooked in restaurant
kitchens for almost five years before starting work at The Cookbook Store
two months after Fryer. "Ideally, each recipe in a cookbook should be tested
by a professional and a home cook," offers Grange, who concedes that's an
expensive proposition. "Writing a recipe is difficult," Fryer adds. "People who
think they're great cooks assume they can write recipes." She lists some pit-
falls: "Saying 'reduce liquid' is not enough. You have to know how much and
how long." Sometimes, she continues, ingredients are omitted, an error that's
becoming more common because of computer glitches in which "whole
chunks of copy have been known to disappear."

According to one publisher, she continues, an average 200-page cookbook
contains 350,000 to 400,000 facts: "That's lots of room for problems." "The
worst mistakes are usually in baking recipes," says Grange, "because of chemical
reactions." In the case of a dessert garnished with poisonous lily of the valley

that appeared in the original *Great Cakes* by American author Carole Walter, such reactions can be deadly. The unprecedented result: all copies were recalled. "That error should have been caught in editing," says Fryer.

When it comes to prolific authors like the unstoppable Emeril Lagasse and British hottie Jamie Oliver, a.k.a "The Naked Chef," she notes that "first and third books are usually their best."

I ask the pair which cookbooks they trust to serve up recipes that work.

HERE ARE FRYER'S FAVOURITES, IN NO PARTICULAR ORDER:
- "Anything by Diane Rossen Worthington. Her *Cuisine of California* (Chronicle) came out in 1984 and is still one of my favourites, especially for chicken recipes."
- "Julia Child's books, especially *The Way to Cook* (Knopf)."
- "I still use the *Joy of Cooking* (Scribner) by Rombauer and Becker for family meals."
- "Likewise for books by Canadian authors Anne Lindsay, Elizabeth Baird, Bonnie Stern and Rose Murray."
- "For baking, I like *Classic Home Desserts* (Houghton Mifflin) by Richard Sax."

GRANGE'S LIST SHOWS A PENCHANT FOR BRITISH AND EUROPEAN TOMES:
- "The first cookbook I ever bought was by Marcella Hazan. I constantly use the new compendium of her first two books: *Essentials of Classic Italian Cooking* (Knopf)."
- "All books by Patricia Wells, in particular *Bistro Cooking* (Workman)."
- "Books by British food writer Nigel Slater, especially *Real Cooking* (Penguin)."
- "Nigella Lawson's *How to Eat* (Knopf Canada) and *How to Be a Domestic Goddess* (Knopf Canada)."
- "Peter Gordon *Cooks at Home* (Headline) by British chef Peter Gordon."

HERE ARE FRYER'S AND GRANGE'S POINTERS ON WHERE TO FIND POPULAR RECIPES:
- BEST HOMEY DISH: Three-Cheese Meat Loaf from Ontario author Rose Murray's book: *A Year in My Kitchen* (Prentice-Hall Canada).
- BEST POUND CAKE: *The Cake Bible* (Morrow) by Rose Levy Beranbaum.
- BEST RICE PUDDING: *New Classics* (BBC) by British chef Gary Rhodes.

- BEST POTATO RECIPE: Gratin Dauphinois Madame Cartet from *Bistro Cooking* by Patricia Wells.
- BEST COOKBOOK BY EMERIL LAGASSE: His first: *New Orleans Cooking* (Morrow).
- BEST MAGAZINE FOR DO-ABLE RECIPES: *Food & Wine*.

Lemon Herb Chicken

Use fresh lemons for this wondrous dish from The Cuisine of California.

2 tbsp (30 mL) grated lemon rind
½ cup (125 mL) fresh lemon juice
¼ cup (50 mL) olive oil
¼ cup (50 mL) finely chopped fresh or 2 tbsp (30 mL) dried herbs (rosemary, thyme, parsley, basil and oregano)
½ cup (125 mL) dry white wine
1 tsp (5 mL) liquid honey or maple syrup
½ tsp (2 mL) salt

¼ tsp (1 mL) freshly ground black pepper
4 whole large chicken breasts, skinned, boned, halved
2 tbsp (30 mL) unsalted butter
6 tbsp (90 mL) whipping cream
Salt and freshly ground black pepper
¼ cup (50 mL) finely chopped fresh parsley
1 lemon, sliced

1. In bowl, combine lemon peel, lemon juice, 2 tbsp (30 mL) of olive oil, herbs, wine, honey, salt and pepper.

2. Arrange chicken breasts in single layer in large, shallow non-metal dish; pour on lemon mixture. Let marinate in fridge 4 hours to overnight.

3. Remove chicken from marinade; pat dry with paper towels. Reserve marinade.

4. Melt butter and remaining olive oil in large skillet over medium-high heat. Add chicken breasts in single layer; cook about 5 minutes per side until browned and just cooked through. (You may have to do this in two batches.) Transfer to plate. Add reserved marinade, scraping up browned bits from skillet. Bring to boil; reduce heat and cook 1 to 2 minutes. Add cream; cook 2 to 3 minutes, stirring. Add salt, pepper and 2 tbsp (30 mL) of parsley.

5. Return chicken to skillet; cook in sauce until heated through. Transfer to warmed platter. Garnish with lemon slices and remaining parsley.

MAKES 6 SERVINGS.

Gingerbread with Lemon Icing

From How to Be a Domestic Goddess *by Nigella Lawson (North American edition—the British one uses only metric) comes this super dessert recommended by Grange who adjusted amounts for the icing.*

½ cup plus 2 tbsp (155 mL) unsalted butter

½ cup plus 2 tbsp (155 mL) brown sugar

¾ cup plus 1 tbsp (190 mL) corn syrup

¾ cup plus 1 tbsp (190 mL) molasses

1 tbsp (15 mL) fresh ginger root, finely grated

1 tsp (5 mL) ground cinnamon

1 cup plus 2 tbsp (280 mL) milk

2 large eggs, beaten

1 tsp (5 mL) baking soda dissolved in 2 tbsp (30 mL) warm water

2 cups (500 mL) all-purpose flour

LEMON ICING

3 tbsp (45 mL) lemon juice

2 cups (500 mL) icing sugar, sifted

About 2 tbsp (30 mL) warm water

1. Preheat oven to 325°F (160°C).

2. In saucepan, melt butter with brown sugar, corn syrup, molasses, ginger root and cinnamon. Remove from heat; add milk, eggs and baking soda mixture.

3. Place flour in large bowl. Beat in liquid mixture until combined. (Batter will be very liquid.) Pour into greased 9 x 13-inch (23 x 33 cm) baking dish or pan. Place in oven; bake 45 to 55 minutes, or until risen and firm. (Do not overbake; this tastes best when slightly sticky.) Place dish on wire rack to cool.

4. For lemon icing: In bowl, whisk together lemon juice and icing sugar, then just enough water for thick spreading consistency. Spread over cooled gingerbread; cut in squares.

MAKES ABOUT 20 SQUARES.

COUSCOUS KING

✳ No DOUBT ABOUT IT, COUSCOUS IS UP there with the fringed velvet scarf and asymmetric hemline. In a nutshell, it's hot, hot, hot. Some telltale signs: I caught two of my favourite TV chefs—Emeril Lagasse and Ming Tsai—dishing up this trendy carb on Food Network in the same recent week. My local supermarket, which is not one of your giant, one-stop stores, sells six versions of the stuff—including one with "wild forest mushrooms"—in its health food section. And when I told a couple of friends I was dedicating a column to this fashionable food, they immediately demanded the recipe.

Enter Omar Houmani, who came to Toronto from his native Algiers, the capital of Algeria, six years ago. I met this charming young man at Casa Acoreana, the busy bulk food store-cum-coffee shop located at the corner of Baldwin St. and Augusta Ave., at the hub of Kensington Market. Here, he serves up what I consider the best cappuccino in town—the result of using top-notch coffee, cleaning the espresso machine daily and, most important, of having that special knack.

Two evenings a week, Houmani—a talented, mostly self-taught chef who operated his own downtown restaurant called Le Roi du Couscous, featuring his homeland's cuisine, for three years—cooks Italian fare at La Forchetta on College St.'s busy strip in Little Italy. It was here we arranged to meet one recent Tuesday night when the eatery was closed so I could watch him prepare couscous, as he insists it must be done, the authentic way. "The quick couscous people make from the instructions on the package is nothing like *couscous,*" Houmani says, adding adamantly: "That is the wrong way." He explains that the dish, which must be steamed twice, is a staple in the North African countries of Algeria, Morocco and Tunisia where it is eaten in homes at least several days a week and differs slightly according to region.

Having done some reading on this topic, including *Couscous and Other Good Food from Morocco* by Paula Wolfert, I already knew that the word "couscous" can have two meanings. First, there's the couscous itself which is made from semolina: ground wheat grains that are by-products of flour milling. Sometimes, the word is also used to describe a duo of dishes that go well together: cooked couscous and *tagine*, a North African stew made with lamb, chicken or fish.

Deftly juggling pots and pans, Houmani is making both of these along with a lentil-based soup and our dessert: a luscious dried fruit compote laced with orange blossom water. To cook the couscous, he uses his version of a couscousiere: basically, a two-pot steamer. In it, steam produced by water, stock, sauce or a *tagine* boiling gently in the bottom half (he used stock on this occasion; I later used water when making it at home) cooks the couscous in the steamer section which fits tightly on top.

Luckily, I was spared the job of drilling holes in a cheap pot from Chinatown, as Houmani cleverly did, to create the top steamer, which he sets over a large stockpot. Instead, I found a six-litre couscousiere—they're sold at many good houseware stores. You could use a fine sieve set in a deep saucepan. Fill the lower pot about half-full of water, let it boil steadily but not too rapidly and don't let it touch the steamer on top. Also, the couscous should not be covered during cooking.

Houmani's recipe produces such delectable results you'll never revert to cooking couscous the quick way again. I've used his method with packaged supermarket couscous and the bulk kind from Casa Acoreana, both with excellent results.

This goes well with any stew but particularly with the Lamb Tagine, similar to one Houmani made for me, that follows. Serve *harissa*, a traditional North African, chile-based condiment sold in specialty food shops and larger supermarkets, on the side with this meal for extra heat. You could add a spoonful to the *tagine*.

Omar's Couscous

Accompany with any dish that has lots of sauce. I spoon raisins or currants on top of the couscous during second steaming and serve it garnished with toasted slivered almonds and chopped parsley.

3 cups (750 mL) couscous
1½ tsp (7 mL) kosher or sea salt
1½ tbsp (22 mL) olive oil
1½ cups (325 mL) warm water

1. Using hands, combine all ingredients in large bowl. Let sit about 15 minutes. Rub mixture gently but thoroughly with hands to separate grains. Transfer to top (steamer) section of couscousiere. Steam 30 minutes over boiling water or stock. Do not cover.

2. Return to bowl. Add 1 cup (250 mL) cold water. Stir well. Let sit 5 to 10 minutes. Break up any lumps with spoon. (Couscous can be made ahead up to this point.) Return to steamer; cook about 15 minutes, or until tender and fluffy.

MAKES 4 TO 6 SERVINGS.

Lamb Tagine

You could use chicken or beef. To toast almonds and sesame seeds, cook sepa-rately in a dry skillet over medium-low heat until browned, 3 to 4 minutes. Serve with couscous, rice or orzo pasta, braised or grilled vegetables and/or salad.

3 lb (1.5 kg) lamb shoulder, cut in
   1½-inch (4-cm) cubes
1 tsp (5 mL) salt
½ tsp (2 mL) freshly ground black
   pepper
3 tbsp (45 mL) vegetable oil
2 medium onions, halved, sliced
2 cloves garlic, chopped
1 tsp (5 mL) saffron threads
3 to 3½ cups (750 to 825 mL) water
4 tbsp (60 mL) liquid honey

1 cup (250 mL) pitted prunes
1 tsp (5 mL) cinnamon
½ cup (125 mL) warm water
Salt and freshly ground black pepper
   to taste
½ cup (125 mL) toasted whole
   blanched or slivered almonds
   (optional)
2 tbsp (30 mL) toasted sesame seeds
   (optional)

1. In large bowl, toss lamb with salt and pepper.

2. Heat 2 tbsp (30 mL) of oil in large saucepan or dutch oven over high heat. Add lamb; cook in single layer, in batches if necessary, until browned all over. Transfer to bowl.

3. Reduce heat to medium-low. Add remaining oil to saucepan; add onions, garlic and saffron. Cook, stirring at intervals, until soft and gold-en, about 5 minutes. Return lamb to saucepan. Add water, just enough to cover. Bring to boil over high heat; reduce to low and simmer, partially covered, 30 minutes. Stir in 2 tbsp (30 mL) of honey; cook about 1 hour or until lamb is tender. (Check at intervals to make sure lamb does not overcook and fall apart.)

4. Meanwhile, in bowl, toss prunes with remaining 2 tbsp (30 mL) of honey and cinnamon. Add warm water. Let sit while lamb cooks. Drain prunes; add to lamb mixture. Cook about 15 minutes. or until prunes are soft but not falling apart. Add salt and pepper. Serve garnished with toasted almonds and sesame seeds.

MAKES 6 TO 8 SERVINGS.

MARION'S BASICS

✳ WHEN IT COMES TO FOOD SHOPPING, I vote with my teeth. These principles are my guide:

Flavour comes first. Food that's rich in taste and texture satisfies both body and soul. To that end, seeking out fresh, wholesome ingredients is a must.

Whenever possible, I buy locally grown, organic produce—in season—for two reasons: to help save the environment (pesticides and fertilizer play havoc with our soil and water table) and because such foods taste better. Schlepping produce from far-flung places uses valuable energy, pollutes the environment and doesn't put money in the pockets of Ontario farmers. These fruit and veg have likely been picked before they're ripe causing them to resemble either a hockey puck or wet wash-cloth. The organic stuff does cost more but, if more of us buy it, the price will go down. I find good organic produce at my local health food store but most supermarkets now also have a decent selection. I'm not a purist and certainly make an exception for imported mangoes and their ilk.

I try to buy meat and poultry from animals raised without hormones and/or antibiotics—practices that are the norm on factory farms and which, I believe, are a long-term hazard to health. Naturally raised meat is tastier.

When cooking, I try to make meals from scratch as I'm not fond of the preservatives in your average convenience food, or of its taste.

Healthwise, I try to include plenty of fibre, minimal hydrogenated fats, a balance of those trusty food groups and, in general, enough variety to keep tastebuds hopping and my kitchen skills honed.

My favourite dishes are spur-of-the-moment stir-fries; roasted or grilled chicken, fish and veggies; whole grains like wheat berries, barley and brown rice accompanied by a protein hit of beans, tofu or a little meat; simple pastas laced with garlic, herbs and olive oil; slow-cooked stews, soups and braised dishes that can be made ahead, and main dish salads comprised of mixed greens tossed with dressing and topped with grilled meat or seafood.

Here are items I almost always have on hand:

ASIAN: Patak's wonderful line of Indian curry sauces, chutneys and pickles. Asian Home Gourmet spice pastes, sold at some supermarkets and gourmet shops, are great for Thai dishes.

COFFEE AND TEA: I belong to Cameron's Coffee club. They mail me 2 pounds of excellent Fair Trade organic beans each month (call: 1-866-793-3301). I buy green tea and yummy Provence Rooibos from Great Cooks and the Tea Spot on The Bay, Queen Street's lower level.

BREAD: I do a mini-milk-run to pick up baked goods like Ace Bakery's baguette and focaccia; Pita Break's muesli or flax pitas (sold in some supermarkets and gourmet shops); the lemon croissant at Zane, 1852 Queen St. E.; Portuguese pada buns at Caldense, 1209 Dundas St. W.; and twister bagels at Harbord Bakery.

CEREAL: A toothsome breakfast combo I've created is equal parts Kashi Puffed Seven Whole Grains & Sesame, Kellogg's All-Bran Buds and Kellogg's Vector.

SWEETS: I usually have fruit, raw or cooked, for dessert. However, I always keep good dark chocolate such as Lindt around for cooking and the odd snack. I like two—and only two—cookies made by local New Moon Bakery sold in health food and gourmet shops: crispy oatmeal ones called Bite Me! and their chocolate chip.

FRESH HERBS: I toss these into salads and stews—especially curly parsley, basil and coriander—and for garnish. I use them generously, very coarsely chopped. I store them as a chef showed me: Wash and cut off stems, line a large, shallow, airtight, plastic container with damp paper towel and store, covered, in fridge.

MAPLE SYRUP: A boon poured on French toast, as a baste for roasted or grilled meat or fish, to sweeten thickened yogurt and to brush on squash before roasting.

MEAT: I shop at Cumbrae's, 481 Church St., or Whitehouse Meats in the St. Lawrence Market. I pay more but tend to eat less as their naturally raised meat has fantastic, satisfying flavour. In this genre, Rowe Farm chicken is also good and beef from Beretta Organic Farms (both sold in some health food and gourmet stores).

RICE, PASTA AND GNOCCHI: I keep arborio, carnaroli or other short-grain rice on hand for risotto and like to try interesting new shapes of dried pasta. Refrigerated, ready-made gnocchi are easy to find and are great tossed with homemade or store-bought sauce.

SALAD DRESSINGS: I keep two dressings in my fridge made by and sold at All the Best Fine Foods, 1099 Yonge St.: Mustard Vinaigrette and Miso Dressing. Renee's Lite Caesar, sold in supermarkets, is another staple.

SALT: I use kosher salt for grilling and roasting, fine sea salt for everything else.

SEASONING BLENDS: I like to make my own rubs and mixes but have found two good store-bought ones: Barberian's Steak Seasoning (I also use it on chicken) and chef Paul Prudhomme's Seafood Magic. I've found both at gourmet shops and some Loblaws.

STOCKS: I like the cartons of Imagine ready-to-use chicken and vegetable broth sold in most health food stores and supermarkets.

WHOLE GRAINS: I serve brown rice with stir-fries and in pilafs. Wheat berries, sold in health food stores, are delicious. Kashi makes a terrific blend of seven grains that's called a cereal but I use it as a sidekick for main courses.

Here are two recipes using ingredients I usually have on hand.

Sweet Potato Bean Soup

Simple, seasonal, healthful and yummy, this meatless soup made with a few simple ingredients was inspired by Jill Dupleix, food columnist at the Times *in England. Puréeing half the beans thickens the soup; leaving the rest whole gives a nice, chunky texture. Beans' bonus: A protein boost that makes this soup a meal. The flavouring—curry, balsamic vinegar and maple syrup—sounds quirky, but it works. Orange-hued* Imagine *vegetable broth is perfect for this recipe; I use one 946-mL carton and add water for the extra liquid.*

1 tbsp (15 mL) unsalted butter
1 tbsp (15 mL) vegetable oil
1 small onion, coarsely chopped
1 rounded tsp (5 mL) curry powder
2 medium sweet potatoes, peeled, diced
About 5 cups (1.25 L) boiling hot vegetable stock and/or water
19 oz (540 mL) can white beans (navy, kidney, cannellini), rinsed, drained

1 tbsp (15 mL) each balsamic vinegar, maple syrup (optional)
Sea salt and freshly ground black pepper to taste
Plain yogurt for garnish
Chopped fresh parsley or coriander for garnish

1. Add butter and oil to large heavy saucepan over medium-low heat. Add onion; cook about 5 minutes until soft, but not brown. Add curry powder; cook, stirring, about 1 minute. Add sweet potatoes; cook, stirring, 1 to 2 minutes. Add hot stock. Bring to boil; reduce heat to low and simmer, covered, about 20 minutes or until sweet potato is soft. Add half the beans. Purée until smooth using hand blender, food processor or blender. Add remaining whole beans, salt and pepper.

2. Taste; add vinegar and maple syrup, if using, and salt and pepper.

3. Reheat to serve. Garnish each bowl with a dollop or swirl of yogurt and parsley or coriander.

MAKES ABOUT 6 SERVINGS.

Grilled Chicken Salad

This bare-bones outline for a wonderfully versatile dish is delicious made with a combo of pre-seasoned, grilled chicken, steak and shrimp. Sometimes I use roast chicken. I use the store-bought miso dressing and steak seasoning (yes, even on chicken) mentioned above. I sometimes add grilled or sautéed mushrooms, big homemade croutons, cubes of crispy, browned potato and/or coarsely crushed tortilla chips on top. Serve with crusty bread, a baked potato or whole grains.

2 boneless (skin on or skinless) chicken breasts, about 1³/₄ lb (875 g) total
1 tsp (5 mL) seasoning mix
1 tsp (15 mL) olive oil

5 to 6 cups (1.25 to 1.5 L) mixed salad greens
1 cup (250 mL) coarsely chopped fresh herbs (parsley, coriander, basil)
About 2 tbsp (30 mL) salad dressing

1. Sprinkle chicken with seasoning mix. Place on broiler rack or grill pan. Drizzle with olive oil. Broil or grill about 7 minutes per side or until browned and just cooked through. Cut in strips or chunks.

2. In bowl, toss salad greens and herbs with dressing. Divide greens between two plates or large shallow bowls. Arrange chicken on top.

MAKES 2 SERVINGS.

─◌ *Chapter Eight* ◌─

CHOCOLATE: FOOD OF THE GODS

❋ IT WAS THE MID-1980S AND THE EDITOR of a major food magazine was addressing a large gathering at one of the conferences I regularly
attend for food writers from across North America. I clearly recall the lively
intro to her speech. She claimed that, according to surveys, if her popular
glossy contained nothing but chocolate recipes, readers would be happy.
Writing about things culinary for almost 30 years has connected me food
wise with thousands of Canadians on a weekly basis. From their feedback,
word on the street and my own observations, I agree: Chocolate is universal-
ly beloved.

When my brothers and I were young, our mother, a high school biology
teacher with some strong opinions on nutrition, would give us chocolate—
Swiss bittersweet, to be exact—saying it contained vitamins and minerals.
This was more than she could say for other "sweets," as candy is called in the

U.K. To this day, I have a soft spot for Swiss, Belgian and other high-quality dark chocolate and always keep a bar or two stashed in a kitchen cupboard for when a sugar hit is in order—almost every day after dinner.

Some of my best and most vivid food memories involve chocolate. There was an exquisite, deeply dark chocolate cake I ate in the early 1980s at a restaurant—long gone, of course—called the Black Banana in downtown Philadelphia. I was a fledgling food writer at the time on what's called a "fam trip" hosted by the tourist board of that city for Canadian food and wine journalists. I can still taste the richness of that dense, fudgey yet delicate-crumbed cake—and here's the brilliant part—its divine contrast of texture cleverly contrived by baking a crisp layer of crumbled Italian almond cookies called *amaretti* in the middle. Today, I would move heaven and earth to get the recipe. At that early stage of my career, I was too busy swooning from the experience to seize the moment. However, I plan to sit down with a stack of dessert cookbooks some lovely day, then get baking to re-create my version of that sublime chocolate concoction.

On home turf, I can still remember the day I first tasted Canada's own out-of-this-world confection: the Nanaimo Bar. It was the summer of 1966 and I had recently arrived to join my parents in Edmonton after my father took a job as head of the University of Alberta's physiology department. Talk about a shock to the system and a step back in time. My brother Eric and I couldn't believe there were real cowboys in the airplane hangar-sized bars we occasionally frequented, where irate rednecks regularly picked some pretty awesome fights. Many aspects of life were new to us. Some were downright shocking—one month of 30-below during our first Prairie winter tops the list.

However, when my friend and fellow university student Nancy, who came from a farm near Edmonton, produced a batch of Nanaimo Bars one memorable afternoon in the kitchen of a house we shared with several other girls, I thought I'd died and gone to heaven.

What a taste sensation: layer upon layer of deliciousness with its crowning glory a glossy coating of dark chocolate. Like all good things, these bars had luscious taste. But better still, there was an array of textures: a crunchy cookie crust laced with chewy coconut and crisp nuts, then a layer of sweet, silky smooth custard topped with a thin, shiny coating of rich chocolate glaze.

My mooching methods garnered the recipe for the best Chocolate Truffles I've ever eaten. The source: my longtime friend and ace home cook Amanda Cameron who has been hosting fabulous potluck gatherings at her home for many years. The truffles are a mandatory goodbye gift for guests.

And the list goes on. Like that *Gourmet* editor, I know what readers want. Read 'em and eat!

Brownies

I experimented several times to come up with a brownie that's just the right combination of fudge-like and cakey. One trick is the baking time—between 25 and 30 minutes—so they come out dense and moist but with an identifiable crumb.

1 cup (250 mL) unsalted butter
3 oz (90 g) unsweetened chocolate
3 oz (90 g) semisweet or bittersweet chocolate
1¾ cups (425 mL) granulated sugar

1 tsp (5 mL) vanilla extract
4 eggs
1¼ cups (300 mL) all-purpose flour
½ tsp (2 mL) salt

1. Preheat oven to 350°F (180°C).

2. Melt butter and chocolates in heavy saucepan, stirring until smooth. (Or microwave in glass bowl on High for 30 seconds. Stir, then continue to microwave and stir at 30-second intervals until melted and smooth.)

3. Add ¾ cup (175 mL) of sugar and vanilla extract to chocolate mixture. Stir until smooth. Pour into large bowl; cool at least 5 minutes.

4. In separate bowl, whisk together remaining 1 cup (250 mL) sugar and eggs. Slowly add half of this to chocolate mixture, stirring until combined.

5. Using electric mixer, beat remaining egg mixture until pale yellow and thick, 2 to 3 minutes. Gently fold into chocolate mixture.

6. In small bowl, combine flour and salt. Stir into chocolate mixture until combined. Pour batter into ungreased 9-inch (2.5 L) square baking pan.

7. Bake 28 minutes. Cool in pan on wire rack. Refrigerate before cutting into bars or squares.

MAKES ABOUT 25 BROWNIES.

Nanaimo Bars

Walnuts are traditional in the base but are often rancid when you buy them; pecans are more reliably fresh. Use an offset palette knife to spread both filling and icing evenly. Although semisweet chocolate is usual in the icing, bittersweet helps cut the sweetness of the other two layers. A sublime state of Canadiana!

BASE
3 cups (750 mL) graham cracker crumbs
2 cups (500 mL) sweetened shredded coconut
1 cup (250 mL) finely chopped pecans or other nuts
1 cup (250 mL) unsalted butter, melted
2/3 cup (150 mL) cocoa powder
1/2 cup (125 mL) granulated sugar
2 eggs
1 1/2 tsp (5 mL) vanilla extract

FILLING
1/2 cup (125 mL) unsalted butter, softened
3 tbsp (45 mL) milk
2 tbsp (30 mL) custard powder (e.g. Bird's)
4 cups (1L) icing sugar, sifted

ICING
8 oz (250 g) semisweet or bittersweet chocolate, chopped
2 tbsp (30 mL) unsalted butter

1. Preheat oven to 350°F (180°C).

2. Line 9 x 13-inch (23 x 33 cm) baking pan with parchment paper.

3. For base: In bowl, stir together graham cracker crumbs, coconut and pecans.

4. In another bowl, whisk together butter, cocoa, sugar, eggs and vanilla extract; stir into graham cracker mixture until well mixed. Press mixture evenly into prepared pan. Bake in centre of oven about 10 minutes. Cool on wire rack.

5. For filling: In bowl and using electric mixer, beat butter with milk and custard powder until creamed. One cup at a time, beat in icing sugar. Spread evenly over base. Chill until firm, about 30 minutes.

6. For icing: In bowl set over (not in) saucepan of hot (not boiling) water, melt chocolate with butter. Whisk until smooth. Spread evenly over filling. Chill until icing is set. Cut into bars. Store in fridge but bring to room temperature before serving.

MAKES ABOUT 48 BARS.

Martha's Ne Plus Ultra Cookies

Yes, some of Martha Stewart's work is done with smoke and mirrors. Worse still, many of the recipes from her glossy, gourmet tomes don't work. However, when I came across this one in a book by Stewart called Holidays—*one of a series based on three years of* Martha Stewart Living *magazines—I almost forgave the cuisine ice queen her other foibles. These are, like the name says, "ne plus ultra." Big and loaded with goodies, they get the serious thumbs-up.*

½ cup (125 mL) unsalted butter, at
   room temperature
⅔ cup (150 mL) packed brown sugar
¼ cup (50 mL) granulated sugar
1 tsp (5 mL) vanilla extract
2 eggs
1¼ cups (300 mL) all-purpose flour

½ tsp (2 mL) salt
½ tsp (2 mL) baking soda
1 cup (250 mL) semisweet chocolate
   chips
1 cup (250 mL) raisins
1 cup (250 mL) pecans, coarsely
   chopped

1. Preheat oven to 350°F (180°C).

2. In large bowl, using electric mixer, beat butter with sugars until light and fluffy. Stir in vanilla extract and eggs.

3. In separate bowl, sift together flour, salt and baking soda in separate bowl. Beat into butter mixture. Stir in chocolate chips, raisins and pecans.

4. Form dough into 2½-inch (6 cm) balls, then press to 1-inch (2.5 cm) thickness with palms of hands (dough is quite sticky). Place on lightly greased cookie sheets, spacing cookies about 3 inches (8 cm) apart. Bake 18 to 20 minutes or until golden. Cool on wire racks.

MAKES ABOUT 1 DOZEN LARGE COOKIES.

Amanda's Truffles

President's Choice Rich Dark Bittersweet Chocolate works well in these delectable confections that are a specialty of my friend and fellow foodie Amanda Cameron. She makes this big batch and hands them out to guests in gift bags after dinner parties. She and I both store them in the freezer; they're delicious eaten frozen or you can let them thaw.

2 lb (1 kg) good quality bittersweet
  chocolate
8 oz (250 g) unsalted butter
6 large egg yolks
1/3 cup (75 mL) dark rum

1. Chop 1 lb (500 g) chocolate finely, into about 1/4-inch (5 mm) dice.

2. In heatproof bowl set over (not in) saucepan of hot (not boiling) water, melt chocolate with butter, stirring occasionally, until smooth. Remove bowl from saucepan. Whisk in egg yolks, then rum. Cover with plastic wrap. Refrigerate until mixture is firm, about 3 hours. Check after 30 minutes. You may need to whisk the mixture once or twice if it separates during chilling.

3. Roll mixture into rough balls in rounded teaspoon amounts (Cameron uses a melon baller). Place on a plastic wrap-lined baking sheet. Place baking sheet in freezer until truffles are hard, about 1 hour.

4. Chop remaining 1 lb (500 g) chocolate finely. In heatproof bowl set over (not in) saucepan of hot (not boiling) water, melt chocolate, stirring occasionally, until smooth. Leave bowl over saucepan. One at a time, roll frozen truffles in melted chocolate, letting excess drip back into bowl and placing dipped truffle onto waxed paper-lined baking sheet. Freeze dipped truffles until coating is set. Place in airtight container and store in freezer.

MAKES ABOUT 7 DOZEN.

All-in-the-Pan Chewy Chocolate Cake

From In the Sweet Kitchen *by Regan Daley. Use an American-style cocoa like Hershey's or Ghirardelli, not Dutch-processed. Line the bottom and two sides of the pan with parchment paper. Be careful not to disturb paper while mixing; use it to lift cooled cake from pan. If you prefer shiny icing to a light-coloured, matte one, make this: Melt 6 oz (175 g) semisweet chocolate in microwave; stir in 1 cup (250 mL) sour cream.*

1½ cups (375 mL) all-purpose flour
1 cup (250 mL) granulated sugar
¼ cup (50 mL) cocoa powder
1 tsp (5 mL) baking soda
½ tsp (2 mL) salt
6 tbsp (90 mL) vegetable oil
1 tbsp (15 mL) white vinegar
1 tsp (5 mL) vanilla extract
1 cup (250 mL) cool water

ICING
¼ cup (50 mL) unsalted butter, softened
2 cups (500 mL) icing sugar
2 to 3 tbsp (30 to 45 mL) milk or water
1½ tbsp (22 mL) cocoa powder
1 tsp (5 mL) vanilla extract

1. Preheat oven to 350°F (180°C).

2. For cake: Sift flour into 8-inch (20 cm) square metal cake pan.

3. In small bowl, combine sugar, cocoa, baking soda and salt. Add to pan; stir well with fork. With back of spoon, make three wells in mixture: one large, one medium and one small. Into large well, pour vegetable oil; into medium well, vinegar; and into small well, vanilla. Pour water over everything. With fork, stir mixture until well blended, reaching into corners for any dry pockets. Don't overmix but stir until most lumps are gone.

4. Pour mixture into cake pan. Bake in centre of oven 30 minutes, or until top feels springy and tester inserted in centre comes out clean. Cool completely in pan on wire rack.

5. For icing: In bowl, using an electric mixer, beat butter with half the icing sugar until smooth. Beat in 1 tbsp (15 mL) of milk or water. Sift cocoa on top; beat in. Beat in vanilla, then remaining icing sugar. Beat in enough remaining milk or water to make a thick, creamy icing. Spread over cake.

MAKES ABOUT 8 SERVINGS.

Chocolate Apple Cake

I ran this recipe one year to celebrate apple season. I knew this snacking cake was a hit when I left squares of it at the reception desk of the Star newsroom. They disappeared in seconds; then the requests for the recipe came fast and furious. It comes from a nifty book called Apple Desserts *by Joie Warner.*

1½ cups (375 mL) all-purpose flour
½ cup (125 mL) cocoa powder
1½ tsp (7 mL) baking powder
½ tsp (2 mL) baking soda
½ tsp (2mL) salt
½ cup (125 mL) unsalted butter, melted
½ cup (125 mL) buttermilk
1¼ cups (300 mL) granulated sugar
2 large eggs

1 tbsp (15 mL) vanilla extract
½ cup (125 mL) semisweet chocolate chips
2 cups (500 mL) peeled, coarsely chopped, tart apples (about 2)

GLAZE
¼ cup (50 mL) water
⅓ cup (75 mL) granulated sugar

1. Preheat oven to 350°F (180°C).

2. Sift flour, cocoa, baking powder, baking soda and salt into large bowl.

3. In medium bowl, whisk together butter, buttermilk and sugar until smooth. Add to flour mixture. Stir with spoon until well combined. Stir in chocolate chips and apples. Spoon into greased 8-inch (20 cm) square baking pan.

4. Bake 50 to 55 minutes, or until cake tester inserted in centre comes out clean. Remove from oven; place baking pan on wire rack.

5. For glaze: Combine water and sugar in small bowl. Pierce cake in several places with toothpick. Slowly drizzle glaze over cake. Let stand 15 minutes. Turn cake on to rack; cool completely. Cut in squares.

MAKES 8 TO 10 SERVINGS.

Oatmeal Cherry Chocolate Chippers

Here's the crunchy, yummy cookie I came up with after several tries. It has fibre from the rolled oats, is fairly low in fat and sugar and tastes yummy. Somewhat pricey dried cherries, sold in most bulk food stores and some supermarkets, add delicious tang; so do cranberries. In a pinch, you could use raisins.

3/4 cup (175 mL) unsalted butter, at room temperature
3/4 cup (75 mL) packed brown sugar
1/4 cup (50 mL) granulated sugar
1 egg
2 tsp (10 mL) vanilla extract
1 tbsp (15 mL) water
3/4 cup (175 mL) all-purpose or whole-wheat flour
3/4 tsp (4 mL) baking soda

Pinch of salt
2 cups (500 mL) quick-cooking (not instant) rolled oats
1 cup (250 mL) cornflakes
1 cup (250 mL) crisp rice cereal
1 cup (250 mL) dried cherries or dried cranberries
1 cup (250 mL) semisweet chocolate chips or chopped semisweet chocolate

1. Preheat oven to 350°F (180°C).

2. In large bowl on medium speed of electric mixer, cream butter, sugars, egg, vanilla and water until light and creamy.

3. In small bowl, combine flour, baking soda and salt. Add to creamed mixture, beating on low speed until blended. With wooden spoon, stir in rolled oats, cornflakes and crisp rice cereal, then dried cherries and chocolate chips.

4. Using round ice cream scoop or spoon, place balls of dough on Silpat- or parchment paper-lined cookie sheet about 2 inches (5 cm) apart. Flatten each ball with fingers until cookies are about 1/2 inch (1 cm) thick. Bake 12 to 15 minutes, or until nicely browned. Cool a few minutes before transferring to rack to cool completely.

MAKES ABOUT 30 COOKIES.

LIST OF RECIPES

INDEX

INDEX

INDEX

INDEX